AF884488

PRAISE FOR PAUL ZANE PILZER

"I'm amazed at your business capacity and, as well, your ability to put into laymen's terms the alchemic process. I know it [Unlimited Wealth] will be well received and a huge success."

— Sam Walton, Chairman
Wal-Mart Stores, Inc.

"[Unlimited Wealth] A must-read—Paul Zane Pilzer has helped to shift our thinking from scarcity in resources to one of a cornucopia of economic abundance and richness."

— Anthony Robbins, Bestselling author of
Awaken the Giant Within

"The Reagan-era economist turned Wellness Guru."

— ***New York Times***

"Paul Zane Pilzer's new book [Unlimited Wealth] makes you understand how and why the world will be getting ever richer materially. He gets it right."

— Julian Simon, Professor of Business Administration, University of Maryland
author of ***The Ultimate Resource***

"Pilzer and Unlimited Wealth can give you the equivalent of a college education in just a few hours. He explains not only where the greatest economic opportunities lie today, but what you can do to take advantage of them."

— Dexter Yager
Yager Enterprises, Inc.

"His theory is crystal clear and applicable to anyone ... Unlimited Wealth is bound to revolutionize the way we view the nation's economy, if not our own lives. Pilzer challenges us to scrap not only the way we think about our daily affairs but the way we prepare ourselves for the future."

— ***Newark Star Ledger***

"Paul Zane Pilzer's unique gift is to tame the mysteries of making money and put you in the saddle. God Wants You To Be Rich will set your mind racing with new ideas."

— Scott DeGarmo, Editor-in-Chief and Publisher, ***SUCCESS Magazine***

"In God Wants You To Be Rich, bestselling author Paul Zane Pilzer provides an original, provocative view of how to accumulate wealth and why it is beneficial to all of humankind. A theology of economics, this book explores why God wants each of us to be rich in every way—physically, emotionally and financially—and shows the way to prosperity, well-being and peace of mind."

— ***Boston Herald***

"Like any machine, our body runs best when operated according to its design principles. Noted economist Paul Zane Pilzer shows how to promote—and profit by—the wellness revolution."

— Michael J. Behe, Professor
Lehigh University
author of ***Darwin's Black Box***

"In The Wellness Revolution, Paul Zane Pilzer reveals the most important secret for tomorrow's successful entrepreneurs: where to invest your dream. Step by step, Pilzer shows entrepreneurs how to find where they fit in the mega-industry of the future."

— Randy Fields, Co-founder
Mrs. Field's Cookies

"Paul Zane Pilzer has paid great tribute to J. I. Rodale, founder of Prevention magazine and the organic industry in the United States, by showing how Rodale traditions of individual and environmental health make sound economic investment sense in today's world."

— Ardath Rodale, Chairman of Rodale, Inc., publisher of
Prevention and ***Men's Health***

ALSO BY
PAUL ZANE PILZER

Other People's Money
Unlimited Wealth
God Wants You To Be Rich
The Wellness Revolution
The Next Millionaires
The Next Trillion
The Fountain of Wealth
The New Health Insurance Solution
The New Wellness Revolution
The Entrepreneurial Challenge
The End of Employer-Provided Health Insurance
The New Roaring Twenties 2023-2033

BECOMING AN ENTREPRENEUR

PAUL
ZANE
PILZER

Becoming An Entrepreneur (Expanded Edition)

Published by ZCI, Inc.

For ordering information or special discounts for bulk purchases as well as booking Paul Zane Pilzer to speak at your event, visit www.paulzanepilzer.com or email reed@paulzanepilzer.com.

Cover design by Zeljka Vukojevic, Kim Baker, and Lisa Dang Pilzer

Interior book design by Reid Kirby

Editing by Hilary Jastram, Paula Phelps, Judith Emmert and Zachary Primo

Publishing management by Reed Bilbray

ISBN: 978-1-7379916-0-1 (Second Impression)

BUSINESS & ECONOMICS / Entrepreneurship

DEDICATION

This book is dedicated to you. Especially if you are just getting started on your first adventure as an entrepreneur.

BECOMING AN ENTREPRENEUR

PAUL ZANE PILZER

CONTENTS

DEDICATION

PREFACE

PART I: SCHOOL (1966–1976)

CHAPTER 1: DISCOVERING PASSION 1

ADDITION A: SINGING ALEINU AT THE ALTNEUSCHUL 15

CHAPTER 2: HOW I BECAME AN ECONOMIST 23

CHAPTER 3: FINDING A WAY TO TAKE CARE OF TONY 37

CHAPTER 4: GOD LOVES SAVERS 45

CHAPTER 5: ART, CREATIVITY & BUSINESS 53

CHAPTER 6: MY FIRST HERO–J.I. RODALE 65

ADDITION B: J.I. RODALE 77

CHAPTER 7: REVELING IN REJECTION 85

CHAPTER 8: TYPING: MY PERSONAL KEY TO SUCCESS 99

CHAPTER 9: MY FIRST DAY AT WHARTON 107

CHAPTER 10: MY FIRST MACROECONOMICS CLASS. 117

ADDITION C: ECONOMIC ALCHEMY AND UNLIMITED WEALTH. . . 123

CHAPTER 11: THE WHARTON GUIDE TO THE STOCK MARKET . . . 131

PART II: CITIBANK (1976 - 1981)

CHAPTER 12: MY FIRST DAY AT CITIBANK 145

CHAPTER 13: HAPPINESS = REALITY MINUS EXPECTATIONS 157

CHAPTER 14: ELEANOR RIGBY–ALL THE LONELY PEOPLE 165

CHAPTER 15: MY CAREER AT CITIBANK TAKES OFF 175

CHAPTER 16: TEACHING AT NEW YORK UNIVERSITY 191

CHAPTER 17: DOING WINDFALL DEALS AT CITIBANK. 221
CHAPTER 18: HOW I MADE MY FIRST $1 MILLION 241
CHAPTER 19: LEAVING CITIBANK WITH $100 MILLION 265

PART III: ENTREPRENEURSHIP (1981 - PRESENT)

CHAPTER 20: MY FIRST $10 MILLION DEAL 291
ADDITION D: A BRIEF HISTORY OF THE S&L INDUSTRY 335
CHAPTER 21: MEMPHIS: MY FIRST $100 MILLION DEAL 341
CHAPTER 22: OTHER PEOPLE'S MONEY. 391
CHAPTER 23: PRESIDENT REAGAN CALLS ME DISHONEST 409
CHAPTER 24: MY LITIGATION WITH APPLE COMPUTER 419
CHAPTER 25: CUTTING IN LINE 439
CHAPTER 26: FIXING THINGS THAT AREN'T BROKEN 449
CHAPTER 27: ADVENTURES IN PROGRESS 455

ACKNOWLEDGMENTS
ABOUT THE AUTHOR

Entrepreneurs and revolutionaries are the same kinds of people born into different circumstances. Both see the status quo in need of change, and both are willing to take the risks and reap the rewards of changing it.

Paul Zane Pilzer

The Wellness Revolution

BECOMING AN ENTREPRENEUR

PAUL ZANE PILZER

PREFACE

I am deeply grateful for the adventures I've had as an entrepreneur, especially when I think about how I didn't know what I didn't know when I started out. I am writing this book to be for my readers the mentor I wish I had when I began my entrepreneurial journey.

In reflecting on their careers, entrepreneurs typically tell of their quantifiable end results, such as how much money they've earned, how many employees they've hired, and how many customers they've served. Yet, the real reward that comes from being an entrepreneur derives from what numbers can't measure: how happy you've been serving your customers and how happy you've been on your journey to become an entrepreneur.

Most successful entrepreneurs will say that their happiest time was when they were just starting out, or the first time their startup failed, and they had to retool—although they didn't realize it back then because they were under such intense pressure to survive.

Many new businesses fail in what they originally set out to do but succeed when they apply what they've learned in real-time to fix their product or distribution. When you fail, remember that the process of fixing failures builds synapses between you and God, your employees, your suppliers, your investors, and your customers, turning a collection of disparate individuals into a cohesive organization where each stakeholder's success depends on the contribution of the other stakeholders.

Speaking of failing and retooling in real-time, I'm reminded of the first time I embarrassingly had to ask an investor for permission to scrap and rebuild the business plan. His reply: "Of course, Paul. We're backing you, not some idea whose time may have already come and gone."

The Stories I've Never Shared Outside Before

Today, 45 years after I became an entrepreneur and a college professor, my former associates and students tell me their most important learnings came from the personal stories I shared with them on the late nights after we closed a big deal or after class. These were confidential stories I shared about my family, schooling, college, Citibank, colleagues, the White House, and working for myself.

This book is the compilation of those stories, what I learned from each story and how you can apply my lessons to create and manage your own entrepreneurial stories.

The stories are divided chronologically into three parts of my life: School (Chapters 1 - 11), Citibank (Chapters 12 - 19), and Entrepreneurship (Chapters 20 - 27). They include:

1. How, when Apple Computer had to pay my startup $250,000 cash for stepping on our trademarks, we turned their mistake from a $250,000 earnings expense on their income statement into a $250,000 asset on their balance sheet, calling it a non-refundable deposit on a $1.25 million purchase order—a purchase order that jump-started our company and brought me my first $3 million in venture capital (see *Chapter 24: My Litigation with Apple Computer*, page 419).

2. How I got rejected at Wharton Graduate Business School as an MBA candidate on April 10, 1974, but was accepted on April 17, 1974, and what you need to do to turn your rejections into acceptances (see *Chapter 7: Reveling in Rejection*, page 85).
3. How there is a business opportunity almost every time you are an unhappy customer serving similarly situated unhappy customers (see *Chapter 18: How I Made My First $1 Million*, page 241).
4. How I learned the formula for happiness at Citibank (see *Chapter 13: Happiness = Reality Minus Expectations*, page 157).
5. How I became an entrepreneur while still working at Citibank and learned to use the resources of my employer to start my real estate, teaching and writing careers (see *Chapter 16: Teaching at New York University*, page 191).
6. How I got my first book published by Simon & Schuster after being rejected for three straight years (see *Chapter 22: Other People's Money*, page 391).
7. How I reexamined my professional life when my hero questioned the integrity of my business dealings (see *Chapter 23: President Reagan Calls Me Dishonest*, page 409).

Should You Quit Before You're Fired?

My father was not an entrepreneur by choice—no one would hire him. He never attended high school and didn't speak English until after arriving in the United States as a refugee from Eastern Europe.

My dad was a great coach and encouraged me through my overlapping careers. Sometimes, he wanted me to work for someone else, like Citibank, NYU, or the government; and sometimes, he wanted me to be an entrepreneur. Still, other times, he wasn't sure what I should do. But as you'll see in *Chapter 15: My Career at Citibank Takes Off* (page 175), if he were alive today, he'd probably want me to be an entrepreneur, but not for the reasons you might suspect.

He'd want me to be an entrepreneur for the job security that comes from employing yourself.

Today, when it comes to the question, "Should you quit before you're fired?" the only item remaining to be considered by many employees is "when?" This is a question I hope to help you answer for yourself by examining my experiences as a serial entrepreneur versus as an executive working for a bank, where my career path was not straightforward. In some cases, I was following corporate culture as an employee, and in others, I was an "intrapreneur," carving out startup businesses within the existing corporation—essentially bucking corporate culture with permission and encouragement from my boss.

How to Make the Most of This Book

This book is not written like a conventional non-fiction book; it's not always linear, nor are the stories always chronological. The narrative follows my experiences as an entrepreneur and intrapreneur, starting with my first job in middle school at age fourteen. You'll notice that although the venue and time change with each story, the people

I meet along the journey and what I learn from each of them are cumulative. The greatest reward from a career in business comes from the lifelong friendships you develop along the way.

Depending on where you are in your own entrepreneurial journey, you may want to start at the Table of Contents and read first the stories of immediate relevance to your career. I've written them so you can jump in at any point.

In the pages that follow, you'll meet some of the fascinating people I've had the honor of calling my friends, colleagues, teachers, students, and mentors through the years. You'll join me in learning valuable life lessons from them and from my own mistakes.

And, like my students and business associates, I hope that by the end of this book, you'll feel as if you've found a new mentor or made a new friend—or hopefully both!

BECOMING AN ENTREPRENEUR

PAUL ZANE PILZER

PART I

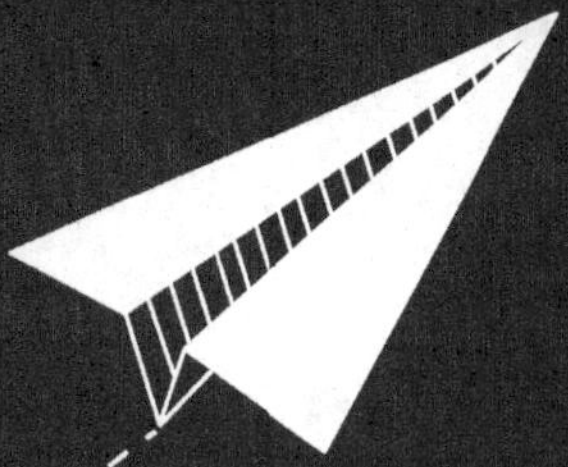

SCHOOL (1966–1976)

BECOMING AN ENTREPRENEUR

PAUL ZANE PILZER

CHAPTER 1

DISCOVERING PASSION

Let your passion lead you in everything you do.

Amateur radio, more popularly known as "ham radio," was *the* big thing for electronics enthusiasts and science nerds from 1920 until the late 1990s when the internet, email, and cell phones took over. I remember the first time I discovered ham radio. It was 1965 and I was 11, visiting my cousin in Brooklyn with my dad. When my cousin showed me his ham radio station setup and demonstrated how to communicate with people all around the world by tuning-in on ham radio frequencies, using radiotelegraphy (Morse code or CW), and single-sideband (SSB) modulation (voice)—I was *blown away*.

At home, we had a short-wave receiver that played the BBC, Radio Moscow, and original source material on the Cold War. Listening to those political broadcasts made me feel important.

I began reading everything I could get my hands on about ham radio. I subscribed to magazines and catalogs like *QST*, *Popular Electronics*, and *CQ Magazine*, and stayed up all night reading them over and over. In order to become a ham radio operator, I first had to obtain a Novice license by passing a radio theory test and a Morse code test. The Novice test was given at the headquarters for *CQ Magazine*, which was located across the street from my high school in Port Washington. I flunked the test the first time I took it and was devastated.

After studying hard, I passed on my second try and received my Novice ham radio license with the call sign WN2DDR, a unique code that identified me and my location. The "N" in WN2DDR stood for Novice, the "W" meant the United States, and the "2" meant New York and New Jersey.

Although my Novice license restricted me from using voice outside of very high frequency bands (VHF), it was still very exciting for me to communicate with others in Morse code. If we did not speak the same language, we used Q-codes, a standardized set of radio shorthand composed of 3-letter combinations that begin with "Q" to communicate. For example, "QTH?" means "What's your location?" Over the next four years, I passed the tests for the higher-level licenses—General and Advanced—and was issued a new call sign, WA2DDR (which meant that I was no longer a Novice!) and could use *my voice* over the airways.

In junior high I was a social outcast. I was too short to play sports and wore thick-rimmed glasses. I was desperate for a different life. Ham radio gave me a new identity, a window into the broader world, a social network, and a *community*—I loved it.

When ham radio operators made contact for the first time, they often mailed each other QSL cards, or *QSL* for short—a custom-designed postcard containing their call sign, time of contact, and other technical details to confirm their on-air contact and to commemorate the event. "QSL" is technically the Q-code used to confirm receipt of a message.

I combined ham radio with my love of chess and played games

A QSL card from call sign UW3EH, located in Moscow, Russia, on September 1, 1969

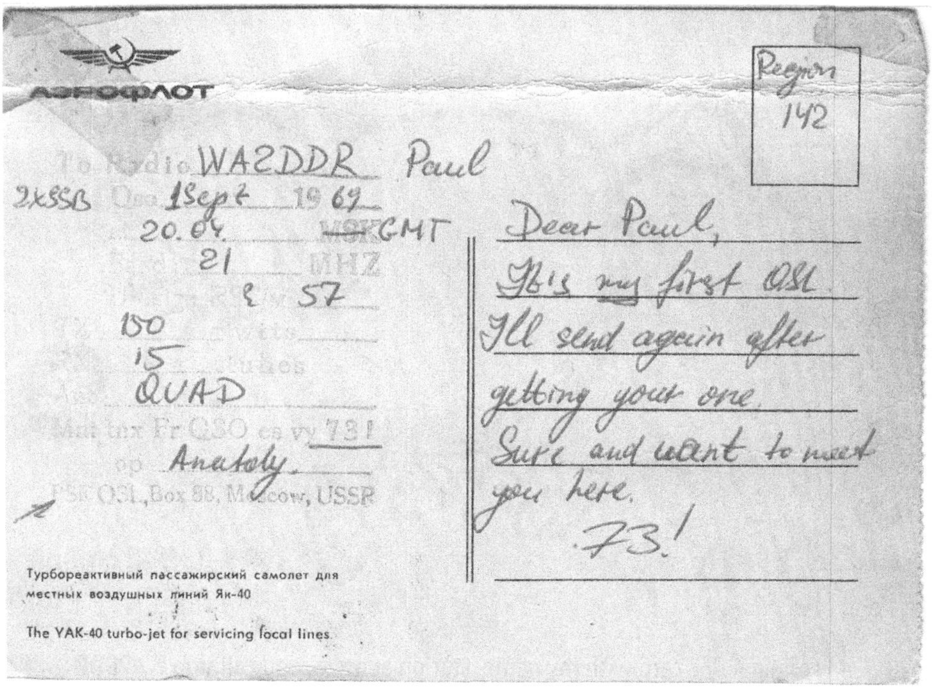

The back side of the QSL from Moscow, Russia, showing details commemorating our on-air contact—date, time, signal report, frequency, location—and a typical message hoping to meet in person one day

My original QSL card with my name, station address, and call sign WA2DDR over the air with chess players *everywhere,* mostly from the former USSR. By the time I was 14, I had already exchanged QSLs with hams from more than *100* countries. When I traveled to Moscow for a student chess tournament in high school, I was able to invite several Russian friends I met through ham radio to come watch me compete in person. It was 1968, and I felt like a spy in the Cold War.

Since I was obsessed with ***CQ Magazine*** and other industry publications, I considered myself an electronics buff and kept up with everything that was happening in the world of radio, ham radio, and electronics. I learned how to design and build ham radio equipment from tinkering with tubes, telephone wiring, and electronics parts from busted radios, TVs, and telephones my neighbors threw out. Later in high school, with friends I met through ham radio, we built our own blue box to hack telephone companies for free long-distance calls. I even wrote an article about modulating an FM signal with a two-meter rig that was published in ***CQ Magazine.***

My passion for ham radio landed me my dream job in high school at Frank's TV and Radio in Port Washington, New York. From the time I was in eighth grade around age 12, while other kids my age were busy with sports, I would hang out at Frank's afterschool, asking questions and talking to Frank, the owner, about electronics. Frank launched his business repairing radios after World War II and expanded to selling and repairing TVs when they became a household essential in the 1950s. In the late 1960s, Frank further grew his business and began installing and fixing car stereos.

I loved hanging out at Frank's and I tried to impress Frank with my extensive knowledge and interest in car stereos. I diligently paid attention to how his employees replaced car stereos and installed new speakers in different models of cars. It was thrilling to watch each employee problem-solve through the various custom installations when a new car rolled in.

When I turned 14, the minimum age to obtain working papers in the State of New York, Frank finally offered me a job and started me at $1.60 an hour, the then-federal minimum wage. Turns out my small stature was my biggest asset and gave me an unfair advantage at work. I easily climbed into trunks to install rear speakers and comfortably slid under dashboards to swap out car stereos. I took great pride in working at Frank's and was eager to do all the petty tasks that no one else wanted to do like sweep the floors, be the runner, and take out the trash.

The adults working for Frank in the repair shop were making $3-$5 an hour. Soon enough, Frank made me his go-to guy for car stereo repairs and one day, out of the blue, he gave me an unsolicited raise to $3 an hour, which was considered an enormous amount back then. There I was at 14 and earning almost *twice* the minimum wage. I didn't know of anyone in our high school making that kind of money.

We were at a turning point in automotive sound history with the rise of the aftermarket stereo system. Before 1968, most cars were equipped with only a standard AM radio and basic speakers, but as more and more drivers desired more from their sound system, they upgraded to aftermarket FM car stereos, high-quality speakers, 8-track players, and, by the end of the 60s, cassette players that let you play your own mixtape you made at home.

We started carrying a limited line of audio equipment at Frank's which we used to upsell customers who came in to get their car stereo fixed. Our salesmen would say, "Sure, we can fix that, but *maybe* instead of just fixing it, how would you like this new 8-track player with an FM radio? And look at this woofer and these tweeter speakers!" It was the first time in history that cars could be customized to have exceptional sound quality and drivers could not resist the phenomenal listening experience.

At Frank's, I learned how to focus on what the customer may need, and not necessarily what they came in for. I watched and learned as Frank greeted distraught customers coming in to get their broken car radios repaired, and then convinced them to spend substantially more money to upgrade to a brand new car stereo with the latest features. These customers were overjoyed and *grateful* when they drove off with their new car stereo installation.

Luckily for Frank, we loved working on new custom installations from scratch. It was too early in the evolution of car audio, so fancy installation kits customized for each vehicle did not exist. Instead, I would drill a hole to get started and use a simple handsaw to cut holes in the car's door panels and install the speakers that way.

Frank was a decent man and fair to work for. My parents were proud of me for having a paying job, and I loved working. I loved the freedom I had from earning my own money.

One day, a woman brought in her 1965 Volkswagen Beetle, one of the most popular and affordable vehicles on the road. It had an aftermarket Audiovox AM/FM car stereo that was out of warranty and a broken built-in cassette player that needed to be fixed.

Frank told me to be especially careful while working on her car because her 1965 VW Beetle was based on a 6-volt system, *not* a 12-volt system like most cars in those days. VW made 6-volt system cars through the 1966 model year and began making 12-volt system cars in 1967. If Frank did not point that out, I probably would have hooked her stereo up to a 12-volt power source without thinking and burned it out completely.

First, I turned over the engine and clicked on the stereo—*nothing.* Then, I pulled the stereo out of the car, put it on my workbench, and hooked it up to a set of speakers and a 6-volt battery eliminator. The radio worked perfectly on the workbench but was completely dead when I put it back in the car. I checked the wiring, the car battery, the ignition switch, and anything that might prevent the stereo from getting power. I performed every test I could think of but could not get the car stereo to play inside the vehicle. For hours I went back and forth, pulling the radio out and testing it on my bench—where it worked perfectly—then putting it back in the car, only to be greeted by nothing. *Not even radio static.*

It didn't make *any* sense!

After about three hours, Frank came out to check my progress. I told him that it wasn't working, and I didn't know what else to try. Frank walked over to the car, leaned inside, and looked under the dashboard. Then he stood up and walked around to the front of the car.

"Paul!" he said, pointing to the front hood, "Did you check the *fuse?*"

Just like a fuse box in a home, every car has fuses that send power to different electrical components of the car, and when one burns out, you simply replace that single fuse. It's easy to tell which fuse needs replacing because the fried part on the exposed metal fuse resembles a burned-out filament inside a light bulb. Back then, fuses cost about 10 cents each.

In most cars, the fuse box was located on the left-side panel below the steering wheel, just above the driver's feet. You couldn't miss the fuse box if you put your head under the steering wheel inside the car—it was right in your face. But in this and every other 1965 Volkswagen Beetle, the entire fuse box was *not* inside the passenger compartment.

Frank popped open the front hood of the 1965 VW Beetle, which, unlike most other cars, did not contain the engine—it was a trunk in the front. Located in that front trunk, right in front of the steering column shaft, was a fuse box with colorful ceramic fuses clearly visible through a transparent plastic cover. I was horrified by my oversight when I looked closely to clearly see inside a burned-out white 15-amp ceramic fuse with the word "Radio" next to it.

We had every fuse imaginable hanging on a wall in the shop. And, Frank had a checklist we were supposed to work through, as standard operating procedure. When a car came in with any kind of electrical problem, the first thing we were *supposed* to do was use a voltmeter to test if a current was being sent from the fuse box. We would know immediately if the problem was likely a fuse and could resolve it in a few minutes for just a couple of dollars.

But in my haste, I had missed that first step entirely. And because the fuse box was not in the car passenger compartment but in the front trunk, it hadn't even occurred to me to check for it there. Out of sight, out of mind. I was embarrassed and disappointed in myself because I wasted half my day on such a basic thing. I knew that I would *never* make that mistake again and tried to move on, but I couldn't help but replay where I went wrong again and again.

If only I had just followed standard operating procedure and used the checklist, I never would have missed the fuse, regardless of the design of the car and the placement of the fuse box.

When the woman came back around 5 p.m. to pick up her car, I overheard Frank tell her that her car was fixed as he handed her the bill.

Her eyes widened as she stared at the amount due.

"Oh, my goodness! Is it *really* this much?" she asked, blindsided by the sticker shock. Frank did not review the bill with me beforehand, so I assumed it would be only a few dollars since all we did was change out a fuse.

Frank had charged her $49—for three hours of labor at $12 an hour, plus $13 for parts—the equivalent of more than $400 today.

Of course, Frank did not tell her that, due to *my* incompetence, we squandered *three hours* by testing her radio repeatedly to find out it was simply a 10-cent fuse that needed replacing, when we should have determined that in the first place. Instead, in a sleazy attempt to justify the bill, not only did Frank bill her for the three hours I foolishly misspent, but he completely made up a list of services and parts to reflect a sizable amount of work we did *not* provide.

Stunned and speechless, she reluctantly paid the invoice. I watched anxiously as she drove off and wondered if she knew she was being duped. Why did Frank decide to charge her so much for such an inexpensive and simple fix? And why did he lie? I needed to know.

"Uh, Frank, did you see the bill for the Volkswagen?" I asked.

"Of course, I did. I'm the one who wrote it up."

I remarked that the woman had seemed upset by how high her bill was, and he responded, "Yeah, Paul, you screwed up on this one."

"I know I did," I said, confused. "But *I* screwed up, and you made her pay for it? It was *my* fault!"

"Well then," he replied facetiously, looking directly at me. "Why don't you go find her and give her back her $49? *Someone* has to pay for those three hours you spent working on her car."

At my wages of three bucks an hour, I thought to myself, the bill should have been $9, plus 10 cents for the cost of the fuse—not more than *five times* that amount!

"It's not *just* your salary, Paul," Frank explained, thrilled at the opportunity to lecture me on business. "It's the overhead, the rent, your training, *all* the expenses that it takes to keep this business running. Our deal is that we charge each customer the same $12 an hour, by the hour, because you don't know what's broken with their radio. They aren't just paying us for our *services.* They're paying us for our *experience* and the years it took us to learn what we do. And this time, because you are still learning, it took you too long to find out what was wrong—*three hours long.*"

I was guilt-ridden and could not get the woman's resentful expression out of my mind. I was unsure about what to do or what to think. I didn't have the money to pay the woman back, and even though it was my fault, I still felt I deserved to be paid for the three hours I did put in. But I didn't think she should have had to pay for my mistake.

At home that night, I presented the problem to my parents. Dad was the person I could trust from both a business standpoint and from a moral perspective, but he was equally perplexed. Dad was less upset than I was about charging the woman for three hours of labor at $12 an hour. After all, the sign on our wall did state our shop rate. He thought our major sin was lying to the woman about the extra parts we had replaced. We talked about it, went over every possible solution, and debated it for several days.

As we wrangled with what should have been done, I wanted Dad to give me the answer that would make everyone happy, and the fact of the matter was, there wasn't one. In the end, the woman was out $49, equivalent to about $400 today, and there was nothing I could do about it.

I never got over my disdain for how the fuse incident went down. Was Frank really a boss I wanted to keep working for and someone I wanted to continue learning from? It is not easy to respect a dishonest person and it is even harder to work for someone you don't respect—especially when you are working so hard to build *their* business empire and knowing deep down the kind of person they *really* are. I finally quit working for Frank a year later when I was 15 to start my own business on *my* terms.

I set up my shop out of my parents' garage and installed new car stereos from scratch. I earned the equivalent of $10-$20 an hour, all for myself, on each installation. The best part about having my own business was that I charged a flat rate between $50-$75 to do a complete installation, regardless of how long it took me. There was no opportunity or incentive for me to pad a bill. My father called that "being on the same side as my customer."

I never forgot about the fuse incident and think about it often whenever I am faced with a moral dilemma. I believe it has shaped the way I treat people, how I design compensation plans, and how I approach problems in business. I didn't realize it then, but I was embarking on a big picture stage of my life. I didn't see myself as just doing my job but contributing to a bigger purpose. Not only was I serving people and making them happy, but I also had a moral obligation to do so with honesty and integrity. When I first started at Frank's, I was thrilled to be a part of a new industry and enjoyed working for him, but I really loved *serving* the customers and working on their behalf. Working for myself was empowering—my big picture had grown to more fully include me. I was shaping and creating customers' experiences as I was feeding *my* passion and learning to orchestrate the events in *my* life.

BECOMING AN ENTREPRENEUR

PAUL ZANE PILZER

ADDITION A

Singing Aleinu at the Altneuschul
Prague, Friday Evening, July 1968

In July 1968, at age 14, I traveled with my mother to Moscow, USSR, where I participated in a high school chess tournament. After the tournament, we flew to Prague on a Friday afternoon and decided to attend Friday evening *Shabbat* services at the Altneuschul, the oldest and most famous active synagogue in Europe (built 1270 AD). My mother arranged with the concierge at our hotel for a car to take us to and from the synagogue. We both dressed that evening the same as we did for *Shabbat* services at home—my mother wore jewelry and a dress, and I wore a sports jacket and tie.

Prague at that time was still recovering from WWII, when the Nazis exterminated virtually all the Jews in what later became The Czech Republic. Everywhere we went that summer in Eastern Europe, people spoke of the Nazi occupation and atrocities as if they had happened yesterday instead of two decades earlier. The area we now call The Czech Republic was liberated by the Soviet Union at the end of WWII, except the Soviets never left. The country (then called Czechoslovakia) became ruled by the local communist party with strong influence from Moscow. In 1967, an uprising by Czech intellectuals against the communists and the Soviets had begun, which eventually led to a full-scale military invasion by the Soviet Union in August 1968. Thus, in July 1968, when we visited Prague, tensions were very high, with many Czech citizens suspecting

Altneuschul (Credit: Øyvind Holmstad, Wikimedia Commons, 2014)

strangers to be spies working for the Soviet Union.

That evening, my mother and I arrived at the Altneuschul in the middle of the Friday night *Shabbat* service. As we took our places in the back row, we each felt the gaze of the congregants, who didn't know what to make of their well-dressed visitors. Everyone but us was very old. A man with a limp came over to hand me a *siddur* (prayer book). As he reached across my face to hand a second *siddur* to my mother, his coat sleeve slid up, and I was shocked to see a six-digit number tattooed on his forearm.

I opened the *siddur* and tried in vain to locate where the congregation was in the service. Even though I had been a *bar mitzvah* only a year earlier, I couldn't recognize any of the prayers in the *siddur*. The text was very small, with words in faded Hebrew without vowels. Not only couldn't I read the Hebrew letters, I didn't recognize any of the words or the melodies of the service. I later learned that the prayers were in Yiddish, written with Hebrew letters.

My mother began a conversation in Yiddish with the old man who gave us the *siddurim*, pausing every few sentences to translate for me what was being said. She explained to the man that we were Jews from New York who had just come from Moscow. While nothing she spoke about seemed consequential, you could feel how suspicious everyone was about who we were and why we were there.

Another old man walked over to me and opened my *siddur* to where we were in the service. Then he cupped his hand around his ear and leaned toward me so he could hear me pray above the din of the other congregants. I was embarrassed that I couldn't read a word or utter a sound.

You could feel throughout the building how untrusted and unwanted my mother and I were in their *shul* during their Friday night service. The lines on the faces of each congregant told us that they each had a fascinating personal history to tell … but we were not going to be hearing any of their stories that evening.

Then, just as my mother was motioning to me that we should leave, everyone stood up and began a new prayer. I recognized the first words and the melody, which I knew by heart. The prayer was *Aleinu*, the most important prayer in the Jewish liturgy after the "*Kaddish*," and a prayer several times older than the Altneuschul itself.

As I finished singing the first sentence, *Aleinu l'shabeach la'Adon hakol*, the man who had cupped his hand around his ear ran over and pointed happily at my face. Then he sang the second sentence, *atet gedulah l'yotzer b'reishit*, with the same melody and pronunciation, only louder. Then I sang the third sentence even louder. By the fourth sentence, the whole congregation had joined in, singing louder and louder and with more and more expression. Everyone was smiling, and when we reached the end of *Aleinu*, we hugged each other.

When the *Shabbat* service ended, we were invited into a room next to the chapel with a large table that was from the Middle Ages. We dined on *challah* and warm schnapps while we spoke for hours. At first, in answer to my mother's questions, we talked about the Holocaust. But our hosts were more interested in talking about the last 700 years than the last 25 years. I learned, and never forgot, how the Jewish community of Prague was once the leading Jewish community in the world.

In the early 1700s, Jews were one-fourth of the city's population, and more Jews lived in Prague than anywhere else on the planet. I also learned how Prague and the Altneuschul itself was the center of Jewish mysticism (Kabbalah) and the residence of The Golem.

We returned to our hotel late that night and realized that we were starving. We had enjoyed our exciting evening so much that we had forgotten to eat dinner and by then all the restaurants were closed.

It has been 49 years since I first visited the Altneuschul in 1968. I've been back to Prague several times and attended *Shabbat* services at the Altneuschul. But no matter where I have been on the 2,500+ *Shabbats* I've celebrated since 1968, every time I sing *Aleinu* on Friday night, I always remember my mother taking me to the Altneuschul.

BECOMING AN ENTREPRENEUR

PAUL ZANE PILZER

Chapter 1 - Learnings

1. Let your passion lead you in everything you do, not just the things you do for compensation. My early passion for ham radio led directly to my getting a high paying job, and that job led me to start my own business. What are your passions, and how can you profit from them?

2. Focus on what your customer needs, not just their initial request. When a customer came in with a broken radio, Frank made them happier by selling them a new stereo. And his employees (like me) loved doing new installations from scratch. How are you serving your customers in your job or business? Is there anything you can do differently to improve your interactions?

3. Take time before starting a task to ask questions, and don't start a new task without a checklist and timetable of how and when you expect to finish. I should have checked for a fuse first and would have done so if I had been following a checklist. What is a task that could benefit from the use of a checklist and timetable?

4. There will always be situations when you don't clearly see the right action—do your best, remedy your mistakes where possible, and move on. Don't get hung up on what you should have done, especially if there's no clear path to correcting yourself. Reflect on the first time you made a mistake that could have been avoided. What was the mistake, and would you do anything differently if confronted with the same situation?

5. Every (and I mean every) transaction and experience can and should be a learning experience. Embrace the learning process versus being overwhelmed by it. Identify your learning style and use it the next time you feel overwhelmed by a learning process.

BECOMING AN ENTREPRENEUR

PAUL ZANE PILZER

CHAPTER 2

HOW I BECAME AN ECONOMIST

Most people spend 90% of their waking lives worrying about money—how to earn it, how to spend it, how to save it, and (hopefully) how to give it away when they die. I originally became an economist to bring home to the people I loved the most the information I felt they needed the most.

I was born to immigrant parents in Brooklyn, New York. They often told me the most important thing in life was family. Our immediate family would get together with my mother's relatives on Saturdays and with my father's relatives on Sundays. My father's family was religious and wouldn't travel on the Sabbath. However, when our extended family got together, I noticed that most of my relatives didn't talk about family; the conversation centered around money—how to earn it, how to get a better job, how to buy a car, how to buy a house, etc. As I watched them argue back and forth, it seemed no one had the right answers when it came to monetary issues.

Before entering college, I never thought much about money. During high school, I was a science and math nerd and always had good part-time jobs that paid enough so I could buy the things I wanted. I applied to engineering schools on the assumption that I'd pursue a career in science and accepted an offer from Lehigh University in Pennsylvania. I began college at 17 and was younger

Paul Pilzer was a "Schreiber Times" editor. He was also President of the Chess Club and a member of the Radio, A.V. and T.V. squads.

This picture is from my 1971 high school yearbook.

than most of my class, not because I was especially smart, but because I was born in January and my parents had enrolled me early in kindergarten. Although I had great jobs throughout high school and college, my father paid for all of my college expenses from his savings and often told me how proud he was of both of us—me for getting into a good college and him for saving enough money so I could attend without student loans. Of course, this was 1971, when a year's expenses at a private college—tuition, room and board, books, and incidentals—cost less than $3,300, equivalent to about $20,000 today.

Flunking Out of Engineering School

At Lehigh, I became the first EE (Electrical Engineering) student in my class to wash out, and I did so in less than four weeks. I told my friends that I had simply changed direction because I didn't like having to learn the physics and math that formed the foundation of electrical engineering. In truth, I found myself woefully behind my classmates, both academically and socially.

Lehigh approved my request to quit EE, and I transferred from the College of Engineering to the College of Arts and Sciences. Nonetheless, my first semester grades were poor: a "C" in economics was the highest grade on my transcript. Years later, I jokingly told my parents that I knew back then that I would have to become a world-famous economist because economics was my best subject.

Learning How to Play the Grade Game

During the second semester, my grades improved significantly, partially because I had studied game theory in my first-semester Calculus class and was able to apply what I had learned. Technically, game theory, the use of mathematics to analyze competing strategies, applies only to two or more rational players, but I figured out how to apply its principles to myself and the university. Here's how it worked:

Each semester at Lehigh was 15 weeks long, and you could elect to take a pass/fail course outside your major for up to six weeks into the semester, as long as you completed at least four courses each semester for a letter grade. You could also drop a course entirely, without having any record you took it, up to ten weeks into the 15-week semester. These rules were designed to encourage students to take difficult courses outside their major without worrying about hurting their GPA or even passing the course. At the beginning of my second semester, I enrolled in eight courses instead of the normal five. When a grade fell below an A, I planned to drop the course or convert it to pass/fail. My goal was to get five A's in the second semester and earn academic credit for as many courses as possible.

But then I stumbled onto what I now call The Most Important Rule for Success.

The Most Important Rule for Success

Once I had signed up for eight courses at the beginning of my second semester, I became concerned about scheduling my time. *How could I physically get to each class and build in time for all of my classes, let alone have time for studying and homework?* Each three-credit course consisted of three one-hour sessions in class per week, plus homework, with some science and math courses demanding four hours of in-class time per week.

I created a large paper calendar, marking the times each week that I would attend each class and noting the hours that I would devote to studying and homework. I didn't expect this challenging schedule to last long because I anticipated I would drop or elect pass/fail in up to three of my eight courses.

When I was done with my calendar, I was sure I had made a mistake; most of my calendar was still blank. I took out a separate yellow pad and began to check and re-check my work. Then it dawned on me what I had done wrong.

I had assumed there were 80 hours in a week, but there weren't. There were 168 hours in a week! That meant even if I slept a generous eight hours a night, seven days a week, totaling 56 hours of sleep, there were still 112 (168 minus 56) hours per week to attend 24 hours of class and do up to 88 hours of studying and homework!

I couldn't believe my good fortune. I felt like an explorer who had started their journey believing there were 80 hours in a week, only to discover 88 *more* hours in a week (168 total) to get them to their destination.

I asked myself: *How come I've never figured this out before?*

Does Everyone Know There are 168 Hours in a Week?

I wondered if I was the only one with the knowledge of the true numbers of hours per week, so I asked a few students in the University Center. After introducing myself and the topic at hand, I said: "Quick, without thinking about it or calculating, how many hours are there in a week?" Almost everyone got it wrong, with most answering somewhere between forty and 100 hours per week.

Take a moment now, call someone you know, or walk up to them, and ask, "Quick, without thinking about it, how many hours are there in a week?" I'm still amazed that word hasn't gotten out about this "discovery" that I made in 1971!

In my second semester at Lehigh, I didn't drop any of my eight courses because I loved the subjects and the professors too much! Looking back, it was my new attitude toward schoolwork, along with my renewed self-confidence in my grades, that made me succeed. With only three hours a week in class to devote to each course and three to six hours spent outside class, the finite time I had left to spend on each course was precious. This made it both challenging and enjoyable. During my first semester at college and in high school, I would typically spend two to three hours procrastinating, aka "getting ready," before spending an hour studying or doing homework.

At Lehigh, with every assignment, I would tell myself: *I only have* X *hours to understand this topic, so I better get working on it right away and not allow any distractions.* I also stopped taking notes in class and instead focused on listening to my professors. *Why learn the material after class from notes when I could learn it the first time during the lectures if I really listened?*

Not only did I finish my second semester with good grades, I kept taking extra courses each semester and graduated from Lehigh with my BA in six semesters over three years, saving a year's tuition. That also translated into starting work and graduate school a year early.

Two years later, when I enrolled at Wharton for my MBA, I convinced the graduate school dean at Wharton to permit me to take extra courses based on my Lehigh undergraduate experience—after all, I had worked hard to graduate college in less than three years. He conceded. His belief in me paid off, and with more hard work, I earned my MBA eight months ahead of schedule.

As I started my second semester at Lehigh and later on, my MBA program at Wharton, I loved my courses, and I began to see the laws of economics ruling everywhere, in every course, internally and externally. Internally, the materials available to study in each class—from labs in science to computers in engineering, to books in English, even to the salary and tenure of my professors—were all determined by laws of economics. Externally, everything in the world outside class was ruled by the laws of economics. In the economics classes themselves, I saw everywhere the famous line of John Maynard Keynes, the founder of modern economics, who said that when it comes to economics, "the world is ruled by little else."

> *"The ideas of economists and political philosophers, both when they are right and when they are wrong, are more powerful than is commonly understood. Indeed, the world is ruled by little else. Practical men, who believe themselves to be quite exempt from any intellectual influences, are usually slaves of some defunct economist."*
>
> *John Maynard Keynes, 1883-1946*

Despite my fascination with economics at Lehigh and Wharton, I didn't major in economics or become an economist—because I knew something was wrong with the underlying concept behind economics.

At that time, most economic theories were based on scarcity. If anyone had any doubts about economics being based on scarcity, all they had to do was spend half a day on a gasoline line during the 1973 oil crisis or watch the cost of heating their home in 1974 soar above $500 a month from less than $100 a month! When it came to solving the big question—how government could improve life for everyone—the underlying belief in scarcity convinced people that you could not improve life for anyone without taking away an equal amount from someone else.

Unlimited Wealth—A Theory of Economics Based on Abundance

During the next 14 years, except for taking a detour into writing ***Other People's Money: The Inside Story of the S&L Crisis*** (Simon & Schuster, 1989), I spent my time developing a working theory of economics based on abundance. It was ready to be published in November 1990 in the form of ***Unlimited Wealth*** (Crown Publishers, 1990). Prior to publication, my publisher had sent out "Advance Reading Copies" (ARCs, also called "galleys") to a chosen list of business leaders, critics, and book publishing executives.

I didn't care about the reception that would come from traditional economists or critics; I wanted to reach the practicing economists—my term for business people who create and manage the companies that are the backbone of the United States—who were out there making a difference every day in our economy.

On Wednesday, August 8, 1990, I received my highest accolade from the biggest practicing economist (i.e., businessperson) in the world. I knew if he found validity in my work, I was on the right track—after all, no one in the world had come close to his quantity of business experiences on which to test my formulas.

The conversation went like this when my secretary, Susie, rushed into my office that day:

"Paul, it's Sam Walton from Walmart, on the phone for you, right now, line one!"

"Susie, get his number, and we'll call him back."

"Paul, I think you want to talk with him now! He's the richest man in the world, and he's calling about your new book ***Unlimited***

Wealth—he saw you on ***Larry King Live*** last night."

"Susie, hang up, now," I said, annoyance creeping into my voice. I explained to Susie that there was no way Sam Walton was on the line; it was either a friend of mine playing a joke or a reporter using Sam's name to get me on the phone.

"I used to do stuff like that all the time," I explained to her dismissively. "That's why I told you to hang up." But Susie wouldn't back down. She insisted it was really Sam Walton, so I asked her for the number she had written down. When she handed it to me, I tore it up.

"If that was the real Sam Walton," I told her pointedly, "he's now waiting for our call. So, look up the main switchboard number for Walmart in Bentonville, Arkansas, and give them a call."

After a few minutes, Susie said she had Sam Walton on the line. I picked up the phone and said, "Hello, Mr. Walton, what can I do for you?"

"Hello, Professor Pilzer," he began. "This is Sam Walton from Walmart. I want to tell you that my sons and I enjoyed your new book. We don't typically have much time for you economist types, but your book, ***Unlimited Wealth***, makes sense to us. We just go out every day and do what we think God wants us to do."

He went on to say that my book had explained to him why certain things had worked for his business in the past and why others had not—especially when it came to improving total sales by focusing on sales per square foot of the existing stores versus just opening more stores.

"Likewise," he continued, "your book explains why some of

what we're doing now is working. But most importantly, your book is the first book I've seen that we can use to help guide our future. I wanted to thank you and congratulate you on it!"

I was amazed that I was having this conversation and told him I was happy he had enjoyed the book, and then I asked, "Would you put that in writing?"

"Of course," he replied. "But I'd also like to put it (the book) in Walmart."

Not only did Walmart carry ***Unlimited Wealth*** in its stores, but the next printing included Sam's quote on the back cover. Sam passed away a year later, at age 74, when there were 1,960 U.S. Walmart stores and 380,000 U.S. employees—there are approximately 10,800 stores today worldwide and 2.2 million employees.[1] ***Forbes*** magazine named Sam the richest person in the world from 1982-1988, and Walmart is, by far, the largest employer in the U.S. Even today, the combined net worth of Sam's children, about $247 billion on December 16, 2020, makes them the richest family in the world and would make Sam the richest person in the world if he were still alive.[2]

Fourteen years later, when I launched my first employee health benefits company, Extend Health, I traveled to Bentonville to meet with the management team at Walmart, and we used Sam's Wholesale Club as the vehicle to introduce defined contribution health benefits to America. Sam would have been proud.

---

1. Walmart. 2021. "Our Business." https://corporate.walmart.com/our-story/our-business.

2. ***Forbes***. "#1 Walton Family." December 16, 2020.

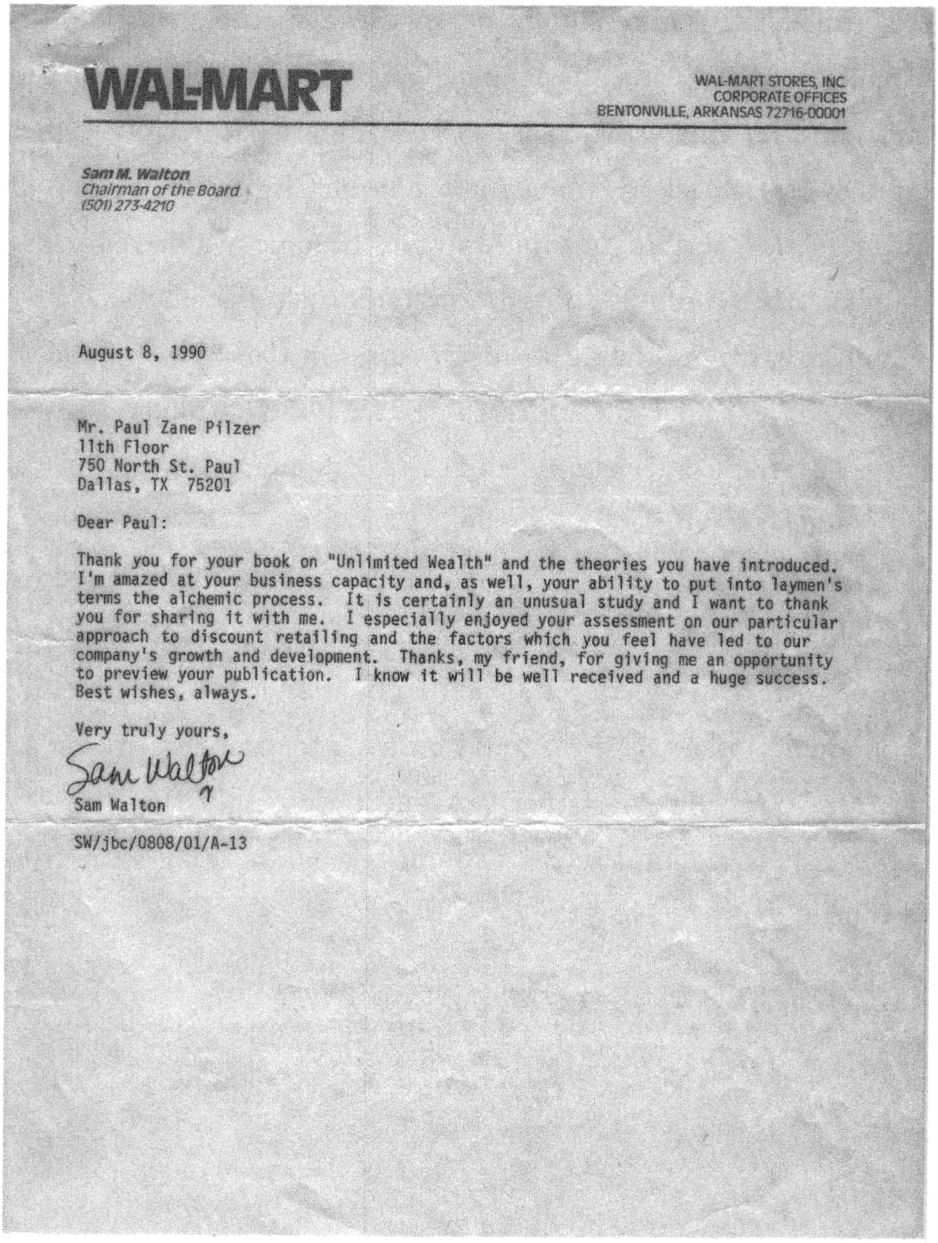

WAL-MART

WAL-MART STORES, INC.
CORPORATE OFFICES
BENTONVILLE, ARKANSAS 72716-00001

Sam M. Walton
Chairman of the Board
(501) 273-4210

August 8, 1990

Mr. Paul Zane Pilzer
11th Floor
750 North St. Paul
Dallas, TX 75201

Dear Paul:

Thank you for your book on "Unlimited Wealth" and the theories you have introduced. I'm amazed at your business capacity and, as well, your ability to put into laymen's terms the alchemic process. It is certainly an unusual study and I want to thank you for sharing it with me. I especially enjoyed your assessment on our particular approach to discount retailing and the factors which you feel have led to our company's growth and development. Thanks, my friend, for giving me an opportunity to preview your publication. I know it will be well received and a huge success. Best wishes, always.

Very truly yours,

Sam Walton

Sam Walton

SW/jbc/0808/01/A-13

Letter from Sam Walton, Founder/CEO of Walmart
August 8, 1990.

Perhaps even more importantly, in the 1980s, Sam Walton established the China supply chain infrastructure, which today supplies Walmart with approximately 90% of $514 billion in annual merchandise. This was no easy task; Walmart had to follow their product orders back to China and teach the Chinese the basic rules of production and finance for China to become Walmart's largest supplier. This enormous amount of trade that went both ways—Walmart has more than 200 major stores in China with 100,000 employees—has paved the path for peace between the two largest nations in the world, who together today represent almost 50% of the world's gross domestic product.

On that day in 1990, when Sam Walton told me he liked my economic theory based on abundance, I began to call myself an "economist." I switched from teaching finance at NYU to teaching economics, and I wished I could go back to Brooklyn to see my relatives, especially my father. I would have taught them how to achieve their economic goals without taking anything away from anyone else.

Chapter 2 - Learnings

1. How can you improve the conversations about money within your family?

2. Look up game theory online. How can you use game theory in your life to benefit your business or personal situation?

3. How many hours in a week did you think there were before you read this chapter? How has the knowledge that there are 168 hours in a week empowered you?

4. Try it yourself! Ask someone near you how many hours they think are in a week.

5. What do you think John Maynard Keynes meant when he said, "Practical men, who believe themselves to be quite exempt from any intellectual influences, are usually slaves of some defunct economist"?

BECOMING AN ENTREPRENEUR

PAUL ZANE PILZER

CHAPTER 3

FINDING A WAY TO TAKE CARE OF TONY

I am the youngest of three sons. All three of us worked together briefly in 1974 in the family business, making curtains and bedspreads. I remember this period as the unhappiest time in my work life and as the happiest time in my father's work life. Every event at work was a new opportunity for him to teach something to his children.[3]

"Elias!" I yelled. I only called my father by his first name when I was angry with him. "How could you give Tony another raise?"

Tony, a Puerto Rican cutter who we had trained and promoted from floor sweeper, had missed two days of work the week before. Since, as a cutter, he provided the material pieces to the people who did the sewing, his absence caused us to have to pay the guaranteed minimum, $2 per hour, to a pair of pieceworkers who had no work to sew.

"I had to," my father shrugged. "His wife had another baby. A boy this time. That's why he forgot to call in."

I was unimpressed. I felt that Tony, at 24 (only four years older than me), shouldn't have any kids—especially four already, and all

3. Parts of this chapter are excerpted from ***Unlimited Wealth*** (Crown Publishers, 1990).

My first business card for the family business at age fourteen.

living with him in the Bronx—when he was only making $200 a week.

"But Dad," I objected, "he cost us $75 last week just by not calling in, let alone what the buyer at Macy's is going to do to us when he finds out we didn't ship his order. Listen to me! Please! We're going broke, and you're going around giving raises to people we should be firing. You don't understand!"

"Don't speak like that," he said sympathetically. "You can't fire Tony … where would he go? He barely speaks English. He'd end up as a floor sweeper somewhere at minimum wage."

"But Dad, we can't make it anymore. You just don't understand, do you?"

"No, Son," he said, "You don't understand. It's not worth being in business if you can't extend a hand to people who haven't had all

Sales 12 Per Cent Ahead of Last Year's at Pilzer Bros.

Sales for the year so far at Pilzer Bros., Inc., are about 12 per cent ahead of last year and their financial statement is better than last year, according to Sam Wilkenfeld, sales manager.

At the end of June when they faced the lull that usually comes in July, August and September, they advertised that they would sell up to $75,000 worth of curtains at actual cost during July. They offered curtain buyers a five-piece novelty valance set or Priscilla set which could be retailed at 44 cents. As a result they have sold between 60,000 and 70,000 pairs, have given their workers steady employment and have cut down overhead while they were making up regular stock for fall.

They regularly carry a stock of $50,000 worth of goods, said Mr. Wilkenfeld, including from 30,000 to 40,000 pairs of curtains and about 1,000,000 yards of various fabrics, as well as bedspreads and pillows. They cut up about 200,000 yards a week, he continued.

"We carry such a big stock of goods because we want no order to stay in the house more than 48 hours," he explained. "In most cases we get the goods out in 24 hours."

Pilzer Bros. do over $1,000,000 worth of business a year, it is said, and all of the factory, offices and salesrooms are located in 20,000 square feet of space. A system of progressive production economizes time and space. Modern equipment and specialized machinery, such as the $10,000 pillow filling unit and the box stitching machines, effect further economies. This firm is said to have been the first to introduce stitched boxes and now buys them in lots of 100,000 in flat form, stitching and shaping them in their own factory. They also maintain their own tool and repair shop. Two hundred workers are employed.

Officers of Pilzer Bros., Inc.

When the partnership of Pilzer Bros. was incorporated in Albany recently with a capital of $125,000, the above officers were elected. Left to right, Manny Pilzer, secretary; Elias Pilzer, vice-president; Max Pilzer, president, and Morris Pilzer, treasurer.

Daily News Record, July 31, 1931. My father and his three brothers.

of your advantages. Go to Wharton next year. Study hard. Figure out how you can make your million bucks and how we can stay in business to make jobs for the Tonys of this world. Then you'll understand."

The "Kaddish"

My father was a religious man. He firmly believed in a true and just God who had a reason for everything. To him, an Eastern European immigrant who had seen his homeland destroyed during the Holocaust, the tragedies and misfortunes of human existence were simply parts of God's plan that we could not yet understand. His philosophy was perhaps best summed up in the "Kaddish," the Hebrew prayer for the dead—the prayer that, as the son of a religious Jew, I recited every morning for a year following his death in 1979.

The "Kaddish" is recited in Aramaic, the spoken language of the Jewish people, and Jesus in ancient times. It was originally written in Aramaic so that every member of the community would understand it. Yet, even more significant than the fact that the Hebrew prayer for the dead is not recited in Hebrew is the fact that this prayer for the dead contains no mention whatsoever of death. Rather, in the midst of sorrow, the "Kaddish" affirms our belief in the meaningfulness of life itself and our faith in a just and true God—even if He moves in what may seem to us to be mysterious ways.

My father, who spent virtually his whole life working to support his family, viewed his own business shortcomings and society's economic problems as one and the same: both were the result of our failure to understand and utilize the tools that God had given us. Even while he was dying of cancer in 1979, my father never wavered for a moment in his belief that God was just and that human suffering was part of a divine plan that we did not yet understand. He firmly believed, as Albert Einstein once said, that "God does not play dice with the universe."

To a man like my father, it was inconceivable that God would allow people to multiply in the billions yet deny them the ability to feed and shelter themselves. Yet like a loving father, God would not simply hand over to his children everything they needed. Rather, He would give them the necessary tools and allow them to discover how to use those tools to take care of themselves.

Scarcity

I began my studies at Wharton Graduate Business School in 1975 with the belief that human suffering and social injustice reflected nothing more than our failure to use the tools that God had given us.

It seemed to me that the science of economics had advanced only to where the science of medicine was at the beginning of the 19th Century. Before we discovered the underlying theories that explained bacterial infections and thus vaccinations and antibiotics, we knew from experience what few medicines and treatments or applications worked. However, without an underlying theory explaining why, we couldn't learn and grow from our experiences, and, more significantly, only a select few could afford what little medical care existed.

Similarly, my professors taught me what worked in applications courses such as marketing, finance, and management, but they couldn't teach me why it worked in theoretical courses such as micro and macroeconomics.

I felt then that the underlying economic theories behind business, which are based on the classical economic concept of scarcity, were wrong, but I did not have a theory to substitute in their place. This began my 15-year quest for a business theory that could better explain the past and predict the future. More importantly, I was on the hunt for a business theory consonant with a just and true God, which would allow everyone, not just a select few, to share in a better world.

Chapter 3 - Learnings

1. Review how my father handled Tony. How would you have handled the situation with Tony?
2. Do you believe that "the tragedies and misfortunes of human existence are simply parts of God's plan that we cannot yet understand?" How do your religious beliefs affect your actions as a manager?
3. How do you feel about my personal views on economics, particularly my belief that there is no scarcity, and why?
4. Is it possible to believe in a just and true God while also believing in the economic concept of scarcity?
5. Do you have strong religious beliefs? Are these different than your employees and/or co-workers? If so, how does this affect your business relationship?

BECOMING AN ENTREPRENEUR

PAUL ZANE PILZER

CHAPTER 4

GOD LOVES SAVERS

I have always been fascinated by money, particularly with how it originates. Money is created when a person earns income but doesn't spend it all right away because they wish to defer their gratification for a higher reward. In 1982, I started writing an academic book on savings for Princeton University Press when the Savings and Loan Crisis began with the Garn-St. Germain Depository Institutions Act of 1982. I transferred my research into my first book, ***Other People's Money*** *(Simon & Schuster, 1989), which played a role in exposing and fixing the S&L crisis.*

Charles Dickens wrote in 1864, "Saving money is a practice that encourages its own success. If you begin [saving] and go on with it for a little time, you come to have a sort of passion for it."

But saving money is more than a commendable habit. It is a personal act of faith, a form of self-denial that expresses confidence in the future. A person who denies current comfort and pleasure for future happiness demonstrates their belief in a destiny that can be controlled and improved.

It is one thing to pray in church for God's favor. It is an altogether different proposition to deny your loved ones food, clothing, and shelter they need now so they will have a better life tomorrow. This is exactly what immigrants in the United States today and in the past have done for generations to take control of their destinies.

Saving is an Act of Faith

As a child growing up in New York in the 1950s, I used to hold onto my father's hand and swing as we entered our synagogue on the Sabbath and the Bowery Savings Bank in the Empire State Building on deposit day. To him, the two institutions were almost one and the same. My father demonstrated devotion to his God by making weekly visits to the synagogue, and he did the same for his children when he made weekly deposits to the custodian savings accounts he had established for our education.

It is more than coincidence that the churches and savings banks built by immigrants throughout America are so much alike. The vaulted ceilings, the echo of your footsteps on the marble floors, the lofty skylights designed to coax your attention upward, all serve the all-important purpose of fostering one's faith: faith in your new nation, faith in God, and faith in your ability to control your destiny.

While the savings of immigrants from about 1890 to 1930 collectively grew to become the largest financial hoard ever known, immigrants were almost always poor people. They were day laborers and domestic servants, teamsters and hod carriers, ship's carpenters, tailors, and cigar makers. Theirs was a dream of an America of golden streets and limitless opportunities, sustained by scrimping on meager wages to allow savings for a better future.

As they saved, they actually financed an economic expansion that eventually would make them prosperous.

A turn-of-the-century journalist observed of the tellers' lines in lower Manhattan savings banks: "Whether you are watching the sad-faced Jew struggling to save the passage money which shall free his family from Russian persecution, or the Greek who has left his beloved Peloponnesus to push a peddler's cart in the city streets, you must be at least conscious that you are standing close to the process of a nation's growth."

The savings of immigrants seeking to improve their lives were responsible not only for the growth of the U.S. savings and loan industry, but for much of the growth of the United States itself. The money deposited in savings banks was invested in homes and municipal bonds used to finance the infrastructure of our emerging nation.

Looking back, the willingness of these immigrants to save may seem prudent, but consider the courage their acts of saving required. The poor, shabby newcomer to 19th Century America, perhaps an Italian peddler from Southern Europe or a peasant farmer from Armenia, had to deprive his family of basic necessities to salt away a few dollars with a nameless banker who operated from a storefront along a crowded, noisy street in Manhattan, Boston, or Philadelphia.

That immigrant, usually a victim of religious, political, or economic repression, could justifiably only have faith in paper money or coins in their possession. Yet the immigrant saver still had sufficient faith in the American dream, and in the durability of the American political and financial systems, to bet that those few pennies and rare dollars would not only be secure but available when he needed them for medicine or a child's education or perhaps the down payment on a modest frame house.

The origins and rich heritage of the savings industry are anchored in a noble purpose—to provide common men and women with a means of accumulating modest wealth to improve their lives and the futures of their children. This heritage bears an indelible religious imprint, rooted in the philanthropic funds accumulated and disbursed by the church in the Middle Ages and the friendly societies organized in Europe during the late 1700s. As explained in ***Other People's Money***, the model for the first modern savings institution was developed in a church in 1810.

The First Modern Savings Bank

In 1810, at Ruthwell Village in Dumfriesshire, Scotland, the Reverend Henry Duncan established the Parish Bank Friendly Society of Ruthwell. The reason that this institution is recognized today as the first modern mutual savings bank is philosophical. Existing friendly societies operated on the principle of charity—people banding together to help a neighbor in distress. In contrast, Dr. Duncan's Ruthwell bank was created to provide a way for one person to accumulate funds for his own benefit.

The Ruthwell institution was not so much a charity as it was a repository for personal savings. In simple charity, a needy person is given help for reasons of mercy. But pride and dignity often reject charity. Avoiding the charitable motivation behind other friendly societies, Dr. Duncan sought to encourage independence, self-reliance, individual pride, and dignity.

Today, conventional wisdom holds that one of the things wrong with our economy is a shortage of capital because consumers don't save enough money. This is far from the truth. Our economy is awash in capital, as is evidenced by the lowest interest rates—the price of capital—ever recorded.

However, reflecting back on Dr. Duncan and his noble intentions with the Ruthwell bank, the conventional wisdom is partially correct. Restated more accurately, one of the things wrong with our society is a shortage of faith because consumers don't *voluntarily* save enough money for their futures. Today, most Americans rely on Social Security, increasing taxation, corporate pensions, and other involuntary savings vehicles to take care of their future.

As a minister first and a banker second, Dr. Duncan's true, noble intention was in providing something beyond economic sustenance in one's old age. He wanted people to experience the real rewards of voluntary savings: pride, dignity, self-reliance, and independence.

BECOMING AN ENTREPRENEUR

PAUL ZANE PILZER

Chapter 4 - Learnings

1. "Saving money is more than a commendable habit. It is a personal act of faith, a form of self-denial that expresses confidence in the future." Consider some ways that saving might express confidence in your future and explore them here.

2. How did my father demonstrate devotion to God by making weekly deposits to his children's custodian savings accounts? Are God and money related?

3. I posit that the immigrant saver had sufficient faith in the durability of the American political and financial systems. Do you think this is true?

4. If an organization were to operate solely on a principle of charity, in contrast with the Parish Bank Friendly Society of Ruthwell, how might that be accomplished and self-sustaining?

5. Have you accomplished your savings goals? Why do you think you have the money-saving behaviors that you do?

BECOMING AN ENTREPRENEUR

PAUL ZANE PILZER

CHAPTER 5

ART, CREATIVITY & BUSINESS

"Art is anything that helps us better see or understand the work of God."

Menashe Kadishman,
Bethlehem, Pennsylvania
September 1971

In September 1971, I was a 17-year-old freshman at Lehigh University in Bethlehem, Pennsylvania, when I joined the school newspaper staff, ***The Brown & White***. I was assigned to cover the installation of a large outdoor work of art by Menashe Kadishman, an Israeli artist. One crisp cold fall Sunday morning, I awoke early, borrowed a car, and drove the three miles from my freshman dormitory to Lehigh's Saucon Valley Fields to see the work.

The Saucon Valley Fields comprised about 550 acres of vacant land adjacent to Lehigh's main campus. The sun was just coming up over the mountains when I arrived. Even without the art, the site was beautiful. Menashe Kadishman was on site working on his installation. I didn't realize it was him at first. He looked like Gandalf, Tolkien's wizard in ***The Hobbit*** and ***The Lord of the Rings.*** Menashe weighed nearly 300 pounds and had a mop of shaggy hair that ran into his long, flowing black beard. As if in defiance of the 50°F temperature, he wore a pair of shorts and a loose T-shirt. I later

Trees by Menashe Kadishman, Lehigh University, 1971. (Credit: Kate Morrell, from Alexa Berliner "Outdoor Sculpture Completes Campus Atmosphere," Lifestyle, ***Brown & White***, March 15, 2017.)

learned that the long, shaggy hair, beard, shorts, and loose T-shirt were his trademark look, regardless of the climate.

The work he was installing consisted of large steel plates about four stories high. The plates were mounted vertically on a grassy hill facing east. The center of each plate featured a two-story cutout of an abstract tree.

I walked over to Menashe and took out my pen and notepad for an interview. "Good morning. Are you Mr. Kadishman?" I asked. "I'm here from the school newspaper to interview you about your installation."

"Call me Menashe," he said.

"Menashe, what is art?" I asked.

He responded, "Art is anything that helps us better see or understand the work of God."

I nodded and wrote as he continued.

"Look down at our shadows on the ground. God created shadows. Shadows are so beautiful. But sadly, they exist for only fleeting moments, seconds, really. And, due to the orbit of the earth around the sun, each shadow will never, ever exist again in its present form. We often fail to see the beauty in shadows, as we take shadows for granted.

"There are two reasons we sometimes don't notice shadows: shadows are mostly dark, and they move slowly. So, I make metal plates like these, which make the shadows of the trees light instead of dark. And, by leveraging the angle of the sun at sunrise and sunset, the white shadows coming through the plates appear much larger and move much faster."

I was dumbfounded.

I stopped writing and asked myself, *what kind of mind notices that shadows are dark and that they've always been dark? And, having noticed, what kind of genius would create something like this to make shadows light? And who would ever think of leveraging the sun's angle to make shadows move faster as the sun rose or set?*

That day was the beginning of a lifelong fascination and friendship with Menashe Kadishman and his work.

I enjoyed him and his art for 44 years until he passed away in 2015. Although I didn't know it then, a Lehigh classmate was the eldest son of one of Menashe's major patrons. I would go on to spend

Menashe Kadishman (1932-2015) (Credit: Wikimedia Commons)

many weekends during college with Menashe at my classmate's family beach house. Moreover, Menashe's words during our first encounter about understanding God through art led me to minor in Art History and eventually become an art collector myself.

In another case of art meeting life, my first job after college and graduate school was with Citibank. The job involved a considerable amount of travel, which allowed me to visit giant Kadishman outdoor sculptures in many world capitals.

Menashe's art provided me food for creativity when I needed to solve a seemingly insurmountable problem in my work. If my friend Menashe could turn shadows from dark to light and make them move at ten times their normal speed, I could surely devise a creative way to finance a new venture or develop a more accurate model to explain abundance versus scarcity in our economy.

Menashe Visits his "Children" in Dallas

On October 21, 1981, ten years after I first met Menashe,[4] I was visiting my college classmate in New York City during the bris of his second child. Menashe was also in attendance. Everyone was dressed in suits except for him. He wore his trademark shorts and T-shirt. Menashe came over to ask me why he hadn't seen me at the family's beach house the previous summer. I explained that I had moved to Dallas, Texas.

"Dallas," Menashe exclaimed, shaking his hair and beard. "I've never been to Dallas, but I have children there. Three of them. When are you going back?" I told him I was flying home on the first American Airlines flight from LaGuardia Airport at 7:00 a.m. the next day. Sure enough, when I arrived at the airport to check in, Menashe was waiting for me in his usual casual dress. He bought a ticket at the gate, and we flew together to Dallas. When we landed, he declared, "Before we do anything else, I must see my children."

I then realized that his "children" were his sculptures.

We drove first to One Nonesuch Lane, the secluded home of Stanley Marcus, the founder and then-CEO of Neiman Marcus. The home itself is a national treasure, having been used by Stanley to entertain countless dignitaries, including Grace Kelly, James Dean, Eleanor Roosevelt, Christian Dior, Lyndon Johnson, and Nelson Rockefeller.

---

4. ***Wikipedia***. 2021. "Menashe Kadishman."

I parked in the circular driveway and headed to the front door. Menashe walked to the side of the home and climbed over a four-foot-high fence, tripping a silent alarm. In the backyard, towering over Stanley's one-story ranch house, was a giant iron Kadishman abstract sculpture.

As Menashe ran toward the sculpture to touch his child, two private security cars arrived in the front, blocking each entrance of the circular driveway. Before the guards could accost me, I heard Stanley Marcus cry out, "Menashe, Menashe!" as he realized his burglar's identity. We met with Stanley for about 30 minutes, planned a dinner at my home for the next evening, and then Menashe asked Stanley for the locations of his other children in Dallas.

The second child graced the home of Elsie and Stanley Pearle, the founder of the 1,000-store chain of Pearle Vision optical stores. Their home was located on Strait Lane, the entranceway marked by a large Frank Stella painting with windows on the side, which looked out to a giant Kadishman abstract sculpture on the back lawn behind the pool.

This time, I rang the doorbell almost immediately, hoping I could preempt Menashe from trespassing to the backyard. Stanley Pearle himself answered the front door, and I said, "I'm here with Menashe Kadishman to see your Kadishman sculpture."

Stanley and his wife Elsie ran to the backyard just as Menashe was approaching the sculpture. We visited with the Pearles for two hours, and they agreed to join us for dinner at my home the following night with Stanley Marcus.

The final and third child was located in University Park at

the home of Ray and Patsy Nasher. Ray was a highly successful businessperson, former White House cabinet officer, and one of the world's largest outdoor sculpture collectors. Unfortunately, the Nashers were in New York, but after receiving calls from Stanley Marcus and the Pearles, the Nasher house staff expected us that afternoon. We visited Menashe's child outside in the Nasher backyard, surrounded by works from Picasso, Matisse, Calder, and Rodin. Menashe, of course, was thrilled that his child had such good neighbors. When the Nashers returned home the following weekend, Menashe and I visited with them in person.

My New Art Friends Become My Business Partners

For the next ten years, from 1981 to 1991, I lived in Dallas. I had many successful personal and career experiences that began on Menashe's first day in Dallas when he introduced me to three of the city's leading families, who had adopted his children.

These patrons of his work, and many others I met through Menashe, became some of my closest friends and regular dinner guests at my home. We would all get together each time Menashe stayed with me in Dallas. Later, when I became a real estate and tech entrepreneur and a candidate for the U.S. Congress, these same families became my earliest investors and political supporters. In 1985, Dr. Pearle invested $6.1 million in my $61 million acquisition of a downtown Dallas office building which was leased to BancTexas. All three of these Dallas families became contributors and supporters of Pilzer for Congress in 1991.[5]

5. Reuters. "BancTexas Group." ***New York Times***, June 13, 1985.

Staircase entering my family's home, May 21, 2021—note the Kadishman (1932-2015) paintings.

The Greek philosopher Aristotle wrote about three overlapping types of friendships:

1. **Friendships of Utility** (you are useful to each other),
2. **Friendships of Pleasure** (you bring good experiences to each other), and
3. **Friendships of Goodness** (you admire and respect each other).

I am forever grateful to my dear, dear friend Menashe, who enriched my life with all three types of friendships, as he enriched the lives of millions worldwide who were touched by his art.

BECOMING AN ENTREPRENEUR

PAUL ZANE PILZER

Chapter 5 - Learnings

1. Menashe explored the world in his signature way. He seized creative inspiration and executed his visions in his work. He was unapologetic in his dress and expression. When was the last time you followed through on a hunch to create or push an innovation into the world? Do you allow others to dictate what you do?

2. Poet Dana Gioia wrote, "The purpose of arts education is not to produce more artists, though that is a byproduct. The real purpose of arts education is to create complete human beings capable of leading successful and productive lives in a free society." Knowing this, do you spend enough time appreciating art? How do you think doing so would help you with your business and/or your career?

3. As a sculptor from Israel, Menashe came from a war-torn background. How do you think this may have affected his work? Hint: He was greatly influenced by the war with Lebanon in 1982.

4. Menashe referred to his works of art as his "children." Have you ever been that passionate about anything in your life?

5. If you don't understand an artist's concepts, do you still feel it is art? What are the criteria of art to you?

BECOMING AN ENTREPRENEUR

PAUL ZANE PILZER

CHAPTER 6

MY FIRST HERO–J.I. RODALE

Change begins with one person who challenges the status quo *with a new idea—an idea they then propagate to create a new status quo. But what would happen to our great nation if we were forbidden from discussing new ideas unless the keepers of the status quo in that field first approved of them? Our economy, and even our democracy, might collapse.*

The U.S. came close to this precipice after World War II. Then one dedicated entrepreneur risked everything to defend our right to freely assemble, write, and speak. I have dedicated four books to this person, and I say a prayer in his memory every time I write a book or give a speech.

In August 1971, when I left home for college, my father gave me some advice: "When you get to Lehigh, everyone around you will be studying the subjects in which they are the strongest—in order to get good grades and a good job after graduation. But you don't have to do that. Your grades won't matter because, after graduation, you're going to work with me in the family business making bedspreads. So, you should study the subjects in which you are weakest; college may be your last chance to improve your skills and knowledge in the areas where you need the most help."

I remember thinking at the time how, with an SAT Verbal score almost 200 points below my SAT Math score, I certainly *wouldn't* be taking this advice. I was terrified of English and history classes—too many papers to write!

Majoring in Journalism

Yet, two months later, in October 1971, when I was flunking out of Electrical Engineering (EE), it seemed that majoring in journalism was one of the few options I had left. If I majored in journalism, which was easy compared to EE, not only could I catch up on the classes I was failing, I could earn credit for my photography and layout work on the school newspaper. Majoring in journalism mostly consisted of attending 3-hour journalism labs (J labs) with the teletype machine noisily banging out printed wire copy facts about a recent event—that you needed to edit into a succinct story before going on to the next one. With each assignment, students were given shorter and shorter deadlines to turn these facts into cohesive articles. I enjoyed competing with other students to write quickly, and I was good at J labs, partly because I had learned how to type almost 100 words per minute in high school. The other journalism students might have been faster at reading and organizing their facts, but I surpassed them when it came to getting each finished story down on paper. Moreover, being fast at writing papers helped me with my other academic work—it was easy to get a professor to raise a grade by offering to "write a paper" on something in which the professor was interested.

The only drawback to majoring in journalism was that the major required writing a senior thesis, a 120-page, heavily footnoted research paper that would count as three academic credits toward my bachelor's degree.

My Senior Thesis

I declared my major in journalism in October 1972, and my department chair suggested I write my senior thesis about J.I. Rodale and Rodale Press, one of the biggest employers in the area and a major benefactor of Lehigh University. My chair scheduled a meeting with J.I.'s son, Robert Rodale, the CEO and publisher of Rodale Press, on February 12, 1973, which happened to be my mother's birthday.

I didn't know back then that the founder of Rodale Press, J.I. Rodale, had died 20 months earlier on ***The Dick Cavett Television Show*** while telling the story that would become my senior thesis. Nor did I know back then that my senior thesis would play an auspicious role in my professional life, even today, decades later, and that it would become a component of J.I.'s legacy.

After calling my mother to wish her a happy birthday, collect from the payphone in the University Center cafeteria, I ran down to the journalism office in the basement. I had a brief early afternoon meeting with my department chair, J.B. McFadden ("Mac," as we called him) and his co-chair Robert J. Sullivan, to discuss my upcoming meeting with Robert Rodale at 2:00 p.m. Mac was an accomplished figure, inside and outside the university, having served in the Kennedy Administration in 1962—he helped resettle more than two million European refugees.

Mac cautioned me to be super polite and even deferential to Mr. Rodale, saying, "These people may look like you and me, but they're a part of one of the richest families in the nation. They probably have some skeletons they don't want you asking about. Stick to the subject of your senior thesis: ***Rodale Press versus the Federal Trade Commission***."

The Road to Emmaus

My meeting with Robert was eight miles away at Rodale Press headquarters in Emmaus, Pennsylvania, but when I left Mac's office I was met with a Pennsylvania deluge. I couldn't read the street signs through the rain and barely made it to Emmaus on time. At one point, I pulled into a gas station to ask for directions. The attendant kept repeating what I had said to him.

"Eee-Mouse? Eee-Mouse? Eee-Mouse, is that what you mean?"

He looked quite perplexed—until he realized I was asking directions to "Uh-Mei-Uhs," and I simply didn't know how to pronounce the name of the city. While most Christian Americans learned how to pronounce Emmaus (Uh-Mei-Uhs) from Sunday school sermons, I had only encountered the name Emmaus on street signs in Bethlehem, Pennsylvania, and thus I pronounced it "Eee-Mouse."

I arrived at Rodale Press headquarters just before 2:00 p.m. and was surprised to find Robert Rodale, the CEO himself, waiting for me, alone in a conference room. He had neatly stacked piles of papers on the table, each chair, and the floor. I certainly hadn't expected Mr. Rodale to clear his entire calendar for me that Monday afternoon, much less every Monday afternoon for the next four months.

Robert explained that Rodale Press had hundreds of third-party articles, legal briefs, and original documents explaining J.I.'s life and his battle with the federal government, which consisted of several different legal cases and procedures spanning 20 years. No one had yet put all this material together into a single document that explained everything. Robert hoped my senior thesis would become that document. He mentioned that he had been looking forward to meeting me ever since Professor McFadden had first discussed the project two years earlier.

So every week for the next four months, I drove my own personal "Road to Emmaus" to Rodale headquarters. Robert gave me free access to everything, including the original source documents, but he wouldn't allow me to take anything outside the building. I was, however, allowed to photocopy anything I wished, and on most afternoons, Robert would come into the conference room to inquire where I was on the project. In June, I told him I had completed enough research to finish my senior thesis off-site, and we met that day to review the ten primary points:

Primary Points of Rodale Press vs. the Federal Trade Commission

1. J.I. Rodale (and his company Rodale Press, Inc.) in the 1950s was a small book and magazine publisher of health

and organic farming information that was sometimes considered controversial when it was first published.

2. In the early 1950s, Rodale claimed that increased physical activity decreased your chance of getting a heart attack at a time when conventional wisdom said physical activity increased your chances of having a heart attack.
3. Rodale also claimed in the 1950s that eating large quantities of red meat and dairy products increased your chances of having a heart attack, at a time when medical experts, including the American Medical Association, claimed exactly the opposite.
4. The Federal Trade Commission (FTC) ordered distributors to stop selling Rodale's publications until the FTC could hold hearings where either the FTC or Rodale could prove the efficacy of their respective claims.
5. The FTC acknowledged that Rodale had the right to publish and distribute this information, but not if the information was contained in a book or magazine sold for money over a state line (in effect, as a "product"). Rodale could give away his information for free but not for commercial sale.
6. Rodale refused to even show up at these hearings, claiming that every American's First Amendment right to freely speak, assemble, and disseminate information was more important to him than the value of his entire company.
7. Rodale fought back, and, for most of the time, it looked as if Rodale would lose. Other larger, richer publishers, such

as Prentice Hall, the world's leading educational publisher, had caved in to similar demands of the FTC.

8. The legal battle took place over 20 years. The FTC, at times fearing a total loss at the Supreme Court, offered to completely back down. But each time, Rodale refused, citing First Amendment issues as more important to him than anything else, including his company.
9. The case never reached the Supreme Court. J.I. Rodale died on June 8, 1971, in New York City while telling this story as a guest on an early evening taping of ***The Dick Cavett Show.***
10. Soon after his death, the U.S. government reversed its position, stating that the FTC would no longer require advertisers of information-based products to establish the efficacy of their claims. This policy change opened the door for the free flow of wellness information, allowing the vitamin, nutritional supplement, fitness, and alternative medicine industries to grow to their current trillion-dollar level, laying the foundation for ***The Wellness Revolution***.[6]

Dedication of My Senior Thesis, May 21, 1974

Although I wrote it almost half a century ago at age 20, the dedication on the cover of my thesis still best expresses how I feel about the great men who guided me through writing my thesis.

6. Readers wanting more detail can read my book, ***The Wellness Revolution*** (Wiley Press, 2002/2007).

Dedication

To Professor Joseph Brendan McFadden, who gave me the motivation and confidence to pursue much of what I have achieved in the past, but more important, much of what I hope to achieve in the future.

And to Professor Robert Joseph Sullivan, who taught me the methodology of effective expression, a tool of invaluable aid throughout my Lehigh career, and one which I know will prove of even greater benefit in the years that lie ahead.

To both of these men, not only for their assistance in compiling this paper, but for their sincere and devoted efforts on my behalf throughout my undergraduate years, I offer my humble gratitude.

In addition, I express my sincere thanks to Robert Rodale, without whose generous cooperation this paper would not have been possible.

Paul Zane Pilzer, May 21, 1974

Epitaph–Robert Rodale (March 27, 1930 – September 20, 1990)

Robert and I kept in touch and, years later, discussed publishing opportunities worldwide. He especially wanted to bring translated versions of Rodale's health and wellness publications to Russia.

On September 20, 1990, when I was coincidentally also working in Moscow, he died in a terrible car accident on the way to the Moscow airport, along with his Russian partner Yevgeni and their interpreter. By the time of his death, he had built his father's company into the largest health-oriented publisher in the world, publishing over 100 new wellness books each year and selling tens of millions of monthly copies of ***Prevention, Organic Gardening, Runner's World, Backpacker, Bicycling, Men's Health and American Woodworker.*** Those of us lucky enough to have known him sorely miss him. But his great work in wellness lives on.

***** **POSTSCRIPT** *****

What Makes You Right and Everyone Else Wrong?

In 1973, it was an exceptional, motivating opportunity for me to work with J.I.'s son and the archives of J.I. Rodale. Even though he had died 20 months before I first arrived in his office, I could feel his living presence when I handled the original documents from his 20-year ordeal.

As I worked on this project with Robert and Rodale Press, this thought ran through my head: *How could Rodale be so sure he was correct, and that he would be able to convince others he was correct, that he was willing to risk his life's work and the careers of his 770 employees?* As explained in my senior thesis, other larger, much more powerful publishers facing a similar fate had caved in to the FTC.

I couldn't answer this question back then, but today I have a better perspective about how J.I. might have felt.

J.I. believed in his own science—he had personally completed much of the biological research that led to his beliefs. And J.I. believed in a higher power setting him up and guiding him to do what he "knew" was right. God had helped him build his company so he could risk it all to accomplish a higher cause—saving the First Amendment.

How many more millions of Americans might have suffered from heart disease if not for J.I. Rodale? Worse, what might have happened in every field, especially civil rights, if our founding father's dream of a free press had been permanently rolled back by federal agencies like the FTC? Imagine what our internet might look like today, for better or worse, if J.I. had not prevailed and if a government agency today had the right to approve the veracity of everything published online.

One year after I completed my senior thesis on J.I. Rodale , in 1975, at Wharton Graduate Business School, I knew something was wrong with my Macroeconomics professor's belief in scarcity. But although I *knew* he was wrong, it would take me 14 more years to come up with an alternative theory that made sense (see *Chapter 10: My First Macroeconomics Class*, page 117).

Two years after completing my senior thesis, in 1976, at Citibank, I knew something was wrong with the banking industry's refusal to pay consumers interest on their checking accounts. This led me to convince my employer to break with 9,000 commercial banks and support giving all financial institutions the ability to pay interest on checking NOW (Negotiable Order of Withdrawal) accounts. I knew I could find a profitable solution for Citibank to support a free market because this was what Adam Smith's Invisible Hand (i.e., God) wanted us to do (see *Chapter 15: My Career at Citibank Takes Off*, page 175).

BECOMING AN ENTREPRENEUR

PAUL ZANE PILZER

ADDITION B

J.I. Rodale

Excerpt from J I. Rodale Press versus the Federal Trade Commission: A Comprehensive Analysis by Paul Zane Pilzer (May 21, 1974).

In 1954, entrepreneur and author J. I. Rodale had a lot to lose. His company, Rodale Press, was just getting his fledgling Prevention magazine off the ground. Prevention was dedicated to teaching readers how to prevent disease versus treating the symptoms of disease.

Rodale had concluded that eating large quantities of red meat and dairy products dramatically increased the risk of heart disease and that physical activity actually decreased the risk of having a heart attack. This was at a time when the U.S. government was spending millions encouraging Americans to eat more red meat and dairy products at every meal, three meals a day. Doctors were telling patients with heart disease to reduce or eliminate physical activity entirely. No wonder heart disease was the leading cause of death in the United States!

Rodale wrote about his new findings in two books: ***How to Eat for a Healthy Heart*** and ***This Pace Is Not Killing Us***. He was convinced that this information could save millions of lives. But, like many writers in the 1950s, he was not on an approved list drawn up by Senator Joseph McCarthy's House Un-American Activities

Committee, so his publisher refused to publish his new books.

This situation forced Rodale to print the books himself and try to sell them through bookstores along with his other Rodale publications. But many booksellers refused to distribute his new books. Undaunted and convinced that the public needed this information as soon as possible, Rodale took [out] full-page advertisements in national publications and offered his new books via mail order at a special price.

The Federal Trade Commission ordered Rodale to stop advertising and selling the books, claiming that the medical advice given in his books was unsubstantiated. The FTC had successfully taken similar action against other publishers who had promulgated then unconventional medical advice.[7]

Rodale was furious! He felt that the FTC action was a blatant violation of the First Amendment, guaranteeing freedom of the press.

The FTC scheduled hearings in 1955 at which Rodale was ordered to present proof that people who purchased the books and followed their advice would, indeed, reduce their risk of heart disease. Rodale refused to attend, claiming that the First Amendment gave

7. Witkower Press, Inc., of Hartford, Connecticut, had published ***Arthritis and Common Sense*** and claimed in their advertisements that it would help arthritic and rheumatoid sufferers. In 1954, the FTC ordered Witkower Press to "forthwith cease and desist from representing, directly or indirectly, that their book was adequate, effective, and reliable in giving relief to arthritic and rheumatoid sufferers." Witkower Press accepted the ruling and did not appeal the case. In a similar case against Prentice Hall, the large publisher agreed to the FTC action because they did not want to enter into costly litigation with the federal government. (Pilzer, Paul Zane, ***Rodale Press vs. the Federal Trade Commission: A Comprehensive Analysis***, senior thesis, Lehigh University, Bethlehem, PA, May 21, 1974.)

him the right to publish any information he wanted, regardless of its efficacy.*

> ***At the original hearing on this case before the FTC examiner, dissenting FTC commissioner Philip Elman foreshadowed the path that the FTC was about to take when he wrote, "Congress did not create this Commission to act as a censor of unorthodox ideas and theories in books, whether they deal with politics or health. We should not forget that, in both fields, today's heresy may become tomorrow's dogma."[8]**

At these hearings, the nation's most respected medical professionals testified that (1) there was no correlation between heart disease and eating large quantities of red meat and dairy products and (2) following Rodale's advice on increasing physical activity to avoid heart disease could be injurious, if not fatal. The FTC ordered Rodale to "cease and desist" from claiming, directly or indirectly, that readers of any of his publications would improve their health.**

> ****FTC commissioner Elman wrote in his dissenting opinion, "It is the glory of a free society that a man can write a book contending that the earth is flat, or that the moon is made of green cheese, or that God is dead, without having to 'substantiate' or 'prove' his claims to the satisfaction of some public official or agency. It is arrogance to presume that in any field of knowledge, whether dealing with health or otherwise, all the answers are now in."[9]**

---

8. *Ibid.*

9. *Ibid.*

Rodale appealed the case, mainly on the grounds that the First Amendment prohibited the FTC from regulating information-based products. His legal battles with the federal government dragged on for almost two decades, at times putting his entire personal net worth at risk. Over the years, the FTC, fearing they would lose their case on constitutional grounds, attempted to settle with Rodale. But despite financial hardship, Rodale refused to back down unless the FTC agreed to acknowledge that the First Amendment prohibited it from regulating books and printed material.

In the later years of the case, Rodale's lawyers introduced new testimony from some of the same leading medical experts that the government originally used at the initial FTC hearings almost 20 years earlier. One by one, these "experts" refuted their original testimony, claiming they "didn't know back then," and admitted that many of Rodale's original claims had since become established medical facts. Rodale felt that there could never be a better example of what our Founding Fathers had in mind when they made freedom of the press the first item in the Bill of Rights.

Then, in 1971, while describing his legal problems with the federal government on the taping of a national television show scheduled to be aired that evening, J. I. Rodale dropped dead. Until he actually stopped breathing and turned blue, everyone watching the taping of *The Dick Cavett Show* thought Rodale was facetiously faking a heart attack in order to make a point about his troubles with the FTC.

The case never reached the Supreme Court.

Soon after wellness pioneer J. I. Rodale passed away, the U.S.

government reversed its position, stating that the FTC would no longer require advertisers of information-based products to establish the efficacy of their claims. This policy change opened the door for the free flow of wellness information, allowing the vitamin, nutritional supplement, fitness, and alternative medicine industries to grow to their current level, laying the foundation for the wellness revolution.

One of the greatest challenges facing Rodale and many entrepreneurs like you today who base their businesses on new technology is the human rejection of the new or unknown. This is especially true when the new technology forces people to rethink established beliefs.

BECOMING AN ENTREPRENEUR

PAUL ZANE PILZER

Chapter 6 - Learnings

1. My father advised me to study subjects that would strengthen my weaker academic areas. What do you think of this advice? If you were in college now, would you prefer to build upon your stronger or weaker areas? Why would you make this decision, and how would it benefit you?

2. J. I. Rodale's legacy is extensive; he invented organic farming, he led the preventative health moment, and he risked everything to protect our first amendment rights. Do you agree with his stance on publishing health-related facts outside of the established medical community?

3. Was it irresponsible for J. I. Rodale to risk his employees' livelihood fighting for a cause he believed in? Should he have been more protective of his business?

4. Considering the climate of the world today, and particularly modern media in the US and politics, is the First Amendment still effective in protecting our rights?

5. Now apply this question to the Internet. Do you think we need more or less regulation? Or are current laws and regulations adequate? If J.I. were alive today, how would his work be affected by social media?

BECOMING AN ENTREPRENEUR

PAUL ZANE PILZER

CHAPTER 7

REVELING IN REJECTION

How I got rejected by Wharton on April 10, 1974; accepted on April 17, 1974, and learned three of life's most important lessons.

In the fall of my third year of college, I decided to pursue an MBA at the Wharton Graduate School of Business of the University of Pennsylvania. Although I was only 19 and a junior at Lehigh University, I told my friends and professors that I was planning to go to Wharton "next year." Then I applied for admission.

On Wednesday, April 10, 1974, at 9:00 a.m., I got rejected. I had called the Wharton admissions office to inquire about the status of my application, and the receptionist read my letter of rejection to me over the phone. The letter suggested that I finish my undergraduate degree, get two years of work experience under my belt, and reapply.

I asked how I could appeal this decision. The receptionist told me that only the director of admissions had the authority to reverse the decision and that he rarely met with individual applicants.

In that moment, I remembered a lesson my father taught me. He said to always "do the math" when faced with a decision—in other words, logically figure out the consequences or reactions of each possible action. Here was the math:

- To get accepted, I had to meet with the director of admissions.
- The director generally didn't take meetings with individual applicants for admission.
- I had nothing more to lose and everything to gain if I got to meet with the director.

This last point was key; I had nothing more to lose, and therefore nothing to fear, from meeting with the director.

I told the receptionist that I had certain "private, confidential matters" regarding the admissions process that I would only discuss with the director or a trustee of the university, and she scheduled a meeting with the director and me for 11:00 a.m. on Wednesday, April 17, 1974.

My work for the next week had begun. I only had seven days to prepare for the upcoming meeting.

Preparation was easy except for the most important part: I had absolutely no idea what I was going to tell the director about my "private, confidential matters" when we met.

Preparing for My Meeting with the Director

During the next week, I contacted the people who had written the three letters of recommendation I had submitted with my application and told them I had a "final meeting" on Wednesday at Wharton. I then asked them to phone or fax any additional information that would support my acceptance to the director before Wednesday morning.

Next, I contacted my favorite professors at Lehigh with a similar message and gave them contact information for the director of admissions. I also scheduled time with my friends to help me role-play different scenarios of what might occur at my upcoming meeting with the director, much like a political candidate would prepare for a debate.

Although I had never met the President of Lehigh University, W. Deming Lewis, I walked to the President's House on campus and explained to his secretary that there was a "final meeting" on Wednesday regarding my application to Wharton Graduate Business School. The secretary told me to write out my credentials and said she would see what she could do to assist with my application and/or get me a meeting with President Lewis. I had written for her the text of a letter about the "outstanding Lehigh student, Paul Zane Pilzer," as if it had been composed by the president.

Each time I completed one of these tasks, I stopped and said aloud to myself: *What else can I do to prepare for my upcoming meeting with the director of admissions?*

Despite having spent every available minute providing more outside support to my application, I still had no idea what I was going to say to the director about my "private, confidential matters" when we met in his office. I felt like Abraham before dawn in the Book of Genesis, leading Isaac up the mountain in the Land of Moriah, wondering where the lamb was for the burnt offering:

> *"And Isaac spoke to Abraham, his father, and he said, 'Here are the fire and the wood, but where is the lamb*

for the burnt offering?'

"And Abraham said, 'God will provide for Himself the lamb for the burnt offering, my son.' And they both went together.

"And they came to the place of which God had spoken to him, and Abraham built the altar there and arranged the wood, and he bound Isaac his son and placed him on the altar upon the wood.

"And Abraham stretched forth his hand and took the knife to slaughter his son.

"And Abraham lifted up his eyes, and he saw, and lo! There was a ram, [and] after [that] it was caught in a tree by its horns. And Abraham went and took the ram and offered it up as a burnt offering instead of his son."

(Genesis, Chapter 22:7-10, 13 KJV)

Meeting the Director of Admissions

I rose before dawn on Wednesday, April 17, the day of the meeting, and began pacing my apartment, still having no idea what I would say in a few hours at my 11:00 a.m. meeting with the director.

Ronnie, my housemate, told me to stop worrying and come with him to Professor Redd's one-hour Art History class at 8:00 a.m. This would still leave me two hours to drive the 90 minutes from

Lehigh to the University of Pennsylvania, so I would have more time to figure out what I was going to say between the Art History class and my meeting.

Professor Redd's class consisted of a fast-paced lecture about the Spanish surrealist Joan Miro. I'd never heard about Miro before then. As the slides of Miro's artwork went by on the screen, I took in every word the professor said but didn't understand anything because I was focused on what I would soon be telling the director.

Although I didn't process Professor Redd's words, I knew I could probably recite much of his lecture from memory. I was born with a degree of eidetic memory, a type of simplified photographic memory that allows me to recite whole lectures or conversations that I've physically heard but haven't yet processed into feelings or understanding. "Eidetikers,"[10] as people with this ability have sometimes been called, can recall visual information, such as pages from books, magazines, and license plate numbers, in great detail after only brief exposure to it. This trait can be found in early childhood (between 2% and 10% of children aged 6-12 show signs) and is unconnected to a person's intelligence. My photographic memory of something typically disappears when I begin to process or understand the material.

After the class, I drove to my meeting at Wharton. Driving down to Philadelphia, I felt confident that I had done everything humanly possible to prepare for it.

I thought of a story my father used to tell me about Joseph, a poor, pious man who prayed every night: "Tomorrow, God, please

10. ***Wikipedia***. 2021. "Eidetic Memory."

Our outdoor entrance stairs made by my wife Lisa from Picasso's ***Girl Before a Mirror*** (1932). I still think of my Art History professor, Richard Redd, whenever I walk these stairs.

let me win the lottery." Finally, after a lifetime of poverty, God appeared to Joseph in a dream, saying, "Joseph, give me a chance! Buy a lottery ticket!"

I felt confident that I had bought all my "lottery tickets" in preparing for this meeting. On a spiritual level, I was ready to ask for God's help because I had demonstrated that I deserved His help by having first done everything I could on my own.

However, despite knowing that I had done everything possible to advance my application, I still had no idea what I was going to say about my "private, confidential matters" to the director.

God Supplies the Lamb—Its name was Joan Miro

When I walked into the Office of Admissions, I was told to wait on a chair inside the office of the director of admissions. The director was on the telephone with the university bookstore. He had just purchased a signed lithograph by artist Joan Miro and was promising to come right over with a $1,500 check to pay for it!

When he put down the phone, and after exchanging niceties, I repeated to him almost word for word everything I had just heard about Miro back at Lehigh. Then I asked him if I could see the print. He jumped up, and we walked quickly together to the university bookstore, continuing to talk about Miro on the way. When we saw the print at the bookstore, I congratulated him on his purchase, and he invited me to lunch.

At lunch, I told him I wanted to get my MBA from Wharton and would probably never attend Wharton if I first had to acquire two years of work experience. He asked about my ATGSB (now called GMAT [Graduate Management Admission Test]) score and grades and told me that, with my interest in modern art and surrealism, I was exactly the kind of well-rounded applicant that Wharton wanted.

After lunch, we went back to his office, and he checked his appointment book. It was then he realized that I was the person who'd had "private, confidential matters" to discuss. He asked what they were. I immediately came clean and told him the truth—I had only told his receptionist that story to get her to schedule this meeting with him.

He asked again about my ATGSB scores and why my math score was so far below my verbal score—the opposite of what my math-versus-verbal scores were in high school. I explained that I had taken the ATGSB without advance preparation and that I hadn't taken any math since high school. But I boasted that I could easily bring my math score up to the level of my near-perfect verbal score.

The director noted that while I had enough credits to receive a B.A. degree from Lehigh, there was uncertainty on my application as to whether I could meet Lehigh's foreign language requirement to receive my degree. I told him if I could get a letter of admission from Wharton, I was confident the Lehigh faculty would not deny me the opportunity to graduate early despite the lack of a few credits in French.

The director called in his secretary, to whom he dictated a letter granting me acceptance (subject to my taking two summer school courses and getting my bachelor's degree from Lehigh).

The letter of acceptance I received from Wharton on April 17,

1974, told me to disregard their letter of April 10, 1974 and offered me admission to the Wharton MBA program. But the letter also stated that I needed to bring my math ATGSB score up to the level of my verbal score and obtain my bachelor's degree from Lehigh before beginning my studies at Wharton. The director did this to save face and provide an empirical explanation for why he was reversing the decision.

When I drove back to Lehigh that afternoon, I was already thinking about my next task. I now had to convince the Lehigh University Faculty Committee to grant me my bachelor's degree without meeting the school's foreign language distribution requirements. And I would have to re-take the ATGSB exam.

Later that month, I submitted a brief to the Lehigh University Faculty Committee arguing that computer programming languages (e.g., BASIC, Fortran, COBOL) were "the new foreign languages." I attached my April 17 letter of conditional acceptance from Wharton, in effect, telling my teachers that if they denied my request to modify my foreign language requirement, they would also deny me the opportunity of a lifetime to attend Wharton Graduate Business School. The faculty granted my request for a bachelor's degree subject to my taking one more course in French and one more programming language course.

In May, I re-took the ATGSB exam after studying day and night. I brought my math score up to the level of my verbal score as required by my Wharton acceptance letter. Then I enrolled in summer school courses at Hunter College, taking French and COBOL to meet the Lehigh University foreign language distribution requirement.

I began my studies as a Wharton MBA student later that year at age twenty.

On my first day at Wharton, I was terrified. The majority of my classmates had graduated from Ivy League schools; Harvard and Yale led the list.

I wrote my mother a letter expressing my concern that while my classmates had been accepted based on their experience, grades and intelligence, I had manipulated my way into the school. Despite these feelings of inferiority, I graduated from Wharton near the top of my class, finishing the two-year MBA program in 15 ½ months and landed a job in New York with Citibank.

Two years after graduating from Wharton, while attending a recruiting event for Citibank, I ran into the director of admissions on campus. I asked him if he remembered me: "Remember you? I will never forget you," he said. "You put me in a tough situation."

He then told me how he'd felt terribly pressured during our initial meeting two years earlier. It seemed that the president of Lehigh University, a former senior official with NASA, had phoned him that morning to talk about my application. While the director had enjoyed our conversation about Joan Miro, he had already decided he would probably have to admit me after his call with the president.

At our meeting, I remember the director telling me: "It's not every day the president of a major university, who had managed the Apollo Space Program, calls you asking to admit a candidate." The director went on to tell me that there had been no need for him to require me to raise my ATGSB math score, but I had been so cocky about my ability to do so that he wanted to see me do it—and he would have waived this requirement if I had been unsuccessful. He added that he had no doubt he would have heard from me again (and again) if I'd been unable to increase my score.

Looking back, I succeeded at Wharton in part because of the inferiority complex that I'd developed thanks to my initial rejection. At the time, I didn't realize that I would soon experience an initial rejection in everything of value that I was to accomplish—starting several businesses, teaching at New York University, working at the White House, and getting my books published.

I realize now that in each case, I was rejected precisely because I had sought out a higher level of success. After each rejection and successful reapplication, I moved up a step on the ladder of success. While others around me rested on their laurels, waiting patiently for what they deserved, I used each success to push the envelope and shoot for a higher objective. It was inevitable that I would at first be rejected with each new challenge.

It wasn't until I reached my 30s that I learned to enjoy and even revel in the process of application, rejection, and reapplication. Now when I experience rejection I smile; it reassures me that I'm on the right track in seeking a higher level. I've also learned to take personal responsibility for rejection rather than blame my prospect—*rejection by a qualified prospect means that you, personally, have failed to accurately communicate the potential of the product or service you are trying to sell.*

Today, I wish I had learned to enjoy rejection earlier in my career, as I might have taken more time to appreciate the application, rejection, and reapplication process that was unfolding.

BECOMING AN ENTREPRENEUR

PAUL ZANE PILZER

Chapter 7 - Learnings

1. Rejection means that you, personally, have failed to accurately communicate the potential of yourself or the product you are trying to sell. When has this happened in your career, and did you overcome it?

2. To reverse a decision, you need to give the decision-maker a way to save face or justify the reversal of his or her initial decision. In the case of the director of admissions reversing his decision regarding my admission, do you feel that I knowingly provided this safe harbor, or did I just get lucky?

3. God helps those the most who first help themselves the most before seeking God's help. Do you agree or disagree with this statement? Do you act this way before turning to prayer?

4. What do you think about the director of admissions requiring that I raise my ATGSB math score even though he had every intention of approving my application to Wharton regardless of that score?

5. Is there an ethically correct way to climb the ladder of success? Do you think I was foolhardy to take each action before figuring out what I would do if I reached the next milestone?

BECOMING AN ENTREPRENEUR

PAUL ZANE PILZER

CHAPTER 8

TYPING: MY PERSONAL KEY TO SUCCESS

Starting at age 12, my career seemed to be a series of lucky breaks where each break led to the next. Was I simply lucky, again and again, or did I make my own luck by the way I took advantage of each break?

In 1965, when I was in sixth grade, my brother Lee, who was in seventh grade, got a Brother (no pun intended) electric typewriter as a bar mitzvah present. My parents considered it to be such a great asset for schoolwork that they purchased the same electric typewriter for me (in a different color) the following year for $79.95, about $640 in today's dollars.

The Brother helped me learn how to type almost 100 words per minute by the time I entered college and indirectly led me to major in Journalism. As I shared earlier, in Journalism Lab classes, I learned how to pre-organize my thoughts and type out organized finished copy at fast speeds. This skill helped me to graduate Lehigh University one year early and earn my MBA from Wharton Graduate Business School early as well. But the best reward for fast typing was yet to come.

When I began work at Citibank in May 1976, I was assigned my first secretary, Rose, who I shared with my boss and Jack, the other management trainee. The three of us would dictate our memos throughout the day on handheld voice recorders, then Rose would type what we'd recorded on an IBM Mag Card Selectric Typewriter. Then we would correct and edit the paper versions, going back and forth with Rose until the final memo or letter was ready to be printed, photocopied, filed in a cabinet, and sent via hand delivery, fax, U.S. mail, or sometimes Overnight Federal Express.

A year earlier at Wharton, I had been given access to a Texas Instruments Silent 745 portable computer terminal and printer with rubber suction cups that, when attached to a telephone handset, allowed me to dial into a mainframe computer from anywhere, such as my dorm room or a payphone. I used this device to type my school papers onto the internal roll of thermal paper and edit them until I was ready to re-type the final versions on normal 8.5 × 11 paper for my professors using the same Brother electric typewriter my parents had bought me in 1966.

In late 1976, Rose and the other secretaries got IBM Mag Card Selectric typewriters. These forerunners to today's personal computers and word processors allowed Rose to edit a memo without having to re-type the entire document again and again on 8.5 × 11 paper. Rose and the other secretaries were sent to two-day IBM Mag Card training courses, and each returned with a spiral-bound notebook of operating instructions and reference codes. After everyone had left the office in the evenings, I would often sit at Rose's desk with the notebook and teach myself how to use her Mag Card typewriter in secret.

It was close to Christmas one snowy afternoon in December 1976 when my boss, Jack, and I were told we all had to stay late that evening to help our boss's boss's boss, Mr. Reed, the Executive Vice President of the Consumers Services Group (CSG), produce an extensive timely report for the Citibank Board of Directors. Each secretary/executive work team was assigned a section of approximately ten pages of the document to type and re-type until their particular document was complete and approved by Mr. Reed.

Rose was annoyed about having to stay late because, in addition to wanting time to shop for Christmas presents, she had a 90-minute train, bus, and walking commute each way to get to her home in southern Brooklyn. Most of the executives, like me, lived near the bank in Manhattan. Whenever we had to work late, the bank would put up executives who didn't live close by at the luxurious Drake Hotel next door, but the secretaries had to fend for themselves.

At approximately 6:00 p.m., we received the first version of our section, which was about 12 typed pages with handwritten changes noted all over the document. It was ready to be typed into the next version on the Mag Card typewriter. Rose entered the changes in 30 minutes, then announced she was "going out for a break" and would be back by 8:00 p.m. I protested, explaining that Mr. Reed's team might edit our changes first and send us our second version to re-type as early as 7:00 p.m. However, Rose was undaunted and walked out of the bank at 6:30 p.m.

Sure enough, our second version to re-type arrived back from Mr. Reed's secretary at 7:00 p.m. Without thinking much about it, I grabbed the second version and sat down at Rose's desk to input the changes into the IBM Mag Card typewriter. I finished the edits, and some later re-edits, by around 7:45 and was told we were done.

Everyone left, but I stayed behind to wait for Rose, who was now no longer needed. When she didn't return by 8:30, I left the bank and walked home.

The next morning, my boss was waiting for me when I arrived at work. He took me into his small office, closed the door, and asked angrily, "What did you say to Rose last night?"

I told him what had transpired. He then told me that Rose had returned to the bank the night before at 7:30, 30 minutes ahead of (her) schedule, but quietly left when she saw me typing away on the IBM Mag Card at her desk. She had then phoned our boss at home, exclaiming, "It doesn't matter if I return since all these new Wharton trainees don't need us because they know how to type on the IBM Mag Cards!"

My boss went on to explain how undignified it looked for an Ivy League executive to sit at a secretary's desk typing. He ordered me never to touch a typewriter again.

In October of 1977, my boss left the bank or was fired, and I was promoted to group staff—the personal staff of Executive Vice President John Reed. Reed became the President of Citibank three years later, at age 39, and the CEO of Citigroup at age 45 in 1984.

I remember a day in 1978 when other group staff members, who were already vice presidents, protested about Mr. Reed taking me on a trip the next day to meet with the Federal Reserve in Washington. He responded to the group that if they wanted to go to Wharton and learn to type 100 words per minute, he'd be happy to take them on the next trip. He added, "When I take Pilzer to a meeting, I get a fully edited memo on what happened that same evening while you guys are just boarding your train home to Greenwich."

BECOMING AN ENTREPRENEUR

PAUL ZANE PILZER

Chapter 8 - Learnings

1. I have always augmented my specialty with skills that others might find useless considering the positions I have held. Do you think there is value in learning a trade, strategy, skill, or process if people are already serving those roles—and you have access to their help?

2. It has been said that a person is only as good as his tools. Is this true in your experience? Does this explain why customers attach so strongly to specific brands, e.g., Apple Computer versus Dell?

3. Rose left the office before she had a chance to explain that she felt useless. Was this the best way for her to handle the situation? Was it necessary for her to call our boss at home at night? How would you have handled this circumstance?

4. My boss essentially shut down my ability to learn additional office skills since they were not a part of my official job description. Was he right to do that? Did he have a right to do that?

5. What do you think about my being chosen to visit the Federal Reserve on the basis that I would hand in a detailed memo about the events of the day? How do you think this contributed to the team morale?

BECOMING AN ENTREPRENEUR

PAUL ZANE PILZER

CHAPTER 9

MY FIRST DAY AT WHARTON

Although I had already experienced the rejection, reapplication, and acceptance process by the time I began the Wharton MBA program, it would take me almost a decade to learn to "revel in rejection" as a sign that I was on the right track.

Thursday, January 2, 1975, was my first day at Wharton. Dean Carroll called the entire MBA class of 540 graduate students together for new student orientation at 8:00 a.m. Like the youthful, blonde-haired dean himself, everyone looked so "white" to me; this was before diversity was a common term at Ivy League schools or employers.

"Welcome to Wharton Graduate Business School of the University of Pennsylvania," he said. "Joseph Wharton founded our school as the world's first collegiate school of business in 1881. And I'm proud to tell you that your class today represents the finest and most qualified student body in our 95-year history.

"You are also the most diversified group of students in terms of race, religion, nationality, sex, age, and prior work experience. Your class is 15% women, compared to just 4% women last year." He called out a few individual names and asked people to stand up one at a time as he mentioned their accomplishments.

Each selected student seemed more impressive than the one

before them. One student, who looked about 25, had produced the 1970 film *Joe*, starring Peter Boyle and Susan Sarandon. Several of the students' last names matched the Fortune 500 list of the world's largest companies. Some had the same last names as American Founding Fathers. Others had last names matching famous politicians, such as the daughter of a political independent who had just been elected the Governor of Maine. "Please tell the Governor hello from me," Dean Carroll said as he asked the daughter of Governor James B. Longley to stand up.

"Look around you," the dean continued. "While your average classmate is 28 years old with five years of work experience, we have students here of all ages. Professor Sigman, are you with us here today?"

A balding man in a white lab coat stood up.

"Professor Sigman is a highly accomplished M.D., research scientist, and professor at the University of Pennsylvania School of Medicine. At age 67, Professor Sigman is the oldest person ever to attend Wharton Graduate Business School, enrolling in our new MBA program in Health Care Management."

Then, I couldn't believe my ears as Dean Carroll called out, "Paul Pilzer, please stand up! Mr. Pilzer's accomplishment is that at age 19, we believe he is the youngest MBA student to ever attend Wharton Graduate Business School."

I sheepishly rose from my chair all the way at the back of the room in the last row, then watched the entire auditorium turn around to stare at me. I wasn't 19 anymore; I was twenty. But physically, I looked 12 years old, and I was certainly the shortest MBA student in the class.

Although I didn't realize it at the time, my career at Wharton was made in that moment. As the class stared at their 12-year-old-appearing classmate, they assumed I was intelligent due to my youth. I would be one of the first students chosen to join the better exam review groups and case studies groups, and eventually, I received some of the best internship and full-time job offers. From that moment on, as I would soon learn, I didn't have to earn my reputation at Wharton; I just had to show up and not blow my undeserved reputation as one of the smarter students.

Nevertheless, despite getting a head start in earning the respect of my classmates, inside, I felt exactly the opposite. I saw my relative youth to be the visible expression of my relative inexperience. And my classmates didn't just have 5-10 years of experience that I lacked, they were from much better undergraduate schools. Forty percent of them had graduated from one of the eight Ivy League colleges—Penn, Harvard, Yale, and Princeton led the list ahead of Columbia, Cornell, Brown, and Dartmouth.

The truth was that I couldn't get into an Ivy League undergraduate school because I had graduated public high school in the bottom third of a class where only the top half went to college. I didn't graduate early from my undergraduate school, Lehigh University, because I was intelligent; remember, I practically flunked out my first semester.

In my second semester at Lehigh, I had to take extra courses, mostly pass/fail, to make up for the classes I had failed in my first semester. Once I realized how easy it was to barely pass a course taken

Me and my classmate's son on my first day at Wharton.

Paul Z. Pilzer
New York City, New York
Lehigh University
Journalism
Sales Manager, Manufacturing

My entry in the 1974 Wharton class directory (before Facebook).

pass/fail, and that the university registrar computers weren't properly programmed to charge for extra credits that were manually added once classes began, it was simple for me to accumulate up to 24 credits a semester (15 is normal) necessary to graduate in three years.

On that first day at Wharton, I felt like Tevye in the song "If I Were a Rich Man" in the 1971 movie Fiddler on the Roof:

> *"The most important men in town would come to fawn on me.*
> *"They would ask me to advise them, Like Solomon the Wise.*
> *'If you please, Reb Tevye?'*
> *'Pardon me, Reb Tevye?'*
> *"Posing problems that would cross a rabbi's eyes!*
> *"And it won't make one bit of difference*
> *"If I answer right or wrong.*
> *"When you're rich, they think you really know."*
>
> *"If I Were a Rich Man,"* ***Fiddler on the Roof,***
> *Lyrics by Sheldon Harnick, 1964*

After I graduated from Wharton Graduate Business School, I began my career at Citibank, still feeling like Tevye. Even with my Wharton MBA, I knew with 100% certainty that I didn't know the answers to the questions most people asked about business and economics. Truthfully, I didn't even know what I didn't know, but the people in my social groups thought I knew because of my

Wharton MBA, my youth, my position at Citibank, and, later on, my outward material success.

Once I got out into the real world of business and government, I found out another secret to success: The knowledge that you don't know something with 100% certainty can be powerful in a world where most successful people believe they do know things with 100% certainty. And the more successful people are, the more convinced they are that what they know is 100% correct.

No one except God knows the future, thus, no one can know anything with 100% certainty. Even if you are correct about something, from how to trade stocks to the exact cause of climate change, the world today changes so fast that it is only a matter of time before you are no longer correct. In *Chapter 19: Leaving Citibank with $100 Million* (page 265), I'll explain mathematically how knowing that you don't know what you don't know can be a great asset.

Later on, I'll also tell you about the last course I took at Wharton, Speculative Markets, where the professor made us promise on the first day of class not to tell anyone what he would reveal to us—how to make a fortune in the stock market.

It wasn't until 1984 when I was 30 years old, nine years after that first day of class in 1975, that I finally had enough confidence to openly tell the story of how I got rejected and then accepted at Wharton. By then, I was already a top-rated teacher at New York University, a former vice president at Citibank, had a net worth of $20 million, and was beginning my next career as an advisor on economic issues in the White House under President Ronald Reagan.

At Wharton I was a student teacher of the APL programing course—on my birthday my students presented me with a birthday cake shaped like a computer terminal.

***** POSTSCRIPT *****

Despite Wharton's desire for more diverse MBA candidates, not much has changed in the past 45 years. In 2013, 36% of the Wharton MBA Class of 2013 came from those eight Ivy League schools, with Penn (7.3%), Harvard (6.5%), Princeton (5.4%), and Yale (3.8%) still leading the list.[11]

In September 1975, I visited my parents' home with a female Wharton classmate. When we sat down to dinner, I was horrified when my mother asked her: "So Pam, did you really apply and get into Wharton, or did you have to apply, get rejected, and then talk your way into the school the way Paul did?"

11. Byrne, J. A. 2011, August 7. "Top Feeder Schools To Wharton's MBA Program." ***Poets&Quants***. https://poetsandquants.com/2011/08/07/top-feeder-schools-to-whartons-mba-program/.

BECOMING AN ENTREPRENEUR

PAUL ZANE PILZER

Chapter 9 - Learnings

1. True or false: The highest valued achievements in life are the ones for which you are initially rejected. Explain your reasoning.

2. True or false: Insecurity is one of the most powerful motivators to achieve success. Have you found that walking toward your fears has been instrumental to achieving success? Do you think society has groomed you to think otherwise?

3. My former business partner, Alan M. May, who you'll meet in *Chapter 20: My First $10 Million Deal* (page 291), used to say, "The secret to success is inspiring confidence in your subordinates and your peers." How have you applied this concept in your professional career?

4. Do you think that the dean introducing notable students at orientation motivated or inspired new students? How do you feel when you meet a former peer who has accomplished more than you have accomplished? Is inciting competition an effective tool for leaders?

5. Throughout my career, I've perceived the people around me as believing that I was smarter than I really was, and I was afraid of being found out. Are you confident in your abilities or overconfident, and how does this affect your work?

BECOMING AN ENTREPRENEUR

PAUL ZANE PILZER

CHAPTER 10

MY FIRST MACROECONOMICS CLASS

I knew theologically that many of the economic theories I was being taught at Wharton based on scarcity were wrong. But at age 20, on my first day in class, I didn't have a theory to substitute for them. I developed Economic Alchemy, explaining business based on abundance, over the next 15 years.

In January 1975, when I was attending my first class as an MBA student, I thought that I might have made a serious mistake going to graduate business school.

The class was macroeconomics, and the professor began his lecture as follows:

"Economics is the study of scarcity. There is a limited supply out there of scarce resources—land, fresh water, oil, labor, and other raw materials. How we distribute our scarce resources for maximum efficiency in capitalism, communism, socialism, or any other 'ism,' is the science of economics."

This was when I realized that I didn't want to be there.

Scarcity, I thought to myself. *There is no scarcity!* I had thought I was going to Wharton to learn how to create unlimited wealth—food, housing, transportation, and entertainment—to ensure that every person on the planet could afford these items.

My Macroeconomics study partner and me outside class in January 1975.

Wharton Contradicted My Religion and Family Experience

My professor's belief in scarcity didn't just contradict my beliefs as an intellectual student—it contradicted my religion and my family's entire experience in the United States.

My father arrived in the U.S. as a refugee in 1914 when he was 11 years old. He went to public school until he was 14 and then joined his three brothers in the textile business making novelty toys and later curtains and bedspreads. Every morning, he thanked God for keeping his family safe, and he blessed the United States for giving him such an incredible opportunity to make a living.

Forty years later, when I was born, he moved our family of five from a three-room, one-bathroom, 600-square-foot apartment in Brooklyn to our own detached 1,200-square-foot home in Long

Island. Our home, along with 23 similar homes, was built by an entrepreneurial developer. He had purchased a small 12-acre farm, demolished the farmhouse, and divided the land into roads and 24 plots, where he built two different model homes to sell—mostly to immigrant families living in Brooklyn.

Our home cost $34,999 in 1954, equivalent to about $350,000 today—I still have the original bill of sale. My father couldn't believe that the banker, who wasn't even Jewish, gave him a 30-year mortgage at only 4% interest with a monthly payment of $143.22. Every Sunday, our relatives from Brooklyn would come to marvel at our abundance with absolute certainty that they, too, could soon own their own home if they worked hard and devoted themselves to God and their new country.

And here I was 20 years later, in 1975, enrolled at the most prestigious business school in the world, with my professor telling me exactly the opposite.

I wished I'd had the courage to stand up and shout at my professor, "My family didn't get our house by kicking someone out of their home. My father doesn't sell curtains to people who stopped buying curtains from someone else."

It was true. Most of our customers had never had any coverings on their windows until people like my father came along. In 1919, he and his brothers discovered how to use new technology like electric sewing machines. They applied that knowledge to manufacture pre-made curtains that people could afford. Moreover, my father and his brothers employed 12 mostly Italian-born workers who couldn't get a job anywhere else because they didn't speak English. My family helped create wealth; we didn't just move it around!

My next class, marketing, upset me almost as much as macroeconomics. In marketing, everyone seemed focused on beating the competition and getting a customer to switch to your brand of cigarettes or packaged food. To me, marketing should have been about educating a prospective customer about a new product or service that would improve their life and health. To many of my fellow MBA students, marketing was about beating the competition by taking away someone else's customer.

My experiences in macroeconomics and marketing were just as bad as what I had experienced in the most popular subject at Wharton: finance. In finance, I learned how to create complex mathematical models to predict the future price of an existing stock and how to run these models on mainframe computers the size of small houses. *Why should I care about the price of an existing share of stock tomorrow? The stock already exists!*

I wanted to learn how new communities could better finance their roads, schools, and hospitals for the betterment of all their citizens. I wanted to learn how companies with new products like affordable restaurants and high-rise apartments could raise money at lower costs to build more units and serve more customers. I wanted to learn how families just starting out could afford to purchase new homes and automobiles without having to save for an entire generation while they lived in a dangerous neighborhood.

In summary, I didn't have a response to marketing courses based on beating the competition versus educating people about products and services that would improve their lives. And I didn't have a response to finance courses based on how to speculate in the stock market versus how to help innovative providers create more affordable homes and automobiles.

Economics Based on Scarcity

At Wharton, while the formulas I learned were technically accurate and could be used to make a lot of money, the underlying premise of traditional economics—scarcity—was all wrong.

It seemed as if I was attending a religious school, but for the wrong religion, one I didn't believe in. The God I knew and prayed to would never have created a world where the only way to get ahead was by taking from someone else.

Too much of Wharton was focused on how to divide an existing pie among a growing population versus how to create an ever-expanding growing pie big enough for everyone to share. No wonder the Scottish writer Thomas Carlyle called economics "The Dismal Science," and no wonder most successful businessmen, like Sam Walton, had rejected much of what they'd studied in an economics class at school.

Other than my theological contradiction, attending Wharton in 1975-1976 was an incredible experience. The mathematical formulas behind each subject made sense and were, frankly, intoxicating. The professors and students were the sharpest I had ever met. And the students, especially the women, were gorgeous; 15% of my class was comprised of women from the best undergraduate schools, countries, and companies around the world. But back then, I was a 20-year-old graduate student who felt intimidated even being at Wharton.

I accelerated my graduation from Wharton by taking additional courses and attending a 6-week summer session and graduated in April 1976.

During my final months there, and over the next 15 years, I developed my own theory of economics rooted in abundance, which was first published in October 1990 in ***Unlimited Wealth*** (Crown Publishers, 1990). I named my new theory Economic Alchemy after the ancient alchemists who believed theologically that they could achieve wealth through science and prayer versus military conquest.

ADDITION C

Economic Alchemy and Unlimited Wealth
(Crown Publishers, 1990)

For the past 400 years, virtually all practitioners of the dismal science we call economics have agreed on one basic premise: namely, that a society's wealth is determined by its supply of physical resources: its land, labor, minerals, water, and so on. Underlying this premise has been another, even more profound, assumption; one supposedly so obvious that it is rarely mentioned: namely, that the entire world contains a limited amount of these physical resources.

This means, from an economic point of view, that life is what the mathematicians call a zero-sum game. After all, if there are only limited resources, one person's gain must be another person's loss; the richer one person is, the poorer his neighbors must be. Over the centuries, this view of the world has been responsible for innumerable wars, revolutions, political movements, government policies, business strategies, and possibly a religion or two. Once upon a time, it may even have been true. But it is not anymore.

Whether or not we ever did, today we do not live in a resource-scarce environment. That may seem hard to believe, but the businessperson and the politician—as well as the butcher, the baker, and the candlestick maker—who continue behaving as if they are operating in the old zero-sum world will soon find themselves eclipsed by those who recognize the new realities and react accordingly.

What are these new realities? To put it simply, we live today in a world of effectively unlimited resources, a world of unlimited wealth. We live in what one might call a new Alchemic World.

The ancient alchemists sought to discover the secret of turning base metals into gold; they tried creating great value where little existed before. But an analysis of their writings show that they were on a spiritual *and* monetary quest. They believed by discovering how to make gold, they could offer unlimited prosperity to all of God's children. And, although in our era, the term alchemy is often equated with "false science" and fraud, the ancient alchemists were successful in their quest in a manner they could not have anticipated.

Consider this: If the ancient alchemists had succeeded in fabricating gold, gold would have become ubiquitous, and thus worthless, and their efforts would have been for naught. Yet, through their attempts to make gold, they laid the foundation for modern science, which today has accomplished exactly what the alchemists hoped to achieve: the ability to create world peace by creating great value where little existed before. We have achieved this ability through the most common, the most powerful, and the most consistently underestimated force in our lives today—technology.

In the alchemic world in which we now live, a society's wealth is still a function of its physical resources, as traditional economics has long maintained. But, unlike the outdated economist, the alchemist of today recognizes that technology controls both the definition and the supply of physical resources. In fact, for the past few decades, it has been the backlog of unimplemented technological advances, rather than unused physical resources, that has been the determinant of real growth. I call this backlog the "Technology Gap."

The Three Principles and Six Laws of Economic Alchemy

Economic Alchemy explains how technology determines the nature and supply of our physical resources, what controls the speed with which technology advances, how technology determines the nature and level of consumer demand, and how we can use the technology gap to see what's ahead around the corner.

1. Technology is the major determinant of wealth because it determines the nature and supply of physical resources.
2. The advance of technology is determined mainly by our ability to process information.
3. The backlog of unimplemented technological advances (the "technology gap") is the true predictor of economic growth for both the individual and society.

The First Law of Economic Alchemy: By enabling us to make productive use of particular raw materials, technology determines what constitutes a physical resource.

> ***Definitional Technology:*** Technology that gives us the ability to define valuable physical resources.

The Second Law of Economic Alchemy: Technology determines our supply of existing physical resources by determining both the efficiency with which we use resources and our ability to find, obtain, distribute, and store them.

Quantity Technology: Technology that determines the available quantity of already-defined physical resources.

> ***Use Technology:*** Technology that determines the efficiency by which we use physical resources.
>
> ***Supply Technology:*** Technology that determines our ability to find, obtain, distribute, and store physical resources.

$$W = P \times T^n$$

Where:

W stands for Wealth;

P for Physical Resources (that is, the traditional measures of wealth such as land, labor, minerals, water, and so on);

T for Technology; and,

n for the Exponential effect of technological advances on themselves.

The Third Law of Economic Alchemy: The rate at which a society's technology advances is determined by the relative level of its ability to process information.

> ***Information-Processing Technology:*** Technology that gives us the ability to distribute information.

The Fourth Law of Economic Alchemy: By providing us with new products and processes that change the way in which we live, technology determines what constitutes a need, and hence the nature of consumer demand.

The Fifth Law of Economic Alchemy: Technology determines the level of consumer demand by determining the price at which goods can be sold.

> ***Alchemic Demand:*** Demand for goods and services in excess of basic physiological needs.

> ***Quantity Demand:*** Demand for more quantity of an existing already-owned product.

> ***Quality Demand:*** Demand for a different quality version of an existing already-owned product.

The Sixth Law of Economic Alchemy: The immediate economic potential for an individual, an industry, or a society can be explained by examining the technology gap—the best practices possible using current knowledge vs. the practices in actual use.

> ***R-I-T (Ready-to-be-Implemented-Technological) advance:*** A fully developed better product or method that is ready to be put to use.
>
> ***User Transparent:*** An R-I-T that, from the standpoint of the user, requires no additional skills or training than the product, method, or practice it is meant to replace.

Chapter 10 - Learnings

1. Do you believe that we live in a world of unlimited physical resources, or their equivalent, due to advancing technology?

2. Do you believe that Economic Alchemy is correct? If yes, do you come to your belief through science or through theology?

3. I provided a formula for creating wealth: $W = P \times T^{n}$. What challenges might you face in accumulating wealth?

4. The technology gap is defined as *"The best practices possible using current knowledge versus the practices in actual use."* Keeping this in mind, where in your business or personal life can you narrow the technology gap? How might you combine the technology gap with the wealth formula to generate greater results in your life?

5. I found it difficult to attend classes that defied or didn't support my personal values: scarcity in economics, a sole focus on making profit in finance, and beating the competition in marketing. Yet, I remained at Wharton until graduation. If you had been in my shoes, would you have chosen the same path I did?

BECOMING AN ENTREPRENEUR

PAUL ZANE PILZER

CHAPTER 11

THE WHARTON GUIDE TO THE STOCK MARKET

When I got accepted to Wharton in 1974, I naively told my parents that I was going to be rich. Why else would someone go to graduate school to study business (versus something more interesting)? In my last class at Wharton, I was disappointed to learn that there is no simple formula to get rich, but by then, I had already fallen in love with studying economics.

The most popular class at Wharton Graduate Business School in 1975 was speculative markets. It was taught by Professor John Perry, who was a funny, brilliant teacher and a consultant to several top Wall Street firms. This highly anticipated class was nicknamed "The Wharton MBA's Guide to the Stock Market."

The class, which promised to teach you how to join a Wall Street firm and make money in the stock market, was so popular that you couldn't get in to take it until your last semester at Wharton. The registrar gave priority to graduating students who wouldn't get a second chance. There was a waiting list, but it never cleared since no one who got in gave up their chance to take this class.

I signed up during my first semester (although I still had to wait until my last semester at Wharton to take it), naively thinking it was going to make me rich.

When I showed up for the first day of class on January 11, 1976, Professor Perry took roll call to make sure everyone in the room was registered, and nobody else had snuck in. One by one, each student in the room stood up and spoke their name while a TA (teaching assistant) checked them off on a list. Once Professor Perry had taken attendance, he apologized that no tape recorders would be allowed and made us promise not to tell anyone outside the class what we were about to learn.

"Each of you must promise not to spoil the surprise by telling your fellow MBA candidates what I'm about to tell you," he began, and we all solemnly agreed.

"Now," he said to his TA, "make sure the doors are closed."

The suspense was building.

Once he ensured the doors were closed, he turned to tell us what we had been waiting so long to hear.

"When you work on Wall Street, your employer expects you to make money for them and their clients and to bring in new clients. Now, here's how a newly minted Wharton MBA can be assured that they will make money for someone on Wall Street …"

This was a time before email, when fax machines were the new hot technology, and everyone had phone and fax numbers on their business cards. But the story I'm about to tell you is even more relevant to today's email and texting environment.

Getting a List of 1,000 High Net Worth Individuals

Professor Perry explained that to get started on Wall Street, we should each buy a list of 1,000 rich people. There were a number of ways to get these lists; we might ask wealthy donors to the opera board, acquire a list of recent purchasers of a luxury automobile, or we could access the members of a church or synagogue in a well-to-do neighborhood. What we needed, to start, he explained, was simply a list of rich people's names and fax numbers.

Once you had that list of 1,000 names, you divided the list into two lists of 500 names each and wrote two different letters on your letterhead. The letter to your first list of 500 names was to go out early on Monday morning before the market opened. It would read something like this:

> Dear RICH PERSON,
>
> My name is Paul Pilzer, and I graduated from Wharton Business School. I would like to meet with you to discuss your portfolio and what we can do together to increase your wealth.
>
> Today, when you see this letter, GM is going to rise. To maximize this opportunity, I recommend that you buy $1,000 worth of call options to purchase General Motors (GM) stock at $50 a share. Each call option gives you the right to buy, but not the

> obligation to purchase, 100 shares of GM stock for $50 a share up until June 30.

Professor Perry told us to fax this letter to our first list of 500 names and then write a separate letter to the second list of 500 names. This separate letter would be almost identical, except for the second paragraph, which should say the opposite:

> Today, when you see this letter, GM is going to fall. To maximize this opportunity, I recommend that you buy $1,000 worth of put options to sell General Motors (GM) stock at $50 a share. Each put option gives you the right to sell, but not the obligation to buy, 100 shares of GM stock for $50 a share up until June 30.

Perry explained, "Assume the market closes on Monday afternoon with GM stock rising $0.50 a share; The GM call options you recommended that the first list buy for $1,000 have doubled in value to $2,000 due to their highly leveraged nature as an out-of-the-money option derivative. The GM put options you recommended to the second list of 500 names, saying GM would fall, became worthless at the opening bell. It is mathematically the same as placing all your chips on red or black at a roulette table."

The body language of the class told the story better than I can describe it. Half the students, mostly the finance majors, leaned in and followed every word, waiting for the next installment. The other half were aghast, sitting up and wondering where this duplicitous action was headed.

Perry continued: "Early the next morning, Tuesday, throw away the second list of the 500 people who got the 'GM is going to fall' letter and divide the first list of 500 people who got the 'GM is going to rise' letter, into two 250-person lists."

Here's the letter you send to the first 250-person list that Ford is going to rise:

> `My name is Paul Pilzer. Yesterday, Monday, I told you that GM was going to rise, and I recommended you buy $1,000 worth of call options, which are now worth $2,000.`
>
> `Today, Tuesday, Ford is going to rise. To maximize this opportunity, I recommend you sell your GM call options and use the $2,000 proceeds to buy $2,000 worth of call options to purchase FORD stock at $30 a share up until June 30.`

And here is the letter you send to the second 250-person list that

Ford is going to fall:

> My name is Paul Pilzer. Yesterday I told you that GM was going to rise, and I recommended you buy $1,000 worth of call options, which are now worth $2,000.
>
> Today, Ford is going to fall. To maximize this opportunity, I recommend you sell your GM call options and use the $2,000 proceeds to buy $2,000 worth of put options to sell FORD stock at $30 a share up until June 30.

"Assuming the market closes on Tuesday afternoon with FORD rising $0.30 a share," Perry said, "the Ford call options you recommended the first list purchase with their $2,000 have doubled in value to $4,000 due to their highly leveraged nature as an out-of-the-money option derivative. The Ford options you recommended to the second list, saying FORD would fall, became worthless at the opening bell.

"Early the next morning, Wednesday, you throw away the second list of the 250 people who got the 'Ford is going to fall' letter and divide the first list of 250 people into two 125-person lists."

Here's the letter you send to 125 people on the 250-person list:

> My name is Paul Pilzer. Yesterday, Tuesday, I told you that Ford was going to rise, and I recommended you buy $2,000 worth of call options, which are now worth $4,000.
>
> Today, Wednesday, GE is going to rise. To maximize this opportunity, I recommend you sell your FORD call options and use the $4,000 proceeds to buy $4,000 worth of call options to purchase GE at $60 a share up until June 30.

And here's the letter you send to the second list of 125 people that GE is going to fall:

> Today, Wednesday, GE is going to fall. To maximize this opportunity, I recommend you sell your FORD call options and use the $4,000 proceeds to buy $4,000 worth of put options to sell GE at $60 a share up until June 30.

"Now," said Perry, "assume the market closes on Wednesday afternoon with GE falling $0.60 a share. The GE call options you recommended the first list of 125 people buy with their $4,000 are worthless, and the GE put options you recommended the second list of 125 people buy have doubled in value to $8,000.

"On Thursday, you send out two similar opposing letters to two lists of 62 people who now each have $8,000 worth of GE options, with each 62-person list betting on the opposite outcome. The people on both of these lists have seen you double their money every day for three days, from $1,000 to $8,000. By the end of the day, the value of each investor's original $1,000 on one list will have risen to $16,000, and the value of each investor's original $1,000 on the other list will be $0.

"On Friday, you send out two more opposing letters to two lists of 31 people. The people on both of these lists have seen you double their money every day for four days, from $1,000 to $16,000. By the end of the day, the value of each investor's $1,000 on one list will have risen to $32,000, and the value of each investor's $1,000 on the other list will be $0.

"On Friday afternoon, you have 15 people who believe you are the Messiah! They have seen you potentially double their money every day for five days in a row, causing their original $1,000 to now be worth $32,000.

"At this point, most of these 15 remaining investors on your list will probably have already picked up the phone and transferred to you a significant part of their family's fortune to manage. But just in case there are some stragglers, if you keep playing the game the following week, you could turn someone's $1,000 original investment into $1,024,000—turning their now-$32,000 into $64,000 on

Monday, $128,000 on Tuesday, $256,000 on Wednesday, $512,000 on Thursday and eventually $1,024,000 on Friday—a 10,000% increase on their original $1,000 in two weeks!"

It was then that Professor Perry summarized the true lesson on how to guarantee success in the stock market: "There is no lesson. When you meet the person who tells you that he can trade your money in the stock market and quickly make money for you, and you watch him do it again and again, unless he's doing something illegal like insider trading, you are merely one person at the tail end of a 1,000-person story like this."

He paced at the front of the class. "No one, except God ... knows what is going to happen at the end of the day in the stock market. The price that an underlying security closes at on Wall Street is that price where half of the traders in that security think the stock is going up and half think it's going down."

He elaborated, "There is a way to make money in the stock market, but it's not something you can do overnight. And that's what this course and your entire major in finance—if you are a finance major—is all about. So, get out your pencils, and let's get to work understanding speculative markets and how they work."

Everyone except me breathed a sigh of relief. Most of the class was made up of second-year graduating finance majors, and they had just invested two years and $100,000 or more in learning sophisticated finance techniques. Understandably, they were relieved to learn that no scheme existed that could put them out of business overnight.

I, on the other hand, wanted a real get-rich-quick scheme when it came to the stock market. And I had naively thought that such a scheme existed when I signed up for the course.

My saving grace, as I was about to find out in a few months, was that while I didn't know what was going to happen in the financial markets, many of the people I was about to meet thought I *did* know—and I could use their incorrect assumptions of my abilities to my advantage.

Chapter 11 - Learnings

1. At the beginning of this chapter, I described Professor Perry's class and his secret with much anticipation. Now that you know the "secret," are you let down by the revelation?

2. Professor Perry's strategy seems plausible but deceptive. Do you think there is any chance it would work today with instant communications and social media?

3. Do you believe there is such a thing as a get-rich-quick scheme for the stock market?

4. If you've worked in retail stock brokerage, list the most effective ways that you have found clients.

5. I talk in this book about using others' incorrect assumptions of my abilities to my advantage. How to Succeed When You Don't Know What You Don't Know: is this honest? Do you have an obligation to reveal any weaknesses in your abilities upfront when you begin a new relationship?

BECOMING AN ENTREPRENEUR

PAUL ZANE PILZER

PART II

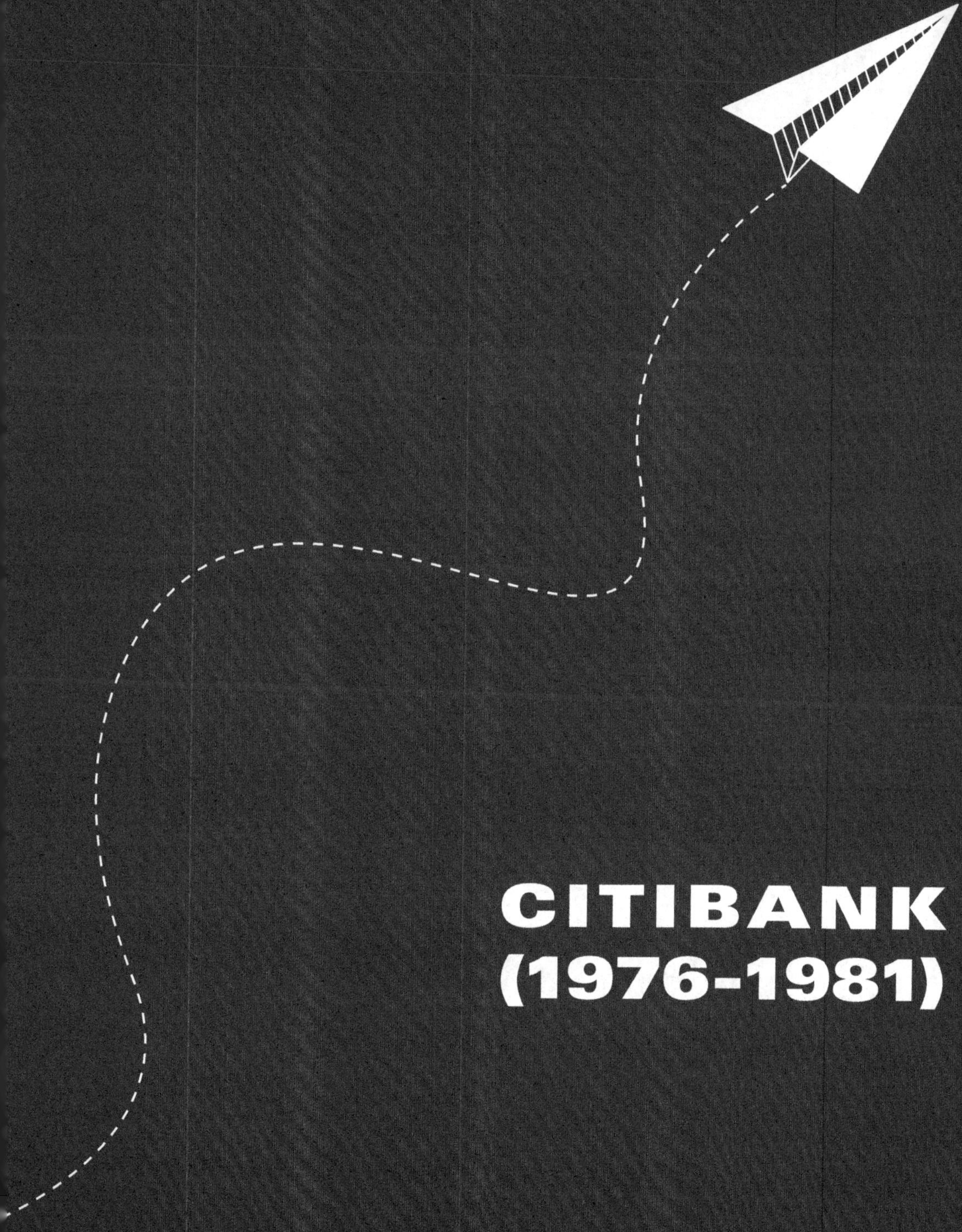

CITIBANK (1976-1981)

BECOMING AN ENTREPRENEUR

PAUL ZANE PILZER

CHAPTER 12

MY FIRST DAY AT CITIBANK

How Citibank recruited me from General Foods before I even started working at General Foods.

In early March 1976, a week after my interview at General Foods in White Plains, New York, I felt confident a job offer was forthcoming. I was set to graduate in April with an MBA in Quantitative Methods in Marketing and had job offers from two of the big three consumer marketing giants: Proctor & Gamble, General Mills, and soon, I hoped, General Foods. I wanted to work in the Main Meal Division of General Foods, which was then headed by J. Brendan Ryan, who I had seen speak at Wharton. Mr. Ryan was smart, funny, and the youngest person I had ever heard of running a multi-billion-dollar division of a major company.

I had no idea back then that Mr. Ryan would have everything to do with my becoming an entrepreneur but nothing to do with my working at General Foods (see *Chapter 18, How I Made my First $1 Million*, page 241).

Mr. Ryan was a Catholic version of me, ten years my senior. He'd been born in the Bronx and had attended Regis High School in Manhattan, the most elite Catholic high school in the U.S., and then Fordham University before going on to Wharton for his MBA. Rumor had it that he was the youngest MBA graduate ever from

Wharton (before I may have taken that title away from him). Later in his career, he became the CEO of Ogilvy and Mather, the largest ad agency in the world. I was waiting for a written job offer from General Foods when I got a phone call one evening in my dorm apartment at Wharton.

"Hello, is this Paul Pilzer?" said the voice on the other end of the line. "This is J. Brendan Ryan. Don't talk; just listen. I am calling to tell you that you will soon be getting an offer from my division at General Foods, but before you accept it, I want you to know that I will be gone before you get here. I'm going to be working on some exciting projects at Citibank, and I want you to interview with Citi before you accept any other job offer. So, write down the number of this recruiter at Citibank; she's expecting your call. Plan on coming in to interview at Citibank when I'm on board there later this month."

The next day I phoned the recruiter and set up a full day of interviews at Citibank, on the last Friday in March. Frankly, I had no interest in joining Citibank, then called First National City Bank, or any other bank. I was expecting to join a large, packaged goods marketing company that would put my advanced marketing and statistical analysis skills to use.

One week before the scheduled interview day, I phoned the recruiter to cancel and tell Mr. Ryan I didn't want to work for a bank. She replied, "You can tell him yourself. He just started here this week—I'll transfer you to him now."

When I told Mr. Ryan I wanted to cancel my upcoming interview day, he asked if I had ever stayed at The Plaza Hotel on

Fifth Avenue near Citibank headquarters, then the most expensive and prominent hotel in New York City. Mr. Ryan told me to check in to The Plaza the next week on Thursday afternoon, invite some of my friends to dinner in the hotel, and plan on being on the third floor at 399 Park Avenue at 8:30 the next morning for my interview day. Even if I hated Citibank, he said, "You'll have a great night at The Plaza with your friends, all paid for by Citibank!" He was very persuasive, and I was already thinking of which friends and female classmates I wanted to invite to my Thursday night dinner party at The Plaza.

The following week, at Citibank's expense, I took the express Amtrak train, first-class, from Philadelphia to New York. The train cost $18 each way, three times the rate of the $6 regular non-express train that I had always taken before from Philadelphia. The express train was almost twice as fast, getting me there in just over an hour instead of the usual two hours and six minutes.

I checked in to The Plaza Hotel at Fifth Avenue and 59th Street, and that evening, my friends joined me for the most expensive meal of my life up to that point, featuring a $300 bottle of 1973 Chateau Mouton-Rothschild. The label on the bottle was designed by Pablo Picasso. I had read about this wine in *New York Magazine* but never expected I would ever get to drink it.

My Interview Day at Citibank

I walked over to Citibank headquarters the next morning and had an incredible day interviewing with some of the sharpest and youngest businessmen and businesswomen I had ever met. One was working on a plastic card, later called Citicard. It had a magnetic stripe that could replace every credit card in the world and would allow you to purchase gasoline anytime without needing an attendant. One was designing an automatic teller machine that would dispense cash 24 hours a day, seven days a week. Another was designing a new "vertical check factory" for an entire building at 111 Wall Street that would automatically process checks five times faster than existing systems at less than 10% of the cost. I didn't know it back then, but these projects and the Citibank executives who ran them were about to become significant in my life, especially Mr. Ryan's boss, Mr. Tozer, who I'll tell you about in a minute.

Everyone but me used their middle name in some fashion and referred to themselves in writing by a three-letter acronym beginning with the first letter of their first name. Mr. Ryan was JBR or "J. Brendan Ryan," and Mr. Tozer was WJT or "W. James Tozer"—just like in the movies! Prior to this day, I always went by "Paul" or "Paul Pilzer," but from that day forward, I started using my legal middle name Zane and became "PZP" or "Paul Zane Pilzer"—I couldn't very well go through life at Citibank as "Pee Pee."

No one I met that day was Jewish or Italian, what people then called *ethnic*—I didn't know an organization could exist in New York and not employ mostly Jews or Italians. At only 22 years old, I wondered if my receding hairline, which I attribute to my Jewish lineage, gave me away. I also wondered if my Jewish background was so obvious that I wouldn't be offered a job. I later found out that most of the executives at Citibank headquarters were WASPs (White Anglo-Saxon Protestant), and almost everyone working at the branches was Jewish or Italian (depending on the ethnicity of the majority of the customers of a particular branch).

At 6:30 p.m., ten hours after we had begun the day, I had my final interview in the corner office of W.J. Tozer, a youthful 35-year-old senior vice president who looked younger than me. Mr. Tozer had a thick head of hair that fell on his forehead 1-2 inches below where my receding hairline hit my forehead. He had spent his entire career, 11 years since graduating Harvard Business School, at Citibank, and was then running Citibank's New York Retail Banking Division (the NYBD), employing 18,000 people in 305 branches.

He wore an impeccably pressed blue shirt with white cuffs, a white collar, gold cuff links, and a gold collar pin, which I later learned was his trademark look (after he left Citibank, I copied him and the look became my trademark). I had no idea at the time that Mr. Tozer would become one of my most important business mentors and lifelong friends for the next 46 years, a position he still holds today as my partner in PeopleKeep (formerly Zane Benefits).

Mr. Ryan came by Mr. Tozer's office around 7:30 to take me out for a drink at Brasserie, a 24-hour restaurant on 53rd Street inside the Seagram's Building, directly across from the Citibank employee entrance to 399 Park Avenue. Brasserie was located underneath The Four Seasons Restaurant, notable for its art collection and celebrity diners.

We sat down at a small high-top table across from the bar and ordered our drinks. Mr. Ryan told me that everyone loved meeting me and that I should expect an offer from Citibank within the week.

I told him that I was absolutely ready to join Citibank, except for one problem: since I'd been so sure I was never going to see anyone from Citibank ever again, I had gone overboard last night and run up a $700 tab for my room, wine and dinner for eight at The Plaza. Mr. Ryan laughed and told me not to worry about the bill, adding, "There's plenty more where that came from. Welcome to Citibank!"

My First Day at Citibank

I began work at Citibank as a management trainee in New York City on May 17, 1976. There were 145 trainees in my "class," mostly recent MBA graduates from what were then the "top five" business schools (Harvard, Wharton, Columbia, Chicago, and Stanford). On the first day of orientation, Citibank gathered us together in the auditorium to meet our Chairman, Walter Wriston, at the time the most powerful banker in the world.

"Before we start," Mr. Wriston said, "if you are in an even-numbered seat, take two minutes now to meet the person on your right." Then, two minutes later, he said, "Now, if you are in an odd-numbered seat, do the same with the person on your right."

After we had finished this exercise, he said, "I hope you enjoyed meeting each other because 24 months from now, only 50% of you will still be working at Citibank. But don't worry, most of you who wash out in our rigorous training program will get a job with one of our clients at up to twice what we're paying you now. And we hope wherever you go, you will remember your time at Citibank and use us as your banker in your new position."

He wasn't kidding.

Traditionally, when you were promoted to an officer title at Citibank—or most any other bank back then—you were given a solid brass heavy name plate which you typically kept for the rest of your life.

Seven months later, in December 1976, I became the first trainee in my class to make 'officer,' possibly the youngest in Citibank history. My new title was Assistant Cashier, and my salary was increased 8% from \$20,000 a year to \$21,600 a year. I started receiving monthly calls from headhunters offering me up to twice my salary to jump ship.

Almost five years later, in January 1981, I became the youngest Citibank vice president at age twenty-six. At that time, I was earning \$39,000. But it wouldn't be long before I accepted an outside offer with a \$100,000 annual salary plus a \$100,000 cash signing bonus.

Ten years later, ***Fortune*** magazine reported that more than half of the CFOs (chief financial officers) at the 100 largest corporations in America had begun their careers at Citibank. For the past 42 years, I've preferred using Citibank in my business transactions and now enjoy special alumni status benefits when I come to New York.

The King David Economy

Looking back on my career and departure from Citibank, I left too early and sold out too cheap.

After I left Citibank in 1981, new technology created the world we live in today, where some CEOs, senior executives, and entrepreneurs now earn 100 times as much as the average employee. These executives are worth so much because they've learned how to use technology to leverage their skills to produce 100 times more in value for their organization than the average employee.

Although I didn't realize it back in 1981, we were moving into an era I now call "The King David Economy."

About 3,000 years ago, the Israelites asked the prophet, Samuel, to appoint them a king.

"Don't you know," exclaimed Samuel, "that a king will take the best produce from your fields and vineyards, take your sons to fight in his army, and take your daughters to work in his palaces?"

"Yes," exclaimed the Israelites, "we know all that, and we still want a king!"

Economically speaking, the Israelites were correct in wanting a king. The 10th Century BC was the beginning of a new technological period, the Iron Age, where people could make iron tools and weapons that were ten times better than the bronze, stone, and wood items they replaced. But the manufacture and use of iron and steel required a strong individual leader to force people to dig irrigation channels, build furnaces, and coordinate military campaigns. The people of Israel were, in effect, saying to Samuel, "Yes, we know that a king may take away half of our Gross Domestic Product (GDP), but that same king will also triple GDP, which means we'll have a 1.5x lift—50% more wealth (GDP) left over even after the king takes 50% of our tripled economic produce."

Today, most of us, as employees and/or investors, are seeking to find our King Davids: people like Steve Jobs (Apple), Elon Musk (Tesla), or Jeff Bezos (Amazon). Some of us are seeking to become our own King Davids in our communities. Few of us are complaining about how much money our King Davids are going to make for themselves, provided that they produce much more in value for our organizations and us.

As a teacher and an economic advisor, this is my goal for my students and clients: To help you find or become the King David you seek to lead you to happiness and prosperity.

BECOMING AN ENTREPRENEUR

PAUL ZANE PILZER

Chapter 12 - Learnings

1. The Citibank officer who left General Foods for Citibank recruited me to follow him to Citibank while he was still working at General Foods. Was this fair to General Foods? Was it ethical? Or was he being scrupulously honest because he didn't want me to expect him to be there when I joined his former department at General Foods? Was this a conflict of interest for him over being loyal to his former employer or me? What would you have done in this situation?

2. Citibank then staffed its branches with employees of a certain ethnicity depending on the ethnicity of most of the customers of a particular branch. What do you think about this practice? Would this be accepted today?

3. In the 1970s, when Citibank hired me at a $20,000 annual salary, the CEO of Citibank only earned about $140,000—seven times my salary. Today, because we live in what I call *The King David Economy*, Citibank management trainees start at about $80,000, and their CEO earns about $20 million—250 times as much! What do you think about CEOs earning hundreds of times more than other employees?

4. I believe that CEOs and other C-suite executives receive such high salaries because of (1) competition for top talent and (2) because they've learned how to use technology to leverage their skills to produce 100 times or more value for their organization than the average employee. Is this an unfair distribution of wealth?

5. What did you think about Mr. Wriston pointing out to brand-new employees that half of them would no longer be working for Citibank two years later?

BECOMING AN ENTREPRENEUR

PAUL ZANE PILZER

CHAPTER 13

HAPPINESS = REALITY MINUS EXPECTATIONS

My father comes to visit me at Citibank. "Is the whole building air-conditioned?"

The best word I could use to describe my first year at Citibank is "wonderment." Everything about Citibank back in 1976 put me into a state of wonder. Even our headquarters building itself, 399 Park Avenue at the corner of 53rd Street in Manhattan, was something to evoke wonder for a first-generation American like myself.

After my first week at work, my father asked if he could take me out to dinner. I told him to meet me at 399 Park, so I could show him my office, a windowless cubicle in the center of the third floor near the elevator. I was excited he was coming and remained in my cubicle that evening until the receptionist called to say, "Mr. Pilzer is here to see Mr. Pilzer."

He arrived wearing his best suit. The receptionist walked him to my cubicle, which was smaller than a prison cell, about 8 × 7 feet, and consisted of my desk, my chair, and one visitor's chair. As soon as she left us alone, he excitedly leaned toward me and pointed to the noisy air conditioning vent in the ceiling. Then he whispered in my ear: "Paul, is the whole building air-conditioned?"

Forty-three years later, I still remember sharing my father's pride that I worked in a building where every office was air-conditioned and that my salary in my first year was greater than my father had earned in his best year.

At Citibank, I was assigned to work with two other management trainees in the marketing department. The three of us reported to an Assistant Vice President (AVP) who reported to a VP/new products manager—one of 670 Citibank executives in Manhattan with the rank of vice president. The five of us worked together designing reporting and operating systems for consumer banking products like checking accounts, savings accounts, credit cards, and home mortgages.

Each day at Citibank was a blast! Breakfast was subsidized in the trainee's dining room and free in the officer's dining room until 9:00 a.m. We were often taken out to lunch and dinner by the bank's vendors, lawyers, and advertising executives to the most exclusive dining spots in the city. On most evenings, if we worked late, the bank would pay for our dinner out as long as we were still at our desks past 7:30 p.m. I called 7:30 our "reverse curfew" since it meant getting a reward, versus a punishment, for staying late at work. Frequently, I would meet up with the other two management trainees on my team, and we'd go out dining and drinking at the unlimited selection of nightspots near the bank.

The three of us were a typical representation of what Citibank, and most other New York City financial employers, then called "diversity." Jack was Irish Catholic. He'd gone to Regis for high school, Georgetown for his BA, and Columbia for his MBA. His father was the president of a major department store chain. Jeffrey, like more than 90% of Citibank's officers, was a White Anglo-Saxon Protestant (WASP). He had gone to Collegiate for high school, Yale for his BA, and Harvard for his MBA. His father was a senior partner at a large law firm. Of course, I was Jewish, had gone to a public high school on Long Island, Lehigh for my BA, and Wharton for my MBA. My father was an immigrant who made curtains and bedspreads on the Lower East Side.

I remember my fellow trainees' backgrounds so well because back then, people seemed more defined by their family background and educational credentials than by their character and accomplishments.

My father had told me to rent an apartment as close to the bank as possible so I wouldn't have to commute, could always arrive early, and could easily stay late. My apartment was a 400-square-foot studio on the 30th floor at 417 East 57th Street. The view, with a 28-foot-wide and 10-foot-high glass wall, was spectacular! My rent, including all utilities, was $475/month, and the take-home pay on my $20,000 annual Citibank salary was $1,191/month.

One night, the three of us trainees were walking by my building, so I invited Jack and Jeffrey up to see my apartment. I was expecting them to ooh and aah at the view and congratulate me on my living quarters. When we arrived, I talked excitedly about how great our careers were for being so young, how proud our friends and families were of our success, how the bank paid for almost all our meals at the best places, how beautiful the girls were in New York City, how incredible it was to live in Manhattan and how much money we were going to be making at Citibank.

Instead of echoing my optimistic thoughts, my two colleagues described the same set of facts with an opposite interpretation. According to them, the pressure to succeed never let them enjoy a moment of success. Each time they accomplished something, they were compared to a friend or sibling who had accomplished more than they had and at a younger age. They complained about earning so little money that they had to get up extra early or work late for free meals. None of the girls they wanted to date would give them the time of day because they hadn't yet accomplished anything on their own. *Wow, what a difference in our perspectives!*

I phoned my father later that evening to tell him how grateful I was that he had raised me without expectations and that he always delighted in my accomplishments.

Dad and I laughed over how he had phoned me four years earlier, long-distance when he first received a letter from Lehigh University saying I had made the "Dean's List." In this call, after he congratulated me, he said, "Now who is this Mr. Dean, and what is his list all about?"

I learned something that night with my fellow trainees that became a lifelong mantra and is now a theme in this book: *Happiness equals reality minus expectations.*

That night, I stopped feeling jealous of friends or strangers from wealthier or more prominent backgrounds. I started saying prayers of gratitude at random moments, such as when the waitress brings a check, and everyone dining wants to and can afford to pick up the entire amount themselves.

I've addressed the subject of happiness in my books and lectures, from the University of Pennsylvania in 1976 to Nanjing University in 2018. In ***Unlimited Wealth*** (Crown Publishers, 1990), I explained how Keynes made his major mistake by "assuming that human satisfaction was related to some absolute level of achievement," and thus the only way to keep the economy growing was to progressively tax (read: punish) society's best producers relative to their success. In 1995, I appeared along with Tony Robbins and Stephen Covey in a Maria Shriver television special called ***Desperately Seeking Happiness.***

In 1776, in his book ***The Wealth of Nations***, Adam Smith stated, "Consumption is the sole purpose of all economic activity." John Maynard Keynes later echoed this view in the 1930s. Today, Smith and Keynes would probably both agree that happiness is the sole purpose of all economic activity.

It is more than a coincidence that Smith wrote this famous line in 1776, the same year our founding fathers wrote the Declaration of Independence. This great document does not grant people the right to seek just economics, rather, it goes beyond economics to what people really need and want: happiness.

> *"We hold these truths to be self-evident, that all men are created equal, that they are endowed by their Creator with certain unalienable Rights, that among these are Life, Liberty, and the pursuit of Happiness.*
>
> *Declaration of Independence, 1776*

BECOMING AN ENTREPRENEUR

PAUL ZANE PILZER

Chapter 13 - Learnings

1. I believe that attaining happiness can be equated to following the formula: Happiness equals Reality minus Expectations. Do you agree with this formula?

2. Do you think too much emphasis is placed on where one attends school, particularly prestigious universities? Why wouldn't a student from a less notable school be able to perform the tasks associated with any job in a competitive field if they were properly trained?

3. When I first started working at Citibank, people were defined more by their family background and educational credentials than by their character and accomplishments. Was this fair? Do you feel this is still true today?

4. The perspective of my fellow trainees and I differed greatly when we reflected on working at Citibank. How is your perception of your current job different than your colleagues?

5. Ask yourself the same question, substituting the concept of gratitude for perspective. Should my formula for happiness be revised to simply read "happiness equals gratitude?"

BECOMING AN ENTREPRENEUR

PAUL ZANE PILZER

CHAPTER 14

ELEANOR RIGBY
ALL THE LONELY PEOPLE

"All the lonely people
Where do they all come from?
All the lonely people
Where do they all belong?"

John Lennon and Paul McCartney, 1966

When I first began working at Citibank, I looked forward each morning to seeing Eleanor, the Citibank mail person who filled the inbox on my desk throughout the day with memos and outside mail. Eleanor sometimes brought me coffee and always kept me informed of the latest office politics. We initially bonded over both being born in Flatbush; she told me she had never met a "future officer" who had been born in Brooklyn and who had attended public high school.

Citibank officers mostly lived in Manhattan and came from a small list of private high schools and Ivy League colleges. Secretaries, tellers, and support personnel were disparagingly called "bridge and tunnel people" because they mostly lived outside the island of Manhattan and had to take a bridge or tunnel to get to work, as my parents and I had done—before Citibank. Eleanor assured me that my "secret" was safe with her.

Eleanor's whole life revolved around Citibank. As the mail deliverer on the executive floor, she knew each secretary by name and everything going on at the bank. She'd been a widow for more than ten years and had worked for Citibank for more than 35 years. She sometimes reminded me of Eleanor Rigby in the Beatles song of the same name.

One day in late 1976, Eleanor didn't show up. In her place arrived an automated, boxy-looking robot that stopped outside my desk and beeped until one of the secretaries took the paper mail from the slot labeled "Paul Z. Pilzer" and placed it in the inbox on my desk.

People started visiting our floor to marvel at the robot, which was quickly named "Robbie the Robot," after a character in the 1956 science fiction movie ***Forbidden Planet***.

One day, when my boss and I were showing off Robbie to some visiting foreign bankers, my boss went into a tirade about how much better Robbie was than the "gossiping overpaid old lady" that the robot had replaced. I remember my boss's sharp tongue complaining, "Before she (Eleanor) was fired, she made almost as much money as some of our junior officers," because she had worked so many years at the bank.

Eleanor was a victim of what economists call "structural unemployment"—that is, unemployment caused by a technological change in the structure of the economy—in her case, a primitive robot.

I wondered what became of Eleanor and if she'd ever found another job, but I never took the time to find out, perhaps because I was afraid of what I might learn.

As the years flew by, I became part of the structural unemployment problem. I made my own fortune helping organizations identify their Eleanors and replace them with much more efficient Robbies.

How I Became the First Automated Teller Machine

Ironically, shortly after Eleanor was displaced by Robbie, I was asked to join a team at Citibank that had developed our first ATM, or Automated Teller Machine. This was a machine destined to replace potentially millions of bank tellers.

ATMs back then were in limited use by our competitors, most notably the Chemical Bank located down the street. They were mostly made by a Texas company called Docutel and were called Docutellers. But Docutellers never caught on because they came hard-wired with a limited number of buttons pre-programmed for specific functions. Each major bank back then had its own customized operating system running on cumbersome mainframe computers that were difficult to change. No major bank was going to force a change in their primary operating systems just to accommodate an unproven technology like ATMs.

At Citibank, our team had developed an ATM that adapted to the needs of the customer and to the needs of the bank's primary operating system. We did this by inventing "soft buttons" that offered the ability to change their labels and their function as a customer worked through each transaction. Instead of fixed, pre-labeled buttons, we put a small television screen at the center of our ATM, surrounded by five mechanical buttons on the right and five on the top. Then with each entry, we would change the text on the screen next to each button to give confirmations and more choices to the customer. At the time, we lacked the technological capability to provide ever-changing text labels on the buttons themselves—touchscreens and LEDs didn't exist.

When I joined the team in 1976, we were ready to test a mock-up of our ATM on real consumers and develop the best text for each of the soft buttons. The mock-up was installed in our bank teller training center, located five stories underground near the Daily News Building on 42nd Street.

To run our mock ATM, we needed a human being to sit inside the ATM and type out responses for each screen. This person would also physically dispense the cash. I volunteered to sit inside the machine, and for the next few months, we ran thousands of consumers through transactions on this underground ATM with no one suspecting there was a real person (me) inside the machine making it work.

In late 1976, the bank spent $100 million to install ATMs all over New York City and developed the ad campaign "The Citi Never Sleeps." Everything paid off in January 1977 when the Blizzard of 1977 struck and cut off millions of New Yorkers from their money—except those who banked with Citibank.

The Branch Visit

One summer morning in July 1976, my boss told me to clear my schedule. I was to plan on leaving the bank at 1:00 p.m. and not being back in Manhattan until around 5:00 p.m. We were going on a "branch visit." I asked what a branch visit was and he replied,

"You'll find out."

A few minutes before 1:00 p.m., my boss told me to join him at the elevator. Already present was one executive I didn't know, Gary Judd, and one that I did: Mr. Tozer, the Senior Vice President in charge of the entire NYBD. This was the first time I had seen Mr. Tozer since my job interview in April, so I knew something big was about to happen. Mr. Tozer announced that we were going to Bensonhurst, which I recognized as the name of an Italian neighborhood in Brooklyn—the largest borough in New York City.

The five of us squeezed into a Lincoln Continental waiting outside. I rode in the middle of the front bench seat, which had no seat belt, with the driver on my left and Mr. Tozer on my right. I wished I had brushed my teeth after lunch before we left.

On the 45-minute drive south, I learned that Gary Judd was the regional manager of all 100 of our branches in Manhattan with more than 5,000 employees. Mr. Tozer explained that we were going to pay a surprise visit, sort of a branch audit, to one of the oldest branches of the bank. The branch had approximately 65 full-time employees, many of whom had probably worked their entire adult lives at this branch. No one, not even the branch manager, was expecting us; the element of surprise was the whole idea. Once there, each of us, "except Pilzer," as Mr. Tozer explained, knew whom to speak to about their operations to ensure they were complying with bank protocol and procedures. "We should all be ready to leave around 3:00 p.m., within one hour after we arrive, except Paul Pilzer."

I was surprised to hear my name mentioned.

Mr. Tozer turned to me even though our heads were inches

apart. "When we get there, Paul, your responsibility is to stick close to me, listen to my conversation with each employee I meet, and take notes." I nodded in the small space. "After we leave, spend a few minutes with the branch manager learning about the employee, and draft a personalized letter to each of these employees for my signature tomorrow morning."

We arrived at 2:00 p.m., and over the next hour, Mr. Tozer shook hands with 25 individuals. In my notes to myself, I described each employee by their glasses, shoes, the dress they were wearing, haircut, etc. My cohort left at 3:00 p.m., but I remained behind until 5:00 p.m. with the branch manager to discuss each of the 25 employees.

The branch manager told me their names, titles, and particulars—how long they'd worked for the bank, if they'd had a recent promotion, if they'd recently completed a difficult task, etc. Then I asked about their personal lives—were they recently married? Had one of their children recently married? Did they have a new grandchild? Had someone in their family recently graduated from high school or college? When I left the branch to take the subway home, I was confident I had enough material to draft a warm, knowledgeable letter to each employee on the personal letterhead of W. James Tozer.

The next morning, with help from my secretary and two other secretaries, including Mr. Tozer's, I had the 25 letters ready for his signature by noon. Each letter congratulated the employee on their contribution to the lives of our customers, noted something personal about their family and/or career, and was CC'ed with the name of their direct supervisor(s) and the branch manager.

"This is one of the great things we do at Citibank," Mr. Tozer told the three secretaries and me when we laid out the letters on the conference table for his signature. "Each of these people has dedicated most of their working lives to serving our customers during their life events: helping a customer buy a car, taking out a school loan, getting married, or purchasing a home. But they've probably never been properly recognized for their service. This letter we send to them today from headquarters tells them, and their family, that we notice and appreciate them, and most importantly, that we appreciate what they do for our customers. Many of them will frame their letter and retain it for the rest of their lives."

BECOMING AN ENTREPRENEUR

PAUL ZANE PILZER

Chapter 14 - Learnings

1. Structural unemployment is inevitable. Share how you would manage a situation like Eleanor's. What is the moral responsibility, if any, of an employer to an employee whose job was terminated by technology?

2. What do you think about openly testing ATMs in front of human tellers who would eventually lose their jobs to these machines? Is this like asking a prisoner to dig their own grave?

3. Today, what do you think of conducting surprise branch visits and collecting accurate personal snapshots of the employees? What would be a better way to recognize their contributions to the organization than personal letters from top executives?

4. How did you feel when I told you that we referred to employees who couldn't afford to live in Manhattan as "bridge and tunnel people"? Was this a cute or cruel joke? Would it be acceptable today?

5. Mr. Tozer sent out 25 letters to his employees and stated that most of the employees would frame them. Was sending those letters important or a waste of my time?

BECOMING AN ENTREPRENEUR

PAUL ZANE PILZER

CHAPTER 15

MY CAREER AT CITIBANK TAKES OFF

I began working at Citibank in May 1976 with the desire to make as much money as possible as quickly as possible, whether or not I made that money working inside Citibank or outside on my entrepreneurial deals. Then, my career at Citibank took off, and I experienced the joy and satisfaction that comes from being a "player" in a large organization that is changing the world.

I joined Citibank in May as a management trainee, and by December, I had been promoted to officer with the title "Assistant Cashier." This may not sound like much, but it was a big deal to me back then. My promotion meant I could sign contracts committing the bank's assets and that I had the authority to make loans. But most importantly, I could now eat free breakfast and lunch in the prestigious Officer's Dining Room and even bring guests—also for free.

It typically took 12-18 months for a management trainee to make officer, and my boss told me I was the new record holder, having made it in eight months at the age of twenty-two. The reason I was promoted so quickly is that I had become a valuable resource to Citibank senior management thanks to something called a Negotiable Order of Withdrawal or NOW account.

The Savings & Loan Industry 1933-1989

In 1976, there were basically two types of financial organizations that took in deposits and made loans: commercial banks for businesses and Savings and Loan associations (S&Ls) for consumers—credit unions were just getting started.

To keep the S&Ls from getting into financial trouble, the U.S. Congress passed the Federal Home Loan Bank Act in 1932, which established the Federal Home Loan Bank Board (FHLBB) and restricted the actions of Federal Home Loan Banks (i.e., S&Ls). Regulation Q, established in 1933 and managed by the FHLBB for the next 56 years, dictated what interest rate S&Ls could pay for consumer deposits and dictated the types of loans and investments they could make with those deposits. Above all, Regulation Q absolutely:

1. Prohibited S&Ls from offering "demand deposit" or checking accounts because giving consumers immediate and portable access to their funds was considered a major cause of bank failures during The Great Depression, and
2. Prohibited commercial banks from paying interest on checking accounts because S&Ls were mostly small mom-and-pop operations and needed protection from the larger commercial banks and their unfair regulatory advantage of being able to offer checking accounts.

The operation of an S&L and its role in the U.S. economy is best explained in the 1946 movie, ***It's a Wonderful Life***, starring Jimmy

Stewart and Donna Reed. During a pivotal scene when there is a bank run on the Bailey Savings and Loan, banker George Bailey (Jimmy Stewart) calms everyone down by explaining that each individual depositor's funds are actually invested in the mortgages on their home and their neighbor's homes.

S&Ls, also called "thrifts" from 1933-1989, primarily served consumers, and commercial banks primarily served businesses. But these lines began to blur when advancing technology allowed each organization to cross the line into the other's regulatory-established territory.

In the 1960s, during a period of rising interest rates, a few commercial banks took advantage of new computer technology that allowed them to automatically cover a checking account depositor's overdraft with funds from that same depositor's interest-bearing savings account—effectively offering almost the same benefit as paying interest on checking accounts. Also, in the 1960s, commercial banks started giving away toasters and other household consumer items in lieu of paying prohibited interest for a consumer's checking deposits. The thrifts panicked because, under Regulation Q, they couldn't offer checking accounts at all, let alone pay interest on them. In consideration of their dilemma, in 1966, Congress gave the thrifts a 50 basis point (one-half of 1%) interest-rate advantage over commercial banks. S&Ls could now pay up to 5.75% for consumer savings deposits while commercial banks could only pay up to 5.25%.

How I Became Citibank's Expert in Savings & Loans in 1976

In June 1976, while I was still a management trainee, I became the marketing product manager of personal deposit products (checking and savings accounts) for Citibank's New York Banking Division (NYBD). The NYBD was comprised of our 305 retail branches and 18,000 retail banking employees in the New York City area.

Back then, a commercial bank could only open branches in counties adjacent to where its headquarters was located—which meant we could operate anywhere in the New York metropolitan area but nowhere else in the U.S. That was the primary reason that Citibank retail banking became so powerful overseas and expanded into national and international credit cards—we had no other place to grow.

At the NYBD, we had about two million consumer checking accounts with an average balance of $110, about $2.2 billion in deposits—a 50% share of the New York City checking account market. We also had about 500,000 consumer savings accounts with an average balance of $200, about $1 billion in deposits, a 10% share of the New York City savings account market. Citibank's retail banking arm, which was then just the NYBD, was the largest consumer bank in the U.S. and fiercely competed with the thrifts throughout the New York City area for customers.

As the new marketing product manager of checking and savings accounts, I set out to learn everything I could about the history of retail banking, checking accounts, savings accounts, state regulations, federal regulations, etc. The list was endless. None of this detailed information was available in books or articles—I had to do original research and frequently request help from the bank's primary law firm, Shearman & Sterling, which occupied the entire floor (under the dining rooms) of Citibank's world headquarters. Like Citibank itself, this law firm ran 24 hours a day—it had attorneys at the Citibank Asian headquarters office in Singapore, exactly 12 time zones from New York. I would sometimes work all night at Citibank New York from, say, 1:00 to 5:00 a.m., which was 1:00 p.m. to 5:00 p.m. in Singapore. I remember once telling a Singapore colleague, "We'll continue this right after lunch at two o'clock your time"—which was 2:00 a.m. my time.

Yet in 1976, the hottest product I worked on every day at Citibank was neither a checking nor a savings account, and it wasn't even offered in New York State. It was a NOW account.

NOW Accounts—Civil Disobedience for Bankers

In 1974, Ron Haselton, the CEO of a small S&L called Consumers Savings Bank in Worcester, Massachusetts, decided to become a criminal—if you consider civil disobedience a criminal act. Ron was fed up with losing customers to commercial banks that could offer checking accounts. He responded by creating an interest-bearing deposit account product he called a NOW account.

Instead of offering consumers a checking account that paid interest, which would have been illegal under Regulation Q, Ron offered consumers a savings account on which they could write checks—except he called the checks "Negotiable Orders of Withdrawal" (NOW). Ron's NOW account looked and functioned exactly, for the consumer, like a checking account that paid interest.

Within a few weeks, S&Ls all over Massachusetts had copied Consumers Savings Bank and offered NOW accounts. The Democrat-controlled Massachusetts State Legislature endorsed NOW accounts. The commercial banks nationwide, led by Citibank and the American Bankers Association, the trade association for all commercial banks, sued. Everyone thought the Supreme Court would have to rule against the thrifts and order the termination of millions of customers' NOW accounts in Massachusetts—Regulation Q was crystal clear.

The case was headed to the Supreme Court until the U.S. Congress jumped in and passed a law in 1974 permitting NOW accounts in Massachusetts and New Hampshire. It passed another law in 1976 permitting NOW accounts in all six New England states. Although clearly illegal at first, millions of consumers liked their NOW accounts, and no politician was going to vote to take them away.

Now, the big question at Citibank was how soon the S&Ls in New York would similarly violate the law and offer NOW accounts—how were we going to stop them?

One Monday morning in late 1976, just before Congress passed the law allowing NOW accounts in all six New England states, I was called into the office of J. Brendan Ryan, the head of marketing for the NYBD at Citibank. Mr. Ryan explained to me what was happening in Congress and how Citibank had been asked by the American Bankers Association to lead the national effort to stop NOW accounts from expanding beyond New England.

"Next Thursday," Mr. Ryan said, "John Reed, who is probably

going to be the next President of Citibank, has to present to the (Citibank) Board of Directors a plan for how we are going to stop NOW accounts. You're going to help me and Jim Tozer write it." I was elated to have the opportunity.

Changing Horses in Midstream

Three days later, one week before the board meeting, I called Mr. Ryan's secretary to request an urgent meeting regarding Mr. Reed's upcoming presentation to the board. I was pleasantly surprised that Mr. Tozer was also present when I entered the meeting.

"Mr. Ryan and Mr. Tozer," I started out, "we're on the wrong side of history here, trying to stop NOW accounts. Consumers like NOW accounts and banks and consumers both save by offering a single account with checking and earning interest combined. We're going to lose this battle anyway—since starting January 3, 1977, the Democrats will have a solid majority in both houses of Congress."

Both of my superiors were silent and looked perturbed—this was clearly not what they expected.

"But most importantly," I continued, "we can make a lot of money by breaking ranks early with the other commercial banks and supporting the thrifts on NOW accounts!"

They both nodded for me to continue.

"No bank or S&L in the New York area has anything close to our retail distribution network." I was on a roll. "That means 305 branches, and customers with checking accounts need branches to make deposits and cash checks. My research shows that when we start paying interest, even at a nominal amount, on checking accounts, consumers leave lots more money for longer times in their checking accounts, raising their average monthly balance from $110 to $400 or more! And all this extra money will come from savings accounts and brokerage accounts—the former of which we hardly have any, and the latter of which we have none!"

Mr. Tozer pummeled me with question after question until I could tell he was satisfied (and worn out) by my answers. I knew that he knew that I knew everything about paying interest on checking accounts. During our meeting, Mr. Ryan had to call in his secretary twice to cancel his next two meetings so our meeting could continue.

"OK, here's the deal," said Mr. Tozer, rubbing his hands together. "John (Reed) is expecting the exact opposite of what you just told us. To change horses in midstream now, with less than a week to go, is above my pay grade. I'm going to request an emergency meeting to present him our new plan, and you're going to help us make the presentation."

I couldn't believe what I was hearing. *Do Mr. Tozer and Mr. Ryan agree with my recommendation? Am I going to attend a presentation with John Reed?*

Mr. Reed, an executive vice president in his 30s, was the third most powerful person at Citibank, legendary for his accomplishments. He had degrees from MIT and became president of Citibank at 41, then CEO and chairman at 45. Eventually, after he left Citibank, he was appointed chairman of the New York Stock Exchange.

The next morning, Friday, I got word to be in Mr. Ryan's office at 6:00 p.m. Sure enough, there were Mr. Tozer and John Reed—

Mr. Reed looked exactly like he did on television. Mr. Tozer made the presentation, deferring to me to answer some of Mr. Reed's questions. We ended the meeting at 8:00 p.m., agreeing to have a written draft on Mr. Reed's desk by 7:00 a.m. on Tuesday morning.

After Mr. Reed left, Mr. Ryan remarked, "Now you've got all our asses in a sling—your report better be good. This meeting cost me not getting out to the Hamptons until tomorrow morning."

I stayed on the top floor of 399 Park Avenue, writing and researching morning to evening Friday and Saturday. I consulted with Shearman & Sterling, the bank's primary law firm, and had them check every fact I wrote. Then, I finished up the report, typed it myself, and placed it on Mr. Ryan's desk just before midnight Sunday evening.

On Monday morning, Mr. Ryan congratulated me on the report, edited it, and had it retyped under his name and Mr. Tozer's. They delivered it a day earlier than expected to Mr. Reed, who presented it on Thursday along with our recommendation to the board of directors. The board bought every word of it. Citibank made headlines worldwide when it reversed its earlier position and announced that it would support NOW accounts being allowed by all depository institutions, even credit unions.

On Thursday afternoon, Mr. Ryan walked down to my cubicle to give me the good news, saying, "At this rate, you're going to be president of the bank by age forty." I thanked him for everything he had done for me and thought to myself, *he's wrong on that one! I'm only 22 today; I'll make president by age 30!*

During the next few months, the debate over NOW accounts

made the local and national news every week. Citibank star executives from Mr. Tozer to Mr. Reed regularly appeared on national news shows and always took me with them for support—I was the go-to guy at Citibank when it came to NOW accounts.

The Empire Begins to Fall

At the end of the July 4th weekend in 1977, I was driving from the Hamptons to my New York City apartment when I stopped over on Long Island to have dinner with my parents. As usual, my father asked me how things were going at Citibank. I excitedly told him how great my job was progressing and that I was thinking of making Citibank my lifelong career.

"Dad," I exclaimed. "They take care of everything: healthcare, retirement, office space, you name it, and I love working there without having any of the risks or pressures of owning your own business."

Boy, was I about to be surprised!

The next week I was stunned when Mr. Tozer, the person I respected the most at the bank, got fired. I remember thinking, *How can they fire Mr. Tozer? He is Citibank!*

Two days later, when I was getting ready to leave the bank at around 11:00 p.m., I noticed the lights on in Mr. Tozer's third-floor corner office, overlooking Park Avenue. He was going through documents and packing up boxes. I cautiously approached the door to his office until he looked up and motioned for me to come inside.

I started to express how sorry I was that he would be leaving Citibank, but he interrupted me, saying, "Don't worry about me,

Paul. I'll do fine. The bank will let me stay in a 'sayonara suite' for as long as I want, and I've already heard from headhunters and great companies wanting me right away."

Then Mr. Tozer gave me a compliment I've remembered all my life.

"The hardest part for me in leaving Citibank is you, Paul, and the thousands of other *sui generis* 'Paul Zane Pilzers' who join us every year. No organization, anywhere, gets to hire the extreme talent we hire to help us improve the world. It has been such a pleasure working with you on NOW accounts, and I know that wherever I end up, you're not going to be easy to replace."

I returned to my office to look up *sui generis*—it means one of a kind, and I left the bank around midnight. I was emotional and had to speak to someone. So, I called my mother, who I knew would probably be up late doing the ***New York Times*** crossword puzzle. Although I was a grown man, by then, 23, I cried when I told her about Mr. Tozer getting fired.

The year before, I had told my mother about meeting Mr. Tozer on our branch visit to Bensonhurst and writing the 25 letters of appreciation to the lifelong employees. To my mother, the name "Tozer" was synonymous with everything good and just about working for Citibank.

My mother asked me what he had done to get fired. I realized then that I didn't know and, frankly, didn't care. It seemed so unfair that someone who had invested so much of his life and contributed so much to our organization could be forced to leave. Today, as I write this paragraph, I still don't know why Mr. Tozer was asked to leave the bank 44 years ago.

As I told my mom what happened, I realized why my father had always wanted me to be an entrepreneur: it wasn't for the money or the fame; it was for the security.

He meant the security that comes from having your own business versus working for someone else. No amount of healthcare, retirement, salary, or any other benefit is worth having if it can be taken away arbitrarily at a moment's notice.

The following week Mr. Tozer was replaced as head of the NYBD by Dick Kovacevich, a new hire from General Mills, who later became the CEO of Wells Fargo. Dick knew a lot about marketing and was great to work with on NOW accounts, but it wasn't the same as working with Mr. Tozer. After everything that had transpired, I no longer saw Citibank as my lifelong career.

Three months later, on a Monday morning in the fall of 1977, the Citibank marketing department headed by Mr. Ryan was dissolved. I was devastated when I was told the news and the additional news that Mr. Ryan was leaving the bank. I immediately began searching for a new "rabbi" at Citibank. The next morning, Tuesday, my secretary, Rose, said, "Mr. Reed wants to see you in his office, stat!"

I walked quickly to Mr. Reed's office, notable for being in the center of the floor, far from any windows, no corner office for him! I was escorted inside by his assistant. Mr. Reed's head was buried in a document laid across a gigantic round table which was his trademark desk—just like King Arthur's round table in Camelot. The assistant cleared his throat to make our presence known.

"Mr. Pilzer is here."

I hadn't been this close to Mr. Reed or even seen him since our Friday evening meeting on NOW accounts three months earlier. Mr. Reed looked up for a moment from his document.

"Pilzer!" He motioned me forward. "There's *something* going on in your department, and you may be getting calls today about your career and your next job. Ignore them. You start next week on my personal group staff. See you in seven days." Then he lowered his head and returned to reading his document.

Later that afternoon, I was summoned to the office of Pei Chia, the number two person at the NYBD. Mr. Chia told me that I was being transferred to Westchester, a suburb of New York City, to run six retail branches. I started to explain what had transpired with Mr. Reed, but Mr. Chia cut me off, saying, "Shut up and be grateful you still have a job, which you won't have if you don't accept this offer." Some "offer"—it was an order!.

An hour later, I sent a memo to Mr. Reed, thanking him for the opportunity to join his staff but explaining that I couldn't accept his offer because Mr. Chia had just told me I would be fired that day if I didn't accept a mandated transfer to Westchester County. Almost immediately, I got a call from Mr. Reed's secretary telling me to ignore anything related to my moving to Westchester or working for Mr. Chia. I should report to Mr. Reed's office the following week as originally planned.

I ran into a colleague that evening who told me she had overheard Mr. Reed telling Mr. Chia, "What are you, stupid? We pay a fortune to find and train these MBAs like Pilzer, and you fire them over staffing your branches in Westchester!"

I began my next Citibank sojourn on the personal staff of John Reed the following Monday, focusing on legal/regulatory issues. The first document I worked on was called Managing the Legal/ Regulatory Environment. It was a report to Chairman Wriston on how much of our Profit Center Earnings (PCE) was dependent on government regulations and what we could do in Washington and worldwide to maximize PCE in New York and in each country around the world. This new position on Mr. Reed's staff eventually led me to Washington, teaching at NYU, and much, much more.

I never met Pei Chia ever again, but I am sure I saw him once in the next few years, going out of his way to avoid walking past me at Citibank. Pei went on to become the vice-chairman of Citicorp and Citibank and one of the highest-ranking Asian American executives in any major U.S. Corporation.[12] Decades later, Pei gave a generous gift to Wharton establishing the Frances and Pei-Yuan Chia Professor of Marketing, a position now occupied by my esteemed colleague, Wharton Professor Peter Faber.

---

12. ***Wikipedia***. 2021. "Pei-Yuan Chia."

Chapter 15 - Learnings

1. I took a big risk in talking Mr. Ryan and Mr. Tozer into supporting NOW accounts without having first done the required research. What if my recommendation had been rejected—what would that have done to my career?

2. Have you ever banked (no pun intended) your career on supporting a position that eventually got rejected—what happened, and how did you handle it?

3. My dad talked about how working for yourself provides you with security, which is exactly opposite of the conventional wisdom that it's safer to work for a large organization. Which position do you believe is safer—working for yourself or someone else?

4. What did you think of the way that Mr. Chia threatened to fire me if I didn't accept his position in Westchester? Today, we call this bullying. What would you do today if your employer ordered you, on short notice, to work somewhere else miles away in your organization?

5. I loved working at Citibank and, being single, didn't mind working weekends and long hours—which to me didn't feel as much like work as it did learning experience. If you want to ascend the corporate ladder today, are there alternative ways to get there without logging so many hours?

BECOMING AN ENTREPRENEUR

PAUL ZANE PILZER

CHAPTER 16

TEACHING AT NEW YORK UNIVERSITY

How my attempted resignation from Citibank led me to a new career at Citibank in commercial real estate investing and to teaching at NYU for the next 21 years.

On New Year's Day, January 1, 1979, just before I turned 25, I decided to quit Citibank and become a full-time real estate entrepreneur and part-time teacher at Columbia University. I had been a teaching assistant in graduate school, and for the past three years, I had missed being around college students. Plus, I knew that teaching college would make my mother more proud of me.

Financially, it seemed like an obvious decision. After almost three years in New York City, I was earning $32,000 a year as an assistant vice president at Citibank and earning about $300,000 a year as an entrepreneur, building and selling beach houses and renting out summer shares in Westhampton and Southampton (see *Chapter 18: How I Made my First $1 Million*, page 241). Meanwhile, according to the bank's latest 10-Q financial disclosure statement, my group head at Citibank, Mr. Reed, was earning $120,000 a year, plus options, as an executive vice president—options that would only have value if the bank's stock price substantially increased. I realized my earnings at Citibank would never catch up with how much I could make on my own.

On Tuesday, January 2, 1979, I waited outside Mr. Reed's office at 6:45 a.m., knowing I could catch him alone when he arrived a few minutes before his secretary did at 7:00 a.m. As he walked toward his office, I wished him a happy new year and told him I was going to resign. He immediately ushered me inside his office and motioned for me to sit down at his enormous round table desk.

"So, where are you going? Which one of our competitors has hired you?" he asked.

I explained that I was earning almost three times his salary working part-time as a real estate entrepreneur in the Hamptons, and I wanted to go full-time as a real estate entrepreneur and part-time as a teacher at Columbia University.

Mr. Reed looked totally surprised. In his world, leaving a position like mine at Citibank to go build beach houses was inconceivable.

Citibank, founded in 1812, was the largest and most prestigious bank in the United States during most of the 19th and 20th Centuries. We had financed the War of 1812, the Civil War, the Panama Canal, movies like ***South Pacific***, and had more branches in more countries than the next three largest banks combined. Moreover, Mr. Reed was the third most powerful executive in the bank, and most people considered him our future CEO.

"Well, Paul. I'm very disappointed. We've put a lot into training you, and I've always thought of you as one of my protégés here at Citibank. There's a lot more to do in this world than just earn more money. I thought you understood that. Who have you spoken to about this, and what's up with you getting a teaching position at Columbia?"

I explained that I had only made the decision the day before, and I wanted to speak with him before taking any action; I hadn't yet reached out to Columbia.

"Good," he said, in a declarative tone that sounded like he considered himself the sole decision-maker in my career. "Here's what you are going to do."

Mr. Reed continued with his monologue on what I was going to do with my life.

"Some of the projects you are working on here at Citibank are too important. I can't support you leaving now, but I can support you teaching part-time and leaving soon. But not at Columbia ... it's too far away. One of our board members, Larry Tisch, just became Chairman of the Board of Trustees at NYU. NYU is heading straight up, Columbia is heading down. I'll help you meet the right people at NYU for you to teach there part-time. As long as you attend my weekly group staff meetings at 9:00 a.m. on Mondays, you can leave the bank by 10:30 and teach Mondays and weekday evenings."

I didn't know it then, but teaching on Mondays was about to become my schedule at NYU for the next 21 years! NYU was located three subway stops away on the F train, only 11 minutes from Citibank.

Mr. Reed continued. "I've heard about your private real estate deals using Citibank executive's employee benefits for capital, and, frankly, this is a waste of your time. If you like real estate investing so much, you should be putting together international commercial real estate deals where you use your brain and don't get your hands dirty. These deals permanently change the landscape and contribute to our world. Citibank has an exciting new international Real Estate Equities Department in the Investment Management Group, located in Citicorp Center. I'm told that every real estate investment banker in the city wants to work there. If you stay with me until March and finish your current projects, I'll do my best to see that you get transferred there by the end of second quarter. You've been with me almost two years now anyway, and you're ready for a new Citibank experience."

Wow, I thought to myself. *This was just a dream on New Year's Day 24 hours ago.* I'd impetuously acted upon it when I'd waylaid Mr. Reed at the entrance to his office. *Now, all of this could actually happen!*

That afternoon things began to happen. Fast!

New York University

A few hours later, Mr. Reed's secretary phoned and told me to contact Professor Ernest "Ernie" Bloch at NYU's College of Business and Public Administration. I first called the NYU switchboard to ask who he was (without giving my name), and they told me Professor Bloch was chairman of the Department of Finance. I called back, spoke with Ernie's secretary, and we set up a meeting for the following week in his office in Tisch Hall, named after the brother of the same Larry Tisch whose office had referred me to NYU the prior week.

Tisch Hall, designed by the renowned architect Philip Johnson, was then the newest building on campus and was located at 40 West

4th Street on Washington Square Park. This was about to become my part-time office in New York City for the next 21 years.

The southwest corner of the park, dominated by outdoor concrete chess tables that were occupied 24/7, was, and still is, the center of chess in New York City—probably the nation. I had played chess there since I was six years old. The southern border of the chess-playing area is Thompson Street, known for its numerous all-night chess shops where you could always get a game going at any hour. When my wife and I were dating, we would often end up there in the wee hours of the morning. Lisa was a great chess player!

Bobby Fischer played at these shops regularly in the 1950s-60s, and once my father paid $5 to have me join a Bobby Fischer Group Match, where Bobby played 60 elementary school students all at once.

During my first two years teaching at NYU, I always arrived after work from Citibank wearing an expensive suit and tie, and I would hustle the local hustlers at their own game; I would come to the chess park one or two hours before class and set up my queen and king on the wrong color spaces, or refer to my knight as a horse, so other players would misjudge my ability and end up betting between $5 and $100 on the outcome of our game.

Back at Citibank in 1979, a few minutes after contacting NYU, Mr. Reed's secretary told me to call two people in the Citibank Real Estate Equities Department: AVP Stephen Furnary and VP James M. Trucksess. I called Mr. Furnary, left a message, and he called me back three days later, January 5. We set aside two hours to meet on Tuesday, January 16. Meanwhile, I began researching what went on at the Citibank Real Estate Equities Department.

Getting Hired at NYU

My meeting at NYU was set for 2:00 p.m. on Wednesday, January 10. On Monday, two days before the meeting, I walked down Fifth Avenue to the New York Public Library on 42nd and Fifth (the one with the gigantic lion sculptures on the steps that came to life in ***Ghostbusters***) to do some card-catalog, paper-based research on NYU and Professor Bloch—remember, this was two decades before the world wide web. I had last visited this library on an elementary school field trip when I was about ten years old. I was impressed, both with the research I was able to do in the library and with the background of Professor Bloch.

NYU, founded in 1831, is one of the largest and most prominent private universities in the world. In July of 2019, its faculty and alumni included 37 Nobel Laureates, 30 Academy Award winners including Lady Gaga, and over 30 Pulitzer Prize winners, along with members of Congress and numerous heads of state. During the New York City fiscal crisis in the 1970s, when the city itself almost went bankrupt after defaulting on its bonds, NYU went through some hard times—but all of that seemed behind them in 1979 when the university took off academically and financially.

Professor Bloch was a Jewish-born citizen of Nazi Germany who had emigrated to the U.S. in 1939, serving General Patton across Europe during WWII as an interrogator of German prisoners of war. He had worked at the Federal Reserve Bank of New York, had degrees from Columbia and City College, and had joined the faculty of NYU in 1962, becoming chairman of the Finance Department a year before I met him in 1979.

I don't know how I ended up interviewing that day with the NYU Department of Finance; I just wanted to teach undergraduate college students, and I hadn't thought much about which subject. I had assumed that I would teach marketing, which I had studied at Wharton, or government/public policy that I had been working on at Citibank. I probably ended up meeting with Professor Bloch because someone at NYU like Larry Tisch, or at Citibank like Mr. Reed, assumed that if I worked at Citibank, I would be better qualified to teach finance than any other subject.

I arrived at NYU for my 2:00 p.m. meeting early, as usual. After a few minutes of exchanging pleasantries and discussing his fascinating experience with General Patton during WWII, Professor Bloch asked what was going on with me at Citibank. I immediately started talking about the Real Estate Equities Department and shared what I had learned about the international real estate deals being put together there.

I explained how the department was buying U.S. preferred equity interests in real estate partnerships on behalf of tax-exempt foreign individuals like Ferdinand Marcos, President of the Philippines, and Adnan Khashoggi, then known as the richest man in the world. I explained how the same preferred equity deal structure for foreign nationals also worked for U.S. pension funds because they were both tax-exempt and that Citibank was putting together a commingled fund for employee benefit plan sponsors (pension funds). Frankly, most of what I talked about I had only learned the last few days while preparing for my upcoming interview on January 16 with the Real Estate Equities Department.

I was about to tell him that I hadn't yet actually done any of these exciting deals because I was only planning to join the Real Estate Equities Department at Citibank later that year. But that's when Professor Bloch leaned forward, and I paused so he could speak without interrupting me.

"Paul, this is perfect! Our business school is dying to offer a course in real estate finance, especially one tailored to our international students, but we can't find anyone qualified to teach it. Your background at Citibank and your knowledge of taxation and offshore investment entities are exactly what we need. Can you put together a syllabus by March, which will allow us to list your class in our Fall 1979 catalog that comes out in April?"

I couldn't believe what I was hearing. I was actually being offered a teaching position to start at NYU! No, it was even better than that; the chairman of the Department of Finance was acting like I had already accepted and would start teaching in a few months! The lesson here is that when it comes to listening to a presentation, you don't know what you don't know and might be about to learn. It can only help you if you give your presenter every opportunity to speak first. Professor Bloch continued:

"I want you to contact Professor Poorvu from Harvard Business School (HBS), who keeps reaching out to me. Bill Poorvu is famous as a real estate investor, but he's also an adjunct professor at Harvard Business School. He has put together the best real estate finance curriculum anywhere, and he sells the entire curriculum, 16 exciting cases per semester, to most of the top business schools—except NYU, because I haven't been able until now to find someone with your qualifications to teach it. I know you probably don't need the money, but we'll pay you $5,000 per semester, plus give you teaching assistants, so you won't get buried in grading exams and administering the course. I know you still have a career to manage at Citibank."

I accepted Professor Bloch's offer on the spot; $10,000 a year for part-time work was almost a third of my Citibank salary.

Citicorp Center

The pressure was now on for me to get hired by the Citibank Real Estate Equities Department, especially because Professor Bloch thought I already worked there. I spoke to everyone I could find at the bank about what the Real Estate Equities Department did and felt confident I had left no stone unturned by the time my interview rolled around the following week, the day before my 25th birthday.

In 1979, the world headquarters of Citibank was at 399 Park Avenue between Park Avenue, 53rd Street, Lexington Avenue, and 54th Street. It was a 41-story, 520-foot tall non-descript glass tower that the bank (then called First National City Bank) built in 1961. The bank sold the building in 2002.

Directly across the street on Lexington Avenue, in 1977, Citibank built Citicorp Center, a spectacular 59-story building that cantilevered over the site and contained many important innovations. One innovation was an 800,000-pound concrete block in the striking 90-story angled roof called a tuned mass damper, which was on tracks so it could move in any direction to counteract the effect of wind sway on the upper floors. Citicorp Center (later renamed Citigroup Center) was the first skyscraper in the United States to feature a tuned mass damper. Another innovation was a double-decker elevator system which saved energy and reduced the amount of elevator space needed to move tenants. I was intimately familiar with the building's features because, as a junior executive on the staff of senior officers Mr. Tozer and later Mr. Reed, I regularly gave tours of Citicorp Center to visiting dignitaries and executives, the highlight of which was always the 800,000-pound concrete tuned mass damper in the open roof.

Although Citibank had originally contemplated using Citicorp Center as its corporate headquarters, it was considered too expensive when completed. Only the Investment Management Group (IMG) of Citibank, which included the Real Estate Equities Department, had moved in by January 1979. The rest of the space had been rented out to third-party tenants at the highest rent prices in the city.

On Tuesday, January 16, 1979, I walked across Lexington Avenue to Citicorp Center for my interview with the Real Estate Equities Department on the 16th floor. I got confused on the way there because the double-decker elevator took me only to the 15th floor, and I needed to take an escalator to the 16th. The 15th floor was the private banking department for overseas individuals, which had extra security because some of these wealthy individuals were heads of state or relatives of these dignitaries.

Meeting Citibank's Real Estate Equities Department

The first person I met on the 16th floor was Stephen Furnary, who was only three years older than me. I asked Furnary how he liked being in Citicorp Center, and we ended up talking about Citibank and the Citicorp Center building for about 20 minutes. He had been hired a few months earlier and was unaware that his group, the IMG, was the only Citibank department lucky enough to be located in Citicorp Center. He seemed impressed by what I knew about the background of many Citibank senior officers and what I knew about Citicorp Center itself.

I learned that the entire Real Estate Equities Department had recently been formed by hiring Jim Trucksess from TIAA, then the leading organization in the U.S. making direct investments in commercial real estate on behalf of tax-exempt U.S. pension funds. Everyone in the department except the secretaries had been hired from outside the bank. If I joined them, I would be the first department hire from inside the bank.

We spoke for another 20 minutes about real estate investing, the Citibank Real Estate Equities Department, and how it operated. Furnary explained how Citibank got the best deals from developers by leaving the real estate tax benefits on the table for them to sell elsewhere and by purchasing preferred interests in real estate versus purchasing entire buildings.

Then Furnary changed the subject and grilled me for one hour about my personal real estate deals in the Hamptons, especially how I structured my beach house deals with Citibank executives and their employee benefit below-rate mortgages (see *Chapter 18: How*

I Made my First $1 Million, page 241). I was, frankly, embarrassed to talk about my outside activities. At one point, I couldn't tell if Furnary wanted to disqualify me or become an investor in one of these deals or if he wanted tips on getting a house in the Hamptons. It turned out to be none of the above.

"Paul, your personality and creative entrepreneurial spirit are exactly what I want on my team here at Citibank. But I'm not the only decision-maker. Go wait outside in the conference room while I see if Mr. Trucksess is ready to meet with us." I went outside and waited about 15 minutes until Furnary came and got me. The two of us walked down the hall to the corner office occupied by Mr. Trucksess.

"Let me get right to the point," Mr. Trucksess said. He was tall, thin, and had silver hair and intense blue eyes that always made me feel like he could see right through me. "You have no experience in commercial real estate investing, foreign equity investing using Netherlands Antilles entities, or any of the other skill sets we need around here to make money for our clients. But that doesn't matter because Furnary thinks you're a fast learner, and he's ready to take you on his team. What our department needs is someone to help me with the crazy politics at Citibank and all these compliance issues that arise every time we want to do something. So, here's your deal."

Mr. Trucksess explained that they would take me on as a junior deal-maker in the Real Estate Equities Department. But during my first six months, I would be on call to help the department establish their equity commingled fund for U.S. pension fund plan sponsors—the first of its kind in the nation. This fund allowed pension funds that wanted to invest large amounts in commercial real estate equities to write checks to the fund, which would invest the money in a diversified portfolio of major real estate investments.

The department was having trouble completing the documents to establish the fund. The bank's compliance officers and lawyers were driving them crazy with a new issue coming up almost every week. This particular week, the lawyers and compliance officers were concerned that: 1) The commingled fund could be viewed as a securities offering and thus subject to impossible-to-meet SEC regulations, and 2) the performance-based compensation agreements that Mr. Trucksess had promised to his new hires might be violating federal and state banking regulations. Mr. Trucksess needed someone who already knew the top executives and top lawyers at Citibank—me—to help him navigate issue after issue with compliance.

Whenever issues like these came up, my responsibility was to meet with whomever I needed to get the bank's compliance officers and lawyers off his back. In return, Mr. Trucksess said he would let me keep my existing AVP title, even though I knew very little about foreign investment entities and commercial real estate investing. Furnary would teach me everything I needed to know.

I was ecstatic, but I tried not to show it to my conservative new bosses. If I could make $300,000 a year on my own, putting together deals on beach houses, I was sure I could one day make $3 million a year, putting together deals on commercial office buildings, industrial buildings, and shopping centers.

The next week we wrapped everything up at Citibank and NYU,

and the arrangement looked like this:

- I would finish my projects for Mr. Reed in March 1979 and transfer to the Real Estate Equities Department in Citicorp Center around March 31, 1979.
- I would start my first class at NYU teaching Real Estate Finance the day after Labor Day, September 3, 1979.
- I would have five months (April-August) to learn enough about commercial real estate investing to stay ahead of my students at NYU and become a contributing deal-maker in the Citibank Real Estate Equities Department.

My First Class at NYU—Real Estate Finance

The following week I visited the NYU bookstore on Washington Square and introduced myself as the new assistant adjunct professor of finance. I had NYU order me a free sample copy of virtually every real estate finance textbook they could find—I had a lot of reading to do. Meanwhile, I visited the NYU registrar, got my picture taken, and was given a faculty ID card that allowed me unlimited use of NYU's extensive athletic facilities.

The next week I phoned Professor Bill Poorvu at HBS and explained that I would be teaching Real Estate Finance at NYU that fall. Bill was elated and overnighted me the complete syllabus of his course and about 30 HBS real estate finance cases. Bill's material was the mother lode that helped structure my course. He told me he visited New York often and wanted to meet in person soon during his next visit. But for the next two decades that I taught at NYU,

My 1979 NYU Faculty ID, which allowed me use of NYU's extensive athletic facilities.

even though Bill became a mentor on the phone who I spoke to at least once each semester, we actually never met in person. Each semester he sent me his latest and greatest new cases. It was a hard choice for me to pick out the 14 or so cases we had time for in my undergraduate class. Years later, a fellow NYU professor told me that my course was known as the "Harvard Business School Real Estate Finance course at NYU."

I completed my learning and research in August 1979 and felt confident, on Labor Day weekend, that I was ready for my first three-hour class the following Monday evening, September 10.

My First Students at NYU

My first class at NYU in September 1979 had 24 undergraduate students from around the world. Every one of these kids seemed extraordinary. Several were already accomplished entrepreneurs, and all of them were between the ages of 19-22, just a few years younger than I was at 25. I have often wondered if Professor Bloch had somehow hand-picked each of them to make my first class extra special.

The first student I remember meeting was Nicolas Bergruen. He had a heavy German accent, asked questions about his personal New York real estate investments, and graduated from NYU when he was 19 in 1981. While at NYU and still in his 20s, Nicolas began buying real estate with a $250,000 trust fund that he parlayed into $2 billion, earning him a coveted spot on the Forbes 400 list. He is today known for his world-changing philanthropic projects—each of which could occupy an entire book by themselves. The press has referred to him as the "homeless billionaire" because he has often lived in hotels without owning a permanent residence.

A second student who made an impression was Bob Petrucello. You'll meet him later in this book as he became the first of my students that I later hired. Today, his financial success eclipses mine. When I first met Bob, he was marked on my class roster as a special type of scholarship recipient who had received free tuition, room, and board in an NYU high-rise apartment—no small feat at a school renown for having the highest tuition and lodging costs in the world. One evening after class, I overheard him tell his case group that he had to leave by 11:00 p.m. to make the last subway home to Bensonhurst. Later, privately, I asked him if his scholarship included a free apartment in a luxury campus high rise. He said,

"Yes, it does, but I rent out my free apartment for $6,000 a year and live at home with my mother in Brooklyn!"

A third student, Peter Derby, was a piece of Cold War history all by himself. When I first met Peter in 1979, he was my student and living in the Russian community known as "Little Moscow" on the Upper East Side of Manhattan. His grandparents had barely escaped the Bolsheviks in 1917 and had relocated "temporarily" to Manhattan. Peter sounded like a crazy person when he described his plans to bring capitalism back to Russia, which was then part of the USSR. After NYU graduation and stellar careers at Chase Manhattan Bank and the SEC, in 1990, he became one of the world's leading American-Russian businessmen and the founder of the first private bank in Russia. He served in Russia for ten years and helped establish the Russian equivalent of the SEC and other Russian financial regulatory entities.

My first class was a big success! Although I received the credit, it was exceptional mostly because of the students.

Teaching at NYU—1979-2000

Almost two years later, just two weeks after the spring semester class at NYU began on January 16, 1981, I resigned from Citibank and moved to Dallas, Texas.

Since I couldn't abandon my students, I negotiated for my new employer to fly me back to New York, first-class, every Sunday night to teach on Mondays at NYU. This arrangement also allowed me to have dinner with my mother every week, which was especially important because my father had passed away in 1979. I continued with this arrangement for the next 19 years, with five subsequent employers and startups flying in from Dallas, Washington, Moscow, Los Angeles, or Utah, depending on where I was based during the week.

One Sunday night, I found myself embarrassedly booked on a first-class flight for $459 with my multi-millionaire employer, who had a $99 economy ticket. This story, and its aftermath, made it onto the Opinion Page of the ***New York Times*** on October 29, 1985, in a piece entitled "Guide to Flying on Other People's Money,"[13] foreshadowing the title of my first book, four years later (see the article in *Chapter 19: Leaving Citibank with $100 Million*, page 265).

My NYU classroom on Monday evenings, 5:30 to 8:30, became my nexus in New York City for putting together business deals and meeting new friends. I often brought guests with me to class—people I had been working with earlier that day or week—from Moscow to Los Angeles. At 8:30, I would announce that as class was officially over, it was now "optional" for students to stay and hear from our guest speaker. Typically, almost everyone stayed. These optional sessions sometimes lasted past midnight and led to late night/early morning dinners at Café Un Deux Trois in Times Square—one of my favorite New York City all-night places to eat and see and be seen before heading over to the discotheque, Studio 54.

After two years, I cut down from teaching both the fall and spring semesters to just flying in on Sunday evenings to teach in the fall semester.

---

13. Pilzer, P.. Z. "Guide to Flying on Other People's Money." Opinion. ***New York Times***. October 29, 1985. Section A, 29.

One day, in the fall of 1980, right before class started, my teaching assistant, Henry Emerson, who also worked for me at Citibank, asked me if the daughter of his mother's boss could visit our class at 6:30, and join us afterward for dinner. I said yes. At 6:30, the door to my class opened, and in walked a stunningly beautiful woman. Upon seeing her, I stuttered and lost my train of thought. Almost as if scripted, the entire class turned around in synchronization to stare at her. It was Donna Rice, then working in New York as a television commercial and sitcom actress—the same Donna Rice who later became known for her alleged affair with presidential candidate Gary Hart. Donna attended many of my classes that semester and we became friends, but lost touch after the Gary Hart Monkey Business Scandal in 1987.

In 1985-1986, the hottest topic in Washington was the Tax Reform Act of 1986, which passed on October 22, and completely changed the tax benefit component of real estate finance. The man at the center of tax reform was Senator Bob Packwood (R-OR), chairman of the Senate Finance Committee and later candidate for President of the United States. Bob was arguably the most powerful man in the Senate back then, and he was also a graduate of the NYU School of Law who loved coming back to campus. He was my guest speaker on several occasions, and his discussions on tax reform and real estate tax benefits provided priceless learning experiences for my students and me.

In 1987, I noticed a baby-faced new student in the back row visiting class, who I later learned was John F. Kennedy Jr., then a full-time law student at NYU. By that time, my undergraduate Real

Estate Finance class was a popular elective for NYU MBA and JD students.

From 1985 to 1992, I spent many weeks each year working in the former Soviet Union, and I attended the Moscow Summit between President Ronald Reagan and General Secretary Mikhail Gorbachev. I had so many Russian contacts that most of my NYU classes featured visiting Russian guests. Teaching part-time was commonplace among Soviet political and business leaders, and several remarked that I was the first American businessman they'd ever met who also taught at a major U.S. university.

In 1989, my friend Tony Robbins was doing an eight-week series of all-day Unlimited Power seminars every Monday at the Marriott in midtown. I originally met Tony because we had the same literary agent (Jan Miller) and editor (Bob Asahina) at Simon & Schuster. Tony learned to ski at my ski house in Park City, and I learned to scuba dive at his island house in Fiji. He came to class after each seminar and, even after being on stage for 12 hours, would captivate my students until late in the night. Tony had just launched his first mega-successful infomercial, Personal Power, in 1988, so everyone knew he was "someone," although most of my students back then were unsure of exactly who he was or what he did. That changed by 1992 when Tony rose to megastardom. Around that time, he featured me in his latest infomercial and in his second book, ***Awaken the Giant Within***.

In 1991, Sony launched the first portable multimedia CD-ROM player and announced they were taking bids from software developers to make discs for the player. I was then the CEO of

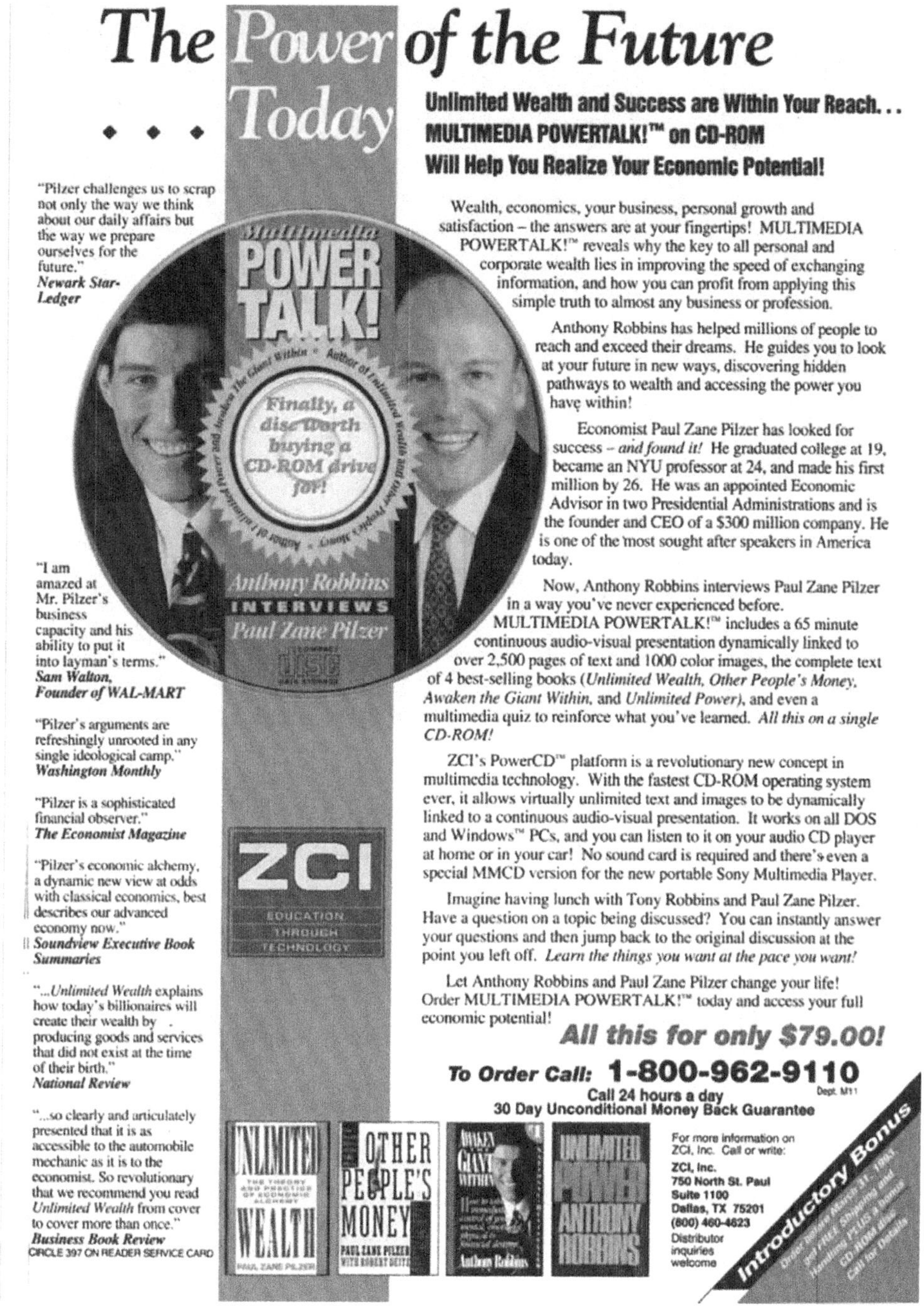

This was a full-page advertisement in ***PC Magazine*** for Zane Publishing's first big CD-ROM—it contained audio-visual presentations by Tony Robbins and me along with the text of our four books that ran on PCs, Apple Computers, and the new Sony portable CD-ROM player.

Productivity In Full Bloom, Two-page inside cover of October 1993 ***Success Magazine*** featuring a Sony portable CD-ROM player. I appeared on the front cover.

a leading educational CD-ROM company (see *Chapter 24: My Litigation with Apple Computer*, page 419). So, I invited the senior Sony CD-ROM executives to meet me at 8:30 p.m. after class to discuss my company, Zane Publishing, making a bid. They arrived three hours early at 5:30 and sat through my entire class, watching me excitedly get my suit covered with chalk as I drew diagrams and keywords on the blackboards to explain what I was teaching.

Afterward, when we sat down for dinner, I asked about the bidding process. They pointed to the chalk on my suit and told me

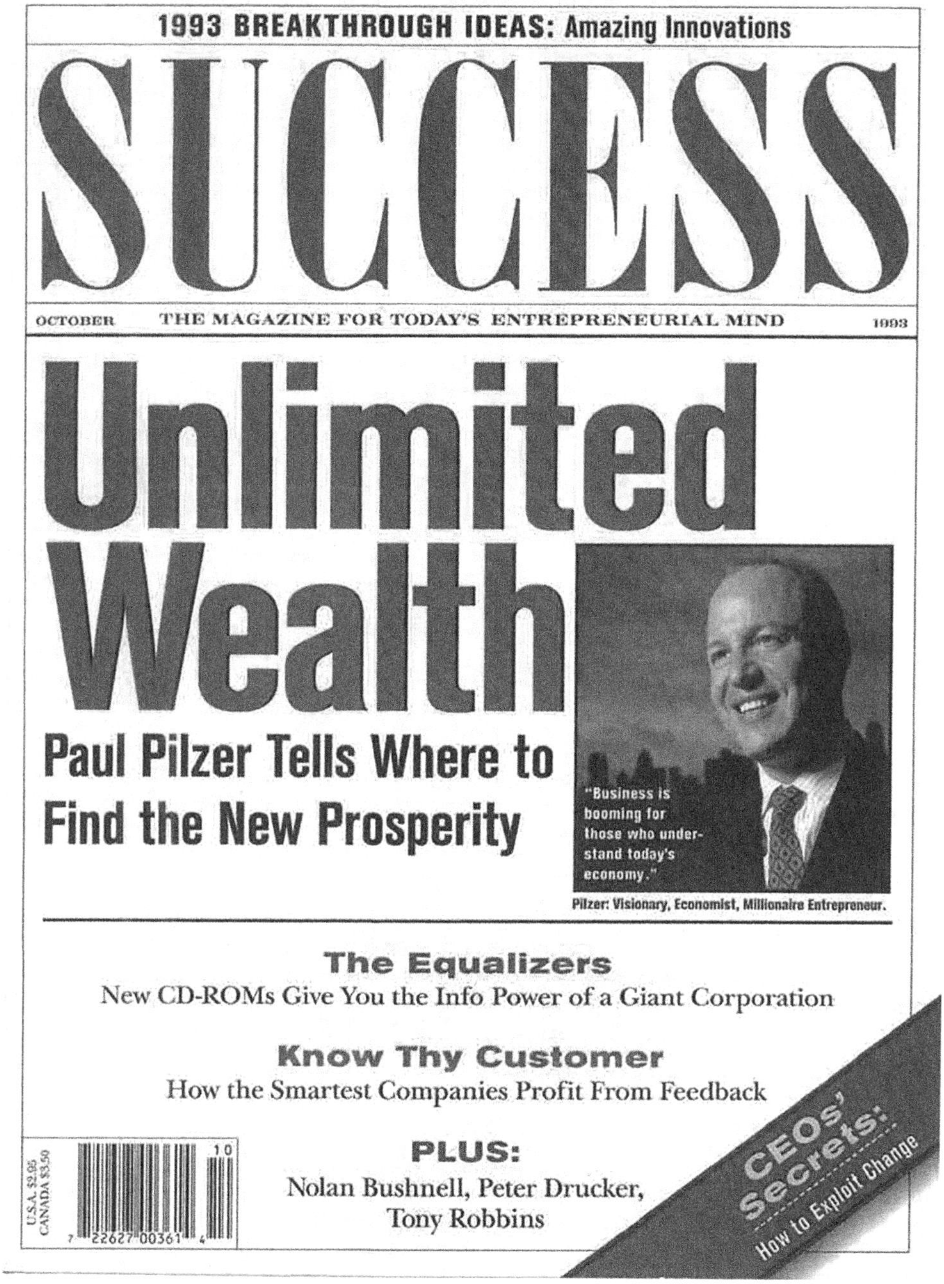

I made the cover of the October 1993 edition of ***Success Magazine***.

In 1997, Amway became the largest distributor of Zane Publishing educational CD-ROMs and ***Success Magazine*** featured me on the cover again. Amway distributors bought millions of CD-ROMs and magazines.

not to worry about the bidding because, after seeing me lecture, they were confident I understood multimedia presentations. They wanted our CD-ROM titles to be bundled with their portable CD-ROM player, and awarded $100,000 outside of the bid process to Zane Publishing to produce a Sony player version of our popular Multimedia Powertalk! CD-ROM. This title contained audio-visual presentations by Tony Robbins and me along with the complete text of four of our books. It also included the entire Zane Publishing CD-ROM catalog.

When Sony launched their portable CD-ROM player, they purchased the inside cover of the October 1993 issue of ***Success Magazine*** to promote it, the same issue in which I appeared on the front cover. Scott DeGarmo, Editor and Publisher of ***Success Magazine***, told me he was grateful that their initial story on me brought them Sony as an advertiser. Over the next 20 years, ***Success*** featured me and my ventures on the cover two more times and in numerous articles.[14]

Beginning A New Chapter at NYU in Shanghai

In January 2000, after 21 years without ever missing a class, I taught my last class at NYU. During the next two decades, I got married, had four children, founded four more startups, wrote six books, and delivered hundreds of keynote speeches.

One of my favorite speeches was on March 6, 2019, at NYU Shanghai, founded in 2012, which is becoming one of the most important educational institutions in Asia. This arm of NYU

14. Anderson, D. M. "Unlimited Wealth." ***Success Magazine***, October 1993.

I delivered one of my favorite speeches on March 6, 2019, at NYU Shanghai, which was founded in 2012 and is now one of the most important educational institutions in Asia.

currently has 2,000 undergraduate students drawn mostly from the People's Republic of China (PRC) and the United States.

I spoke openly at NYU Shanghai about Deng Xiaoping's decision in 1979 to implement the OCP or One Child Policy, which ended in 2016. In terms of GNP (Gross National Product), the One Child Policy may have been the single best decision ever made, leading to China elevating more than one billion people out of poverty. Yet this same decision, in terms of GNH (Gross National Happiness), may have been the single worst decision ever made.

Today, a typical Chinese middle-class couple has their lives limited by having to take care of 12 aging parents and grandparents, what they call the "4-2-1 problem," referring to each working person being responsible for two aging parents and four aging grandparents. China faces enormous social problems ranging from an aging population to a shrinking workforce (see *Chapter 27: Adventures in Progress*, page 455).

Since I began lecturing at NYU Shanghai, the university has broken ground on a new Shanghai campus that will accommodate 4,000 undergraduate and graduate students. I'm looking forward to a long, mutually beneficial relationship with NYU Shanghai.

BECOMING AN ENTREPRENEUR

PAUL ZANE PILZER

Chapter 16 - Learnings

1. When I agreed to teach at NYU, it was assumed by others that I would teach the topic of finance due to my career at Citibank—no one even asked me about my degrees in marketing and journalism. Have you caught yourself assuming the strength or weakness of a person due to their prior career choice or college degree? What can be done to eliminate the labels we put on people?

2. How does knowing I was technically unqualified to teach Real Estate Finance make you feel about the unquestioned trust we have of instructors, professors, and people in authoritative positions?

3. I booked a $459 first-class ticket on the same flight as my employer's $99 ticket. Once I learned how the business allocated their travel expenses and what my employer's expected expenses were, did I have an obligation to reduce my travel costs? Should flying first-class versus coach be considered a taxable perk like an expensive meal (which is taxable income)?

4. Donna Rice was the woman at the center of the Gary Hart affair. Should a politician's personal life be considered in their public office? Will a philandering spouse holding a high office sabotage their professional and political duties? Is much ado about nothing made of this type of behavior, or should society cancel public figures for affairs of the heart?

5. Explain how China's One Child Policy contributed to the "4-2-1" problem. Do you believe that managing their economic problems with this policy was worth their societal detriment in happiness?

BECOMING AN ENTREPRENEUR

PAUL ZANE PILZER

CHAPTER 17

DOING WINDFALL DEALS AT CITIBANK

Windfall:

1) something blown down by the wind
2) an unexpected gain or good fortune
3) accruing unexpected profits

In 1979, I joined the Citibank Real Estate Equities Department as a junior deal-maker, acquiring preferred equity investments in commercial real estate on behalf of international individual clients and domestic tax-exempt employee benefit plan sponsors (i.e. pension funds). Although it only lasted two years, it was one of my happiest work experiences. My official title was senior real estate officer, but they let me keep my officer privileges as an assistant vice president.

There are three types of returns that come from investing in commercial real estate: cash flow, appreciation, and tax benefits. Our department's Unique Selling Proposition (USP) in the commercial real estate world was that we left the tax benefits on the table with the seller or developer—our investors were exempt from U.S. income taxes, and didn't need U.S. tax benefits. Our USP in the investment management world was that we mostly purchased preferred equities, meaning the original developer or seller retained

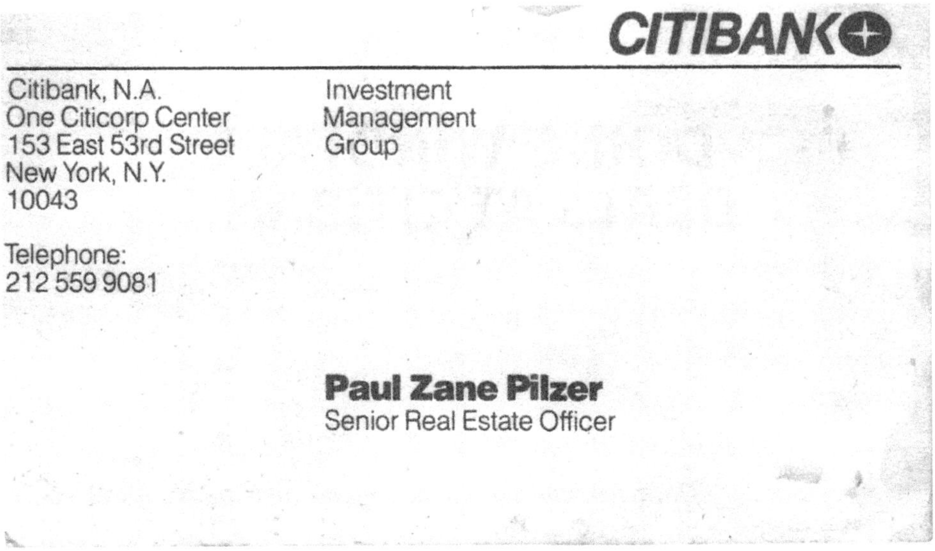
CITIBANK

Citibank, N.A.
One Citicorp Center
153 East 53rd Street
New York, N.Y.
10043

Telephone:
212 559 9081

Investment
Management
Group

Paul Zane Pilzer
Senior Real Estate Officer

I joined the Citibank Real Estate Equities Department in March 1979—acquiring equity interests in commercial real estate on behalf of foreign individuals and U.S. pension funds.

a subordinate 10-50% interest in their property, creating a cushion for our investors in case things went south.

Murray H. Goodman—The First Billionaire I Ever Met

One of the deals I worked on at Citibank later that year was with Murray H. Goodman, a renowned shopping center developer and philanthropist.

I had been working at Citibank structuring real estate investments for tax-exempt pension funds and overseas high net worth individuals. Mr. Goodman asked us to help him solve a tax problem and harvest the equity he had accumulated in 18 retail buildings located in 18 different cities along the Susquehanna River in Pennsylvania. Murray wanted the money to develop shopping malls in Florida but was effectively prevented from selling these retail buildings in Pennsylvania by a tax problem that affects most owners of appreciated stocks and real estate even today.

Under the U.S. tax code, when a person dies, their estate receives permanent forgiveness of taxes on any capital gains. This is why most wealthy taxpayers with large holdings of appreciated stock or property are forced to hold onto these assets until their deaths and is often why older real estate owners refuse to sell their property while they are still alive.

In Murray's case, he had depreciated the 18 retail buildings on his tax returns down to virtually nothing over the years and had borrowed $34 million using the buildings as collateral. If he sold the buildings for their then total value of about $44 million, he would receive about $10 million in cash from the sale after paying off the $34 million in debt and would have to pay capital gains taxes on almost the entire $44 million sales price. At the 1978 capital gains tax rate of 39.875%, a $44 million sale would net Murray $10 million in cash and a federal tax bill of $17.545 million ($44 million × 39.875%). That's a negative $7.545 million before adding in how much Murray would also owe in Pennsylvania state capital gains tax. Ouch!

We solved Murray's tax problem in 1979 by granting him a $10 million long-term, non-recourse, equity participation loan secured by second mortgages on the retail buildings.

In 1980, Murray made a substantial gift to Lehigh to develop buildings on the Saucon Valley Fields land. Today the formerly vacant Saucon Valley Fields contain four buildings serving thousands of students, the Kadishman sculpture, and is called the Murray H. Goodman Campus at Lehigh University. Goodman, age 96 at the time of writing, is the largest living benefactor to Lehigh University.[15]

Citibank Debt-Based Equity-Participation Loan Fund

In 1979, at Citibank, I had also worked on creating an investment fund to give our Citibank investor clients a substantial advantage in competing for investments in U.S. real estate. Instead of purchasing a property outright from a developer, our new investment fund would make the developer a non-recourse, long-term, equity participation loan for 95-99% of the value of their property. The interest on our loan would be all the current cash flow plus 95-99% of the appreciation, almost as if we had purchased the property outright.

The developer would receive the loan proceeds tax-free as a loan, just like money you might net from refinancing a home, as well as an ordinary income tax deduction for the interest paid to our fund from cash flow and appreciation. Our investors couldn't use the ordinary income tax deduction anyway because there were either tax-exempt pension funds or tax-exempt overseas individuals.

At Citibank, we underwrote each investment from this fund, assuming we might eventually foreclose and own the property outright if things went south. But that never happened, partly because if any of our "loans" went into default and got foreclosed on, the IRS would recognize the foreclosure price as a sale at the amount

15. Lehigh University Athletics. 2016. "Venues - Goodman Campus." https://lehighsports.com/sports/2016/9/30/venues-goodman-campus.aspx.

of the debt, and the developer would have to pay capital gains tax on the amount of all the debt (in this case $44 million), even though the developer received no new cash from the foreclosure.

In other words, if, as an example, Murray defaulted on our $10 million loan, he would have to pay the IRS $17.545 million ($44 million × 39.875%) in federal capital gains tax as if he had sold the property for $44 million. This, in effect, made the United States government our partner in ensuring our investment would be solvent at least until the developer and their spouse passed away, getting relief from their capital gains tax obligation.

One reason I remember this transaction is because it was the first investment we made using the investment fund structure that I helped create. It was unusual for a junior officer at Citibank to get the opportunity to raise and structure the monies that they invested.

Another reason I remember the transaction with Murray is that over a two-week period, I had to visit each of the 18 buildings in the cities along the 464-mile-long Susquehanna River and write a report for Citibank on the economic viability of each location.

The Susquehanna River played an important role in transportation in the history of the United States, from the pre-colonial 1600s until the development of railroads in the 1800s. In underwriting these buildings for Citibank, I learned how transportation versus location is the most important factor affecting long-term real estate value, a lesson that serves me today in understanding how Uber and other ride-sharing applications have made communication more important than location as a determinant of long-term real estate valuations.

When I left Citibank in 1981, our department had 63 employees, including eight deal-makers, each leading their own team. We invested about $1 billion in total equity in 40 deals a year, generating about $50 million in annual consulting fees for Citibank. Unlike most other Citibank activities, there was no real risk to the bank because we only invested funds belonging to our clients. Our department earned the bank $42 million in profit per year because we only had $8 million in expenses, which were mostly salaries and bonuses paid to the deal-makers who always complained that they were underpaid.

My First Windfall Investment for a Hong Kong Billionaire

Most of my deal-maker colleagues focused on volume, closing more deals, and generating more consulting fees that dropped straight to the bottom line of our department and the bank. But my personal goal as a deal-maker was to acquire only what we called "windfalls," or investments that made our clients unusually large, unexpected returns. Windfalls allowed us to attract more funds to invest from more clients. Today some investors call windfalls "unicorns," something highly desirable but difficult to obtain.

When we deal-makers got together after work, we would boast of our windfall deals. These deals eventually translated into higher salaries, bonuses, and good stories on our resumes. However, a typical deal-maker at the VP level was lucky if he or she achieved one windfall deal every two years or one every 5-10 deals.

In 1979, I invested $3 million on behalf of a 30-year-old Citibank Hong Kong client named Max Ma. He was the youngest of three sons in a family with about $100 million invested through

Citibank's Investment Management Group, (IMG), the minimum size account Citibank required for clients investing in U.S. real estate equities. I was told that the Ma family's objective was to diversify their family's holdings such that 10% of their portfolio comprised U.S. commercial real estate. We lined up the purchase for his family—a 50% preferred equity interest in an under-construction 120,000-square-foot San Antonio office building. The building cost $12 million to build, and the developer had already secured a commitment for a $9 million first mortgage. We expected it would take up to two years to fully lease up at a rent of $10 per square foot, which was enough to make the mortgage payment and pay an 8% preferred return on our equity. Right after we closed the deal committing to invest $3 million upon completion of construction, a military contractor next door received an unexpected federal contract and desperately needed to lease our entire building.

After we closed on the purchase of our investment, the developer signed a lease with this military contractor at $15 per square foot for 20 years, removing all the leasing risk. This earned us an unexpected $600,000 per year in extra income, which allowed us to increase the $9 million first mortgage to $14 million. When the building was completed one year later, the $14 million mortgage over-financed the $12 million cost by $2 million, producing a tax-free $2 million immediate cash profit on a $3 million potential investment we never funded, an infinite return. We (the developer and the investor) split the $2 million cash profit down the middle, and each of us still owned half the building. Now *that's* a windfall!

One morning in August 1980, before Max had actually signed

and committed his family to this investment, Citibank investment officer, Vice President Roberto Polo asked Furnary and me to drop down to a client conference room on the 15th floor, the headquarters of the IMG, to meet Max and present the investment opportunity personally.

I was elated. I had never met a real centimillionaire (someone whose net worth is at least $100 million). Max, at 28, was only two years older than I was, and we got along famously. He had a big round face framed by square black glasses, was Harvard educated, and spoke the King's English from his years at English prep school. After the meeting, Max insisted that he and I fly immediately to San Antonio in his private plane from Teterboro Airport to see the property.

Even though my apartment was only three blocks from the bank, I always kept a packed overnight bag with an extra shirt and tie at the office for opportunities like this.

While Max phoned his family office from the conference room to arrange the plane, Furnary and Polo summoned me outside the conference room, and Furnary told me under no circumstances should I allow Max to meet anyone else in Texas, especially the developer. Citibank liked to keep its elite clients close to the vest. I could see that my boss was nervous trusting me alone with such an important client. But Max hadn't invited him or Polo to fly to San Antonio—just me.

You'll learn more about Roberto Polo, in *Chapter 20: My First $10 Million Deal* (page 291). Two years later, in 1982, after Roberto and I had each left Citibank, Roberto lent me $1 million over the phone to close my first $10 million deal for my own account.

I was excited to fly in Max's private jet, but I was disappointed when we took off and I realized it was too noisy to continue our conversation. When we got to San Antonio, Max had a Lincoln Town Car with a driver waiting for us. We went straight to the project and met the developer on site. Afterward, when we were alone, Max told me that this was exactly the type of investment his family wanted as protection against inflation, which was running at 13.3% in 1979, the highest rate ever known in the United States.

Max wanted to celebrate and insisted we go out to an early dinner.

He told me that he had heard great things about the Riverwalk in San Antonio and would like to take the developer and me to an early dinner there. I explained that the developer was unavailable to join us for dinner and had my secretary, back in New York, make us a dinner reservation at, according to the developer, the best Mexican steakhouse in the city. Max's driver drove us to the Riverwalk and waited outside while we dined.

The Riverwalk is one of our nation's most beautiful and historic sites; it was developed in the 1920s and features 2.5 miles of upscale restaurants and nightclubs with 20 stone bridges.

When we got to the restaurant, Max ordered a bottle of Dom Perignon champagne for $95 and a tin of beluga caviar for $200, telling the waiter we preferred to pour for ourselves. That was the first time I'd ever seen someone request to pour for themselves at a fine restaurant. Since then, whenever I'm hosting and order an expensive bottle, I remember my dinner with Max Ma and tell my waiter or sommelier that I prefer to pour for my guests. When you're the host, pouring the wine yourself is an act of respect for your guest. In Japan, it's considered impolite if the host allows anyone's sake cup to go empty. Pouring your guests wine makes you pause the conversation and focus on them.

When the champagne and caviar arrived, I gingerly put my small spoon into the tin and filled my champagne glass halfway. Max looked at me through his thick black glasses, poured more champagne to the top of my glass and said, "This is no way to celebrate. When we celebrate, we need to *really celebrate!* Waiter, bring us another bottle of Dom Perignon and another tin of caviar!" Smiling from ear to ear, Max had the waiter open both of them before we had barely started on our entrees. "This way, we won't have to ration it!"

When we left the restaurant, we hadn't even touched the now-open second bottle of champagne. I, on behalf of Citibank, of course, insisted on picking up the $800 dinner check. I knew I would have some explaining to do to my boss, Mr. Furnary when we got back to New York. I justified my action by noting that the dinner check was less than it would have cost me to fly down to San Antonio on a commercial plane, and that the bank was billing Max's family $300,000 in consulting fees for less than two weeks of my time.

Furnary loved busting my chops over my expense report, and I loved defending my actions, entertaining Citibank's clients. Once, I paid $800 in cash to bouncers just to get some overweight clients in suits into Studio 54. Furnary didn't want to approve my expense report on the grounds that I hadn't gotten the bouncers to give me a receipt. He eventually approved it when I reclassified the expense.

A Windfall in San Francisco Shopping Centers

Another windfall deal was created by a seller who became too anxious to close. In November 1980, a deal-maker in our department was almost finished acquiring a portfolio of six net-leased shopping centers outside San Francisco for $80 million on behalf of a Citibank pension fund client. The seller was a billion-dollar public company, set to close on November 21. The Citibank deal-maker unexpectedly resigned from Citibank, and my team was assigned to complete the acquisition. I got a call from the seller's anxious CFO, who wanted assurances that we would be able to close that year. That surprised me since large companies typically don't care whether something like this gets closed in one week or three months.

Frankly, I was moving slowly because I was busy with my own deals, and I had delegated most of the work on these shopping centers to my assistant Carolyn. It seemed as if whenever she brought up an issue to the seller about the properties, the seller would agree with her and lower the price. At one point, Carolyn asked me what to do about one of the parking lots that might need resurfacing, which she guessed might cost about $750,000, but she didn't have time before our scheduled closing date to verify the necessity or the price. I told her, "Tell the seller we want a $1.25 million price adjustment because of the parking lot."

Carolyn protested, saying that she wouldn't lie about the necessity or the price and that it probably wouldn't cost that much. I then told her to say, "My boss wants a $1.25 million adjustment in the price," without saying why, blaming the request on me. I was as surprised as she was when the seller agreed and lowered the price an additional $1.25 million.

After other similar negotiations, we closed on these six shopping centers on December 23, 1980, for $71 million instead of the expected $80 million. I didn't want it to look to the real estate broker or the seller like we had reneged on the original $80 million price or look to our investor like we had overpaid, so I had our investor fund the entire $80 million original price, putting $9 million into a reserve account. I expected we would never need the reserve account because the long-term net leases required the tenants to pay for upkeep and maintenance. This was 1980, a time when U.S. Treasury rates exceeded 12%, which meant our client would earn a higher rate of return on the money in their reserve account in the first few years than on the money they had invested in the properties.

I never found out exactly why the public company was such an anxious seller, although I surmised that it had something to do with the seller owning these properties for more than two decades. After depreciating the buildings all these years, the seller probably had a low GAAP (Generally Accepted Accounting Principles) accounting basis on the properties and had budgeted internally that they would "earn" $40-70 million or more in GAAP profit from this sale. This internal expectation of such a large book profit made the seller too anxious to sell and led to a windfall deal for my Citibank client, who we saved $9 million.

Stand by if you don't know what GAAP is; there's a whole section on GAAP and how you can use it to your advantage coming up in the next few pages and in several more stories in this book.

Regionalization

During most of my time in the Real Estate Equities Department, deal-makers were allowed to do transactions anywhere in the U.S. I personally focused on doing most of my deals in Texas, but on December 29, 1980, I completed an unusual raw land investment for a Filipino investor in Tribeca, then an up-and-coming area of Lower Manhattan on the "south and west" part of Manhattan Island.

Later that day, Mr. Furnary called me into the office of Mr. Trucksess to tell me big news: the deal-making teams were being reorganized based on geography, and I was going to be promoted to vice president, leading my own team focused on the Southwest.

Before Mr. Furnary and Mr. Trucksess could finish congratulating me, I vehemently protested that the promotion was unfair because there were so few deals available in the Southwest. Mr. Trucksess turned to Mr. Furnary and said, "What is he upset about? The Southwest is the hottest commercial real estate market in the United States!"

"Oh. Paul is from Brooklyn," Mr. Furnary explained, "with a narrow-minded view of the United States outside of New York. He thinks the southwest we're promoting him to is the south and west part of southwest Manhattan, Tribeca, versus the entire states of Texas, Oklahoma, Arizona, and New Mexico combined."

Compensation for Windfalls

After our meeting, I calmed down, thanked Mr. Furnary for my promotion, and told him I disagreed with our compensation formula, where deal-makers were paid based on the consulting fees they generated instead of how much money their deals made for clients. I brought up my recent deals in San Antonio and San Francisco and said we should only do deals like that, which had a visible potential to turn into windfalls. Mr. Furnary explained that it was impossible to know which deals would turn out to be windfalls, and the only reason we got to see and do our few windfall deals was because of the extreme volume of deals—$1 billion a year in equity—completed each year by our department.

"If we could identify and only do deals that had the potential to be windfalls, it could result in us cutting back our equity investments from $1 billion to $100 million a year," he explained. "The brokerage community wouldn't keep bringing us the volume of deals that would allow us to statistically get the windfall deals."

I disagreed with Mr. Furnary's explanation but didn't argue any further. I told myself that if I ever ran my own book of deal flow, I would staff the deal-makers at a level where we'd look seriously at ten times the amount of deals we could afford to close, but we'd only close on the few deals that had the potential to make enormous windfall returns that would be partially shared with the deal-maker who made the investment on behalf of the client.

Actively Managing Deal Flow

Most investors in real estate sit back passively and wait until a good investment, driven by the owner's desire to sell, comes to them. We did that in the Citibank Real Estate Equities Department. But later, at my own company, Zane May Interests (1982-1989), we pursued investments aggressively and actively managed our deal flow. We made it our business to bird-dog owners of the commercial real estate we wanted to buy, systematically reviewing their portfolios and discussing when they might be interested in harvesting their profit from each asset. We called on banks and S&Ls for sale/leasebacks (see *Chapter 20: My First $10 Million Deal*, page 291) and insurance companies and pension funds for multi-tenanted commercial real estate office, retail, and industrial (see *Chapter 21: Memphis: My First $100 Million Deal*, page 341).

My father taught me to seek to understand the motivation of the other party in every transaction. This advice served me well through college when I acquired electronic equipment and used cars. But it was difficult advice to follow when acquiring assets where your seller was also simultaneously a buyer of similar assets.

For example, when you are buying a used car, you will likely keep asking questions and doing research until you know why the seller is selling. Hopefully, the seller's desire to sell does not belie something physically wrong with the car. Sellers generally sell things for one or all three of the following reasons:

1. **Utility:** They no longer need it (e.g. they're buying a new car).
2. **Price:** They no longer want it based on a price someone is willing to pay them for it.
3. **Profits:** They need to prove to their investors or a third party that they are earning profits by harvesting some of their investments.

GAAP Accounting

Understanding a seller's motivation gets more difficult when your seller is simultaneously buying similar things. Why would a professional investor who is acquiring, say, office buildings in Houston also be selling similar office buildings in Houston? They obviously like the category Houston Office Buildings, so what aren't they telling you about the individual buildings they are selling to you? Why is a particular seller selling "this asset" while also acquiring similar assets? Is this a sign of caveat emptor, "Let the buyer beware"?

The answer often lies in understanding Generally Accepted Accounting Principles (GAAP) that require large owners of commercial property (or other assets) to carry these assets on their books for far less than their current value. When a publicly traded entity sells a property, even if only for the amount they paid for it (including improvements), GAAP requires them to record a profit of the sales price less accumulated depreciation less cost. This could be a profit of up to 100% of their sales price if they have owned it long enough to have depreciated it down to $0.

***** POSTSCRIPT *****

Looking back on my years at Citibank, I was a real pain in the butt to my superiors. I'm grateful they put up with me long enough for me to have three exciting different careers at the bank: consumer banking, legal/regulatory, and real estate equity investing. Moreover, some of my best friends and active business partners today are people I worked with at Citibank more than four decades ago. Lifelong relationships are the real dividends that come from a successful career in business.

BECOMING AN ENTREPRENEUR

PAUL ZANE PILZER

Chapter 17 - Learnings

1. We all bring personal morals to the workplace. Do you know what yours are? List them, and then consider how yours are different than your colleagues and customers.

2. Do you think it is fair for an employer like Citibank not to pay their employees a bonus based on windfall investments that they bring in—as was the case with my employer, who paid dealmakers based on their consulting fees versus the success of their deals? How do you think our compensation should have been structured?

3. Mr. Furnary believed that the only reason the other dealmakers and I got to see and do windfall deals was due to the extreme volume of deals we did each year. Do you feel he is correct?

4. Do you regularly seek to understand the motivation of each party in a transaction? If not, how can you improve in this area? In the remaining chapters, we'll cover how most financial institutions (legally) keep three sets of books: cash, GAAP, and RAP.

5. "Lifelong relationships are the real dividends that come from a successful career in business." When you interact with clients and colleagues, are you focusing on building relationships, or are you more focused on closing the deal?

BECOMING AN ENTREPRENEUR

PAUL ZANE PILZER

CHAPTER 18

HOW I MADE MY FIRST $1 MILLION

Whenever you are an unhappy customer, there's usually an opportunity to build a business serving other similarly situated unhappy customers.

On my first day at Citibank, I was given an organization chart showing that I reported to an assistant vice president who reported to a vice president who reported to the Vice President of Marketing, J. Brendan Ryan. Thus, I was flattered and surprised when Mr. Ryan came by my office himself and asked what I was planning to do for the summer. Naturally, I replied, "I'll be here, working for your department."

"No, your summer weekend plans," he said. "Where is your house in the Hamptons?"

I looked at him like he was crazy. *The Hamptons?*

I was a kid from Brooklyn, and even though I had grown up on Long Island, I had not known the Hamptons even existed until my wealthy college classmates had invited me to their parents' beach houses on the weekends. Today, of course, everyone knows the Hamptons is the center of the world in terms of movie stars, billionaires, and former presidents who all hang out there during the summer.

The Hamptons

What makes the Hamptons—the 40-mile strip of ocean property on the eastern tip of Long Island—a sought-after location is that it is an exclusive community. You can make the two-hour drive from New York City (four hours with traffic), but you won't find a nice place to stay. That's because zoning laws have restricted the building of hotels in the many beach-front municipalities.

Why? Because with hotels, you get people who do not have notoriety or money or both. The Hamptons is synonymous with fame and wealth.

Homes in the Hamptons today sell for anywhere between $1 million to nearly $200 million. Back in 1976, when Mr. Ryan asked me that question, homes were $100,000 and up, still well beyond the reach of a 22-year-old Citibank trainee earning $20,000 a year.

At least, that's what I thought until I learned the meaning of *share*, decades before Uber and Airbnb made the sharing economy a household term.

Sharing Homes in the Hamptons

"Paul, you need to get a share in a house in the Hamptons," Mr. Ryan said.

In simplest terms, a share was a ticket to the Hamptons' lifestyle for the summer. In an exclusive community, everyone wanted to be there, but unless you belonged to a wealthy family or knew someone who did, you were out of luck. Knowing this, entrepreneurs rented out shares in homes to those who wanted to experience the Hamptons lifestyle during the summer but were either unwilling or unable to rent or buy their own homes.

Let's say an entrepreneur owned or rented a five-bedroom home in East Hampton. If he put two beds in each bedroom, that gave him ten shares to sell. Anyone who bought a share knew that they'd have a place to stay in the Hamptons from Memorial Day (around May 30) through Labor Day (around August 31), which was prime time for seeing and being seen.

If the entrepreneur sold all ten shares for $1,000 each, that meant he could bring in $10,000 upfront for the summer. If someone couldn't afford a full share, they might buy a half share or a quarter share for $500 or $250 respectively, in exchange for two weekends or one weekend a month.

Now, these numbers are from 45 years ago; today, it costs something like $50,000 to rent a home for the summer and $5,000 for a full share.

Once Mr. Ryan told me about the shares and how it worked, my next question was, "How do I locate a share?"

His answer? "Parties."

The people renting out shares would advertise in the classified ads section of *New York Magazine* and in the real estate section of the *New York Times*. For example, an ad would read:

```
Westhampton House on Dune Road.
Tennis court. Pool. Five bedrooms.
10 Shares available. Ages 25-35.
Call 212-758-8549*
```

***This is actually my old New York City phone number from 1976, but if you google it today, it brings up my ads from the 1970s for shares in *New York Magazine*.**

Once you called the number, after answering a few questions, you would get the date and location of a party being held for interested buyers—this was a get-together to see more details of the house and to meet other people interested in buying the shares.

I got a copy of ***New York Magazin***e, found an ad, and called the phone number. I told the person who answered that I was interested in buying a share, and he said, "Great. We're having a party at 239 East 79th Street tonight at 7:00 p.m. Come meet the people who are going to be in the house and see if you like it."

The party was held in a large three-bedroom, three-bathroom New York City apartment where the living room furniture was stacked against the wall to make room for the guests. One wall was covered with pictures of the house being rented out; there were photos of the house from different angles, as well as ones of the pool, tennis court, and the manicured acres of land surrounding the house. There was also a sheet of paper on a clipboard that listed the home's address and the shares available.

There were probably 40-50 people in the apartment at any one time and 150-200 over the course of the evening. Some, like me, were looking to buy a share. The sponsors of the group house were looking to sell shares. And others had already bought a share and wanted to meet their prospective housemates.

I met a lot of interesting people and was amazed by the fact that everyone was so attractive. The women were, frankly, gorgeous.

And smart! It seemed as if everyone had recently graduated from a top college or professional school. I had a great time and wanted in!

The next morning, I called the same phone number and said that I had attended the party the night before and wanted to purchase a share. The guy on the other end of the line asked my name and put me on hold. After a few moments, he came back on the line, requested my name (again) and phone number, and told me someone would get back to me. I could tell he hadn't written down my name and number.

Three days went by, and I had not received a call-back. I didn't think much of it, figuring maybe they had sold out. So, I found another ad and went to the next party. And then another. And another.

That's when I learned the difference between the beautiful people and the nerds.

After a few weeks of doing this and not receiving any call-backs, I finally realized that these parties were like fraternity house interviews: They weren't just selling me on joining their house; they were checking me out to see if they wanted me in their house.

They wanted a cool house with good-looking, smart people, and I was a super-nerd before Steve Jobs made nerds cool. At age 22, I looked like I was 12 years old. I was short and goofy-looking. If you were trying to sell shares in a house to beautiful, smart people, you didn't want me there.

When it dawned on me that I was not going to get into one of these group houses—the cool houses with the cool people—I went to see Mr. Ryan, told him what was happening, and asked if I could buy a share in his big house in Westhampton. He said it wasn't a good idea for a top Citibank executive to have someone working in his department buy a share in his summer home. Then he said something that was about to make me a cool $1 million in the next four years.

Becoming a Part-Time Entrepreneur

"You're too smart for this, Paul. You shouldn't be renting a share; you should be selling shares like I do. You should go rent an entire house."

He handed me a card for Margaret Berwick, a real estate broker with Bellringer Real Estate on Montauk Highway in Westhampton.

"Go visit my broker, Margaret," Mr. Ryan said. "She's cool about grouping. Tell her you're going to rent out shares which is not technically legal, so you want a house located where people won't come down on you for renting out shares and having too many cars in the driveway."

That weekend I drove out to Bellringer Real Estate in the Hamptons and found my first house to rent. It was a five-bedroom home in the middle of nowhere, north of Montauk Highway and hidden in the woods. Because of the poor location and lack of amenities like a beach, tennis court, or pool, it cost only $4,000 for the entire summer. What a bargain!

I did the math: Five bedrooms meant I had ten full shares to sell. If I set the price of the shares at $500 apiece, I'd bring in $5,000. So not only would I get to use the house whenever I wanted, but I'd also make a $1,000 profit!

The bad news was that it was already the second week of May when I rented the house. Shares would stop selling on Memorial Day, May 30, which was less than three weeks away. The day I signed the lease, I was terrified because the rental agreement stated that I must pay one-third immediately upon signing, one-third by Memorial Day, and the final third by July 4th.

I paid the first third, $1,666, and in a couple of weeks, I would have to pay the second third. The problem was I was out of money. So, I started calling everyone I knew to sell the ten shares and asked them who else they knew who might want a share.

My older brother, Lee, was a law student in New York. He bought a share and gave me some leads of other law students. I was in full panic mode, and I was swamped, working at my new job at Citibank.

This was the learning experience of a lifetime, and one of the first things I learned about selling is that *buyers are liars*. Everyone I spoke to about buying shares had a similar line: "Oh, cool. That sounds wonderful." "Oh, I'd love to share in your house." "Oh, that'll be fun." But when I asked for a check, the responses were: "Let me get back to you." "Let me check with my girlfriend." "Sorry, I've changed my mind." "I don't know if I want to rent this summer after all."

In sales, everybody says they're ready to move forward to keep the conversation going or be polite, but buyers are liars until you get their check. Feeling the stress, I even called up prospects who had graduated from Wharton the year before and were working in New York City. I had eight $500 shares left to sell, equaling $4,000, not including the $1,000 from myself and my brother.

By the time Memorial Day came, May 31, I had not sold ten shares—I had sold 18 shares. And I had leads for many more. Because I'd been so afraid of running out of money, I'd completely oversold the shares. I'd taken anybody and everybody who was interested and could afford it.

Now, I had to run back to Margaret at Bellringer Real Estate and find an additional house to rent. Luckily, Margaret had one about a block and half away from the house I was already renting. It was a little more rundown, but it had five bedrooms, and the owner was desperate because summer was just around the corner. I could get it for $3,500—$500 off the asking price—if I rented it that day.

Between the two houses, I sold 20, $500 shares for $10,000 total, and I only had to pay the owners $7,500 total in summer rent. It was a nice $2,500 profit for me.

Over the next five years, I rented, and sometimes purchased, 24 houses. I would rent or buy the houses and then rent out the shares. I was basically catering to the nerds of the world. I didn't care how good-looking my renters were, how rich they were, or if they attended Harvard or an elite prep school—everything that made the Hamptons shares so exclusive. I only cared that they could pay $500 or more for a share upfront.

Of course, I was selling to people who went to good colleges. Those who bought shares were mostly recent law, business, and medical school graduates. Some of them were or were about to become amazing people. One of them was Leon Black, who went on to become one of the richest men in America. He later made the

Forbes 400 list and, in 2012, paid $119 million for Edvard Munch's masterpiece, *The Scream*.

Today, my renting out shares doesn't sound particularly innovative. But keep in mind that this happened long before Airbnb became a multi-billion-dollar business, igniting the vacation home rental market. At that time, in 1976, it was a radical idea to take a home in a luxury neighborhood and rent it out in shares for the summer.

Of course, the people who owned homes and lived full-time in the Hamptons didn't like the idea. They passed ordinances to stop it (and me), but there were always legal ways around local regulations. Moreover, by the time any of the neighbors could get someone to rule on their complaints, the summer would be over, and I'd be gone until the next year.

For example, most of the local municipalities had ordinances saying an owner wasn't allowed to "group" a house. But what proof was there of grouping? The house was rented to one person (me), and my sharers were my "house guests."

In every hamlet there were vocal people who objected to group rentals, and the local municipalities responded to their objections by passing various laws. However, it usually wasn't difficult to find a way around these ordinances. For example, one ordinance specified that no more than four cars could be parked on the property overnight, and the town ordinance already prohibited overnight parking on the street. The solution? We simply worked with the tenants to manage the number of cars that were driven to the property each weekend.

From Renting Homes to Buying Homes

Early the following spring, in 1977, I went searching for more homes to rent. That's when I met Walter Zang, a developer who had an unsold brand-new house on the wrong (north) side of Montauk Highway, with a pool and tennis court all squeezed onto a one-acre plot of land. He wanted $100,000 for this brand-new, five-bedroom, five-bathroom house. I told him I'd buy it if he could wall off the living room and den to create two more bedrooms. *Wow*, I thought to myself. *I could rent out the 14 shares of this house for $1,200 each, bringing in $16,800 a year in sharing income!*

Now, the cheap clay tennis court had to be re-rolled after playing on it every time, and the plastic-liner pool was not the greatest, but the home was far nicer than the other ones I had, and I wanted to rent it. But Zang wasn't interested in my renting the house; he wanted me to buy it.

I didn't have $100,000, but I did have a job that provided me with certain benefits. As a Citibank officer, I could get a no-point, no-closing cost mortgage. At that time, in 1977, mortgage rates were heading up to 15-20%, with the prime rate reaching 21% in 1981. Mortgages were hard to get anywhere and almost impossible to get in New York State, where a usury law set the maximum borrower interest rate at 8.5%. Do the math: If Citibank paid 21% interest to a depositor, they couldn't very well lend that money out to a home buyer at 8.5% interest, the maximum rate they were allowed to charge home borrowers under the New York State usury ceiling.

However, Citibank was required to make a minimum number of home mortgages every year, so they would grant mortgages first to their employees and to friends or customers of their employees. As a junior officer of Citibank, I went downstairs to Employee Benefits, which was literally a windowless room below the basement of 399 Park Avenue, and I sat down with the employee counselor.

She approved me for an 80%-of-value home mortgage. Of course, I didn't tell the counselor that I planned to share the house; she assumed that I was going to live there full-time, and I didn't volunteer any more information. She never asked me how far away (70 miles) the house was from my office.

The math was incredible!

First, I had Zang sell me the house for $125,000 and grant me a $25,000-second mortgage, so I could qualify for a $100,000, 80%-of-value home mortgage. With so many bedrooms and bathrooms and being brand new, the appraiser hired by the bank had no problem appraising the home for $125,000 even though it was cheaply constructed.

Then Citibank granted me a $100,000 mortgage, 100% of what I needed to pay Zang for the house. At 8.5% interest with a 30-year amortization schedule, the mortgage payment was only $768.91 a month, or $9,226.92 a year. Including another $2,800 a year for property taxes, utilities, and expenses, I could own this home for nothing down by simply paying about $12,000 a year, $1,000 a month, linearly over the next 27.5 months.

After I sold the 14 full shares for $1,200 each in May, I would walk away at closing with $16,800 cash ($1,200 x 14 shares) and enjoy a $4,800 cash profit over the coming year. And best of all, since Zang only wanted $100,000 for the house, he gave my company a five-year option to purchase the second mortgage from him for a nominal amount, guarantying my "company" the first $25,000 in profit if and when the house eventually sold for more than $125,000.

Best of all, Zang had 22 more one-acre lots located nearby to keep building what we later came to call a "Pilzer Special," a seven-bedroom, five-bathroom home with a pool and tennis court for $100,000 that would appraise for $125,000 or more.

Financing

Now all I had to do was find up to 22 similarly situated Citibank employees who could qualify for a $100,000 subsidized home mortgage and be my partners in scaling my business. My first such partner was John Alexander, a Citibank vice president who I had never met before the day I strolled into his office.

"Hi," I said, "I'm Paul Zane Pilzer. I work with J. Brendan Ryan in Marketing. Do you have a few minutes?"

Mr. Alexander told me that he had worked at Citibank for ten years, was single, lived in a rented apartment in Manhattan, and didn't own a home, which meant he could qualify for the Citibank employee home mortgage benefit.

"Did you know that, as an employee of this bank, you can get a home mortgage at 8.5%?" I asked.

He replied, "Why would I want a home mortgage at 8.5%?"

"The reason is this house." I opened my briefcase and took out a picture of the Pilzer Special. "You and I are going to buy this brand-new house for $125,000. I'll lend you all the money you need and pay all the expenses of ownership. And we'll split the profit 50/50 when we eventually sell the house."

Remember, I could buy these houses for $100,000 from Zang. All Alexander had to do was come up with $25,000 equity and borrow $100,000 from Citibank, his employer. My company would also lend him the $25,000 in equity, taking back a second mortgage on the property.

He looked at me and said, "Sounds too good." But after making some calls and learning that I had a good reputation, he agreed. We put the home in his name and wrote a partnership agreement saying that when we sold the home, I would get back the $25,000 in equity that I lent him, and then we'd split the profits and tax benefits 50/50.

Scaling My Business

Over the next few years, I kept building more Pilzer Specials, renting out shares in the summer, and locating more Citibank employees who could get an 8.5% no-closing-costs subsidized mortgage from our employer. It sounds exciting, but it was also exhausting. I was the landlord for each of my Westhampton properties and was responsible for repairs and maintenance. As I built this venture into a business, I learned the word scale.

One Thursday night, a preppy Ivy-League tenant of mine called to say the toilet was stopped up and feces was overflowing into his bathroom on the second floor! No matter how many times I instructed him on how to use the plunger, he couldn't figure it out. So, I drove from New York City at 11:00 p.m., arriving in the

The original Pilzer Special from 1978 included a tennis court, a pool, and seven bedrooms, all for $100,000.

Hamptons at 1:30 a.m., where I pushed the plunger down for 30 seconds and fixed the problem. Looking back, I was so cheap and poor that it never occurred to me to even try to find a plumber.

That's when I realized the responsibilities and work involved as a landlord. It sucked. I needed to find some way to scale my business without everyone relying on me to sell the shares and manage the individual shared homes. Fortunately, once again, Citibank, or more accurately the people I met through Citibank, came to my rescue.

Each spring, Citibank would offer positions similar to mine to a new crop of MBA candidates. I would be given a list of a few of these candidates, and my job was to take them individually to dinner and get them to accept their offer. I took them to the best restaurants in Manhattan at Citibank's expense, often finishing up

Over the next few years, I built more Pilzer Specials and rented out shares during the summer to Citibank employees who were eligible for a subsidized mortgage.

at Studio 54—but those stories are for another, different type of book.

At dinner, the first thing I would say to each candidate was, "Great! Congratulations! I hope you'll be joining me at Citibank."

After they accepted their offer, I would ask, "Do you have a share in the Hamptons?"

At that point, I'd pull out my briefcase and show them the picture of the Pilzer Special with, of course, attractive girls and boys in every picture and tell them they could purchase a share in the house.

"Or ..." I would sometimes say, "if you can't afford it now, I have an even better deal for you. I'm going to give you the share in this house for free. All you have to do is find people to buy 14 shares

Summit Blvd., Westhampton. This was the house where my Harvard-educated tenant couldn't figure out how to use the plunger. I bought this house for $39,000 in 1977, added the dormer bathroom and the deck, and sold it in 1978 for $63,500.

Summit Blvd., Westhampton 1977 (under construction). That's me on the roof installing the dormer bathroom.

at $1,200 each."

"Oh, that's easy," they would typically reply. "I know many classmates going to New York who could use a share in the Hamptons."

Sure enough, he or she would go back to Harvard or Wharton and identify the MBAs heading to Goldman Sachs or Bear Stearns in New York. This is exactly what happened with my first protégé, Richard Rowe, an MBA candidate who had been offered a job in my department at Citibank.

Richard had attended Brown University and then Harvard Business School. But he had no interest in purchasing a share for himself; he had school loans from Brown and Harvard Business School and he was adamant about not wanting any more debt.

During our dinner, I said, "Richard, look. You can make a little money. All you have to do is find the 14 sharers." He came back to me with all of them ten days later. And he earned money by managing the house—the role I no longer wanted. I remember making sure he knew what a plunger was and how to use it if a toilet ever got stopped up.

Over the next few years, until I left Citibank in 1981, I kept buying homes in the Hamptons that were designed for summer shares. I focused on finding financial partners like John Alexander, who could qualify for employee benefit subsidized mortgages, and junior entrepreneurs like Richard Rowe, who knew enough people that he could quickly sell 14-24 summer shares for each home.

It was all going well and earning me a lot of money each year. Then inflation and the Hamptons' popularity took off. I sold the first Zang home that I had bought for $100,000 in 1977 for $225,000 in 1980. In 1981, I accepted a job working in Texas for a wealthy family from Chicago. I then sold all my Hampton homes at an average price exceeding $200,000 each, earning me $50,000 to $150,000 in profit from each sale. I walked away with a clean $1 million saved up after five years of hard work.

My net worth and cash flow at such a young age made me feel terrific, especially since I had done all of it on the side as a part-time business while working at Citibank.

It wasn't until years later that I realized the Hamptons business came about because I had been an unhappy customer, a nerd who couldn't get accepted for a share in a summer home. And when you are an unhappy customer, there's usually a business opportunity to serve other similarly situated unhappy customers.

******* POSTSCRIPT *******

Learning How to Borrow Money

In March 1980, I had several building projects going on in the Hamptons. One of my Pilzer Special homes was scheduled to sell for $225,000 in September, after Labor Day Weekend, when the sharers would be gone. I was expecting to clear a $125,000 profit, most of which I had already committed to other projects.

Around that time, I met Harold Copper and his wife at a cocktail party. Harold was the CEO of a Fortune 500 company, and we immediately hit it off, so much so that he invited me to have breakfast at his beach house in Westhampton the next morning.

His house was an iconic glass-walled octagon located on a bluff off Dune Road between the ocean and the bay. I had driven past it hundreds of times over the past few years, wondering who lived there.

Inside, the ocean and bay views were spectacular! The house was filled with centuries-old Buddhist icons that he had personally collected from Thailand, ranging from a 12-foot-tall Laughing Buddha at the entranceway to an enormous gong so loud the entire house shook when he rang it.

Over platters of meticulously laid out smoked salmon, sable, capers, and bagels, I told him about my career at Citibank and the business I was running on the side, buying homes and renting out shares. Later that week, when I was back in the city, his secretary called to invite me to join him for lunch at 21—then a private club and the poshest spot for business meetings in New York. I had read about 21 but had never actually been there or known anyone who had.

Over lunch, he asked me about the challenges of being a part-time entrepreneur while working full-time at Citibank. I told him that I was going to be tight for cash until my upcoming Pilzer Special closing in September.

Although we had just met, Harold ended up personally loaning me $100,000 at 18% interest due on September 30, which meant he'd earn $9,000 in interest over the next six months, even if I paid the loan off early. Today, 18% interest seems usurious, but it was a good deal back then for both of us. This $100,000 would take a lot of pressure off me that summer, allowing me more free time to improve my performance at Citibank while also meeting the financial obligations of my properties.

Then, two months later, on Memorial Day, May 26, 1980, I got bad news. The buyers of my Pilzer Special, who were scheduled to close in September, had backed out. They had planned on renting out shares but got scared after reading an article in the ***New York Times*** on how the local Hamptons' government was cracking down on group houses.

I immediately called Harold and asked if I could come by his house early the next morning before we both headed back to work in the city. Instead, he sensed something was wrong and suggested I come over right away.

"Listen," I told him nervously when I arrived at his house. "I have some bad news about the loan you made me." I told him the whole story of how the buyers had backed out and how now I had to start over to find a new buyer. Harold seemed unconcerned.

"Paul, it's not even June! You don't have to pay me anything until September 30; you have plenty of time to find a new purchaser for this property or any of your other properties."

"I probably will get you your money by then," I said. "But I wanted to let you know right away in case you've promised this money to someone else."

Now Harold started laughing. He said he wasn't desperate to get his money back and that he would not have lent it to me if he'd needed it back so badly. Then our conversation took an unexpected turn.

"I have to tell you, Paul, you're going to go far in life, and it's a pleasure meeting you now when you are so young. It's impressive that you think about the big picture like where a lender gets the money they loan to you."

Harold explained to me how when most people have a problem meeting an obligation, they typically wait until the last date it is due, and then they disappear.

"They run away and hide and pray the money comes in. But here you are, already working your ass off to find a new buyer, and the first thing you do is come to my house to deliver the potentially bad news face to face."

As Harold predicted, I found a new buyer for the Pilzer Special and paid off my loan to him two months early, the first week of August. I tried to pay him interest until September 30, as specified in our loan agreement, but he wouldn't accept the extra $1,500 a month. I didn't know it right away, but I had made a lifelong friend with whom I would go on to do other exciting transactions, including purchasing a gas station and 24 mopeds, which gave my other businesses an edge, being able to buy gas during a gasoline crisis. Our lunch at 21 became a monthly occurrence so much so that one day when I showed up early, the maître d' called me "Mr. Copper," assuming Harold was my father.

My ultimate reward from knowing Harold Copper came years later when his son needed a first job, and I was able to hire him in one of my companies.

On that day, I felt so grateful to God. My career had gone so well that I could help out a friend who I had always thought of as someone who would one day help me out.

BECOMING AN ENTREPRENEUR

PAUL ZANE PILZER

Chapter 18 - Learnings

1. Every person you meet on your entrepreneurial journey, particularly people you meet through a full-time job like working at a bank, can become your customer, financier, or partner. Do you regard your business or job this way? If you don't, how do you think your business would change if you applied this approach?

2. The beautiful people tend to stay with the beautiful people, but nerds can be an exciting group to be in. Is this a true statement or an example of stereotyping?

3. Buyers are liars—until a check is in hand. I found this out when trying to get people to sign up for my shares. In your business, have you found this to be true when it comes to collecting payments? How can you create urgency to receive payments on time from your customers?

4. Employers often do a good job offering employee benefits but don't do a good job telling employees about them. If you are employed and have benefits, do you have a comprehensive understanding of what they are and how to use them?

5. Scaling your business properly allows you to expand while still maintaining a personal life. Have you ever tried to scale a business? How were you successful? How did you fail? If you haven't attempted to scale, and you work for yourself, what is stopping you?

BECOMING AN ENTREPRENEUR

PAUL ZANE PILZER

CHAPTER 19

LEAVING CITIBANK WITH $100 MILLION

The fake news story is that I left Citibank in 1981 when a billionaire gave me $100 million to invest. This is partially true—I did leave Citibank in 1981. The complete story is something else, which couldn't be told until now.

Citibank's Board of Directors met to promote officers in the morning of the third Thursday of each month following the end of the quarter. In January, April, July, and October 1980, I waited anxiously for word that I was finally a vice president. At noon on Thursday, January 15, 1981, two days before my 27th birthday, I finally got the good news. I was technically a vice president for all of about six hours when a short, thin man I had never seen before walked into my office.

"Are you Paul Pilzer?" he asked forcefully.

"Yes, I am—who are you?" I responded in the same tone he had used on me.

"I'm Michael, and you are through f**king me," he growled.

I was stunned because I didn't even know who this guy was, but before I could comment, he said, "No, no, don't get mad. I'm here to figure out how we're going to make lots of money together f**king everyone else!"

I wasn't quite sure what to make of him. But when he introduced himself, I recognized his last name; he was part of a wealthy family from Chicago. Still, I didn't know what he was doing in my office, nor did I understand why he thought we were going to do anything together.

Section 1031 Tax-Free Exchanges

Since 1979, in addition to working at Citibank, I'd worked as a part-time adjunct professor of finance at NYU. One of the topics I taught was Section 1031 Tax-Free Exchanges. Section 1031 of the IRS code allows taxpayers to exchange an appreciated property for a similar property without paying income tax on their gain, provided they follow specific guidelines laid out by the IRS and codified in The Tax Reform Act of 1986.

But back in 1981, structuring a 1031 tax-free exchange was more art than science, and deal-makers had to be careful and creative to ensure their tax-free exchanges would not be challenged by the IRS. I was an expert in Section 1031 exchanges at Citibank and at NYU—and had written articles about tax-free exchanges for NYU's ***Real Estate Review Magazine***.

It turned out that Michael was a significant investor in commercial real estate with hundreds of millions of dollars of (over)financed property, and he desperately needed someone who understood tax-free exchanges. Specifically, he owned equity interests in five shopping centers in Texas that were worth about $100 million, on which he had borrowed $90 million (that he had spent elsewhere).

If his interests in the shopping centers were sold for $100 million, he would have to pay 28% ($28 million) in federal capital gains tax but would only receive $10 million in cash after paying off the $90 million in debt. Even worse, if the lenders ever foreclosed on their $90 million in debt, because the IRS views a foreclosure as a sale at the foreclosure price, Michael would have to pay about 40% of $90 million ($36 million) in capital gains tax, and he would receive no cash at all. Michael needed someone to locate $100 million of similar equity interests in safe, stable properties and structure tax-free exchanges to acquire them.

In addition to Michael's portfolio of over-financed shopping centers, his father-in-law owned a different portfolio of about $200 million worth of unleveraged industrial properties in Chicago in which he had no tax basis. The father-in-law had purchased them decades earlier for a much lower price and depreciated what little tax basis he had down to almost $0. That meant that for every dollar Michael's father-in-law would receive from selling these properties, he would have to pay 40% in capital gains tax. The father-in-law insisted on holding onto these properties until his death which, under IRS code, would allow him to permanently escape paying any capital gains tax due to rules called "Stepped-Up Basis."

But Michael didn't want to wait until his father-in-law's death; he wanted the $200 million now! Michael had convinced his father-in-law that someone like me could figure out how to harvest this $200 million in equity now without paying any capital gains taxes using Section 1031 exchanges.

Michael had hired a headhunter to find a tax-free exchange specialist who also knew how to acquire top properties. That morning, when told I was only 27 years old, he wanted to meet me right away, so he flew to New York without even calling to make an appointment!

Another reason he wanted to meet me was that two months earlier, I had beat him out in acquiring a $36 million shopping mall, Parkdale Mall, in Beaumont, Texas, for a Citibank client. Michael was amazed that I could close on such a large property only three weeks after being introduced to it. That's what Michael meant when he walked in, saying, "You are through f**king me."

The Four Seasons Restaurant

After we talked for a few minutes in my office, Michael said he was thirsty and suggested we continue our conversation at The Four Seasons Restaurant, which was located across the street from Citibank's employee entrance. It was pouring rain, and we had to dodge puddles and double-parked Lincoln Town Cars as we beelined toward the restaurant.

The Four Seasons Restaurant was one of the most famous places to eat in New York since the day it had opened in 1959. It closed in 2019. And it was also the closest eating spot to Citibank's world headquarters at 399 Park. Its regulars included the world's most powerful CEOs, movie stars, U.S. presidents, and Henry Kissinger, who lived a few blocks away and came by all the time. They even had a special small table set up for Henry in an isolated corner of the bar area, so nobody could claim they were just walking by when they tried to introduce themselves to him. This was one of the few places in the world where the famous art on the walls was actually designed for the space by the artists themselves. In other words, the venue for the art was more famous than the art. Featured artists at The Four Seasons Restaurant included Picasso, who designed the curtains, and the architect Mies van der Rohe, who designed the restaurant interior and the Seagram Building that housed the restaurant.

But to me, in 1981, and for the past five years since I'd started working at Citibank, The Four Seasons Restaurant was where I could economically meet my dates and potential business partners. I knew I could always make a full dinner out of the free appetizers at happy hour (5:00-6:30 p.m.), provided I ordered at least one drink. Plus, I didn't mind staying there late because my apartment was located nearby on 57th Street. Even though I wasn't a big spender, I typically tipped 50% of the cost of my one drink, and I often chatted with the waiters who liked that I dressed like a waspy Citibank executive even though I'd actually been born in Brooklyn.

We entered the restaurant, dripping wet from the deluge outside. Michael went in first and asked if there was a high-top table available in the bar. The maître d' looked at me over Michael's shoulder and replied, "We always have a table for Professor Pilzer!"

I could tell Michael was impressed as we followed the maître d′ to our high-top table. He asked, "What can I get you two right away?" and Michael ordered a Stolichnaya martini, straight up, with three olives, shaken, not stirred like James Bond. I ordered a glass of house Riesling white wine, my standard pre-dinner libation, and the cheapest drink on the menu.

"Let me get real straight here," Michael said, looking at his watch. "It's 6:15 now, and my plane has reserved a take-off slot out of LaGuardia Airport at 8:00. It's going to take me 15 minutes to get to the airport from here, so I've got to leave you at 7:30."

He explained that he had a newborn baby girl at home, and if he wasn't there when his wife was ready to put the baby to bed, she was going to give him hell. "So that gives us one hour and 15 minutes more to figure this out."

I asked him what the 'this' was.

He replied, "'This' is whether or not I'm going to hire you, and if so, for how much, and if so, how you are going to resign from Citibank tomorrow morning and come to work for me by next month in Chicago?"

"So," he paused to enjoy his martini and motioned to the waiter for a refill, "That's what 'this' is all about."

When You Don't Know What You Don't Know

Michael asked what I would do if I was given $100 million to invest in commercial real estate. The words came to me easily since I had already taught this lesson many times at NYU.

"Well, if you give me $100 million, I'll take $50 million and buy $500 million in 25 deals, office buildings, and shopping centers, mostly in Texas where I know everyone in commercial real estate. We'll put down an average of 10% on each property, $50 million of equity in total, and we'll borrow $450 million from many different lenders without liability and without cross-pledging our different properties to the lenders. Then, I'll have picked such good properties that over the next five years, our $500 million portfolio is going to go up to $1 billion, so we're going to make $500 million in profit on our $50 million in equity. And I want personally to be paid 2%, $10 million, of our $500 million in profit, plus a salary."

Michael's eyes opened wide, and he nodded his head in agreement. Then he asked what I'd do with his other $50 million.

"Oh, I was afraid you'd ask about the second $50 million," I replied. "I'll buy a second $500 million portfolio, borrowing $450 million, only this time, I'll have picked such bad properties that our $500 million portfolio is going down the drain. Not that we'd care because our equity will be wiped out when this second portfolio falls in value below $450 million."

"Why don't we invest the entire $100 million of equity in $1 billion of only good deals?" he asked.

I looked him right in the eye and said, "Michael, I will not lie to you. I don't know which deals will turn out good and which deals will turn out bad. If there's anything I've learned in five years at Citibank, it's that only God Himself knows the future when it comes to real estate or any other kind of investing. But …" I continued, watching his eyes open even wider, "everyone else in commercial real estate besides me, especially the arrogant lenders like New York Life and some of the other insurance companies, believe that they 'know' good real estate deals that are going to increase in value, no matter what happens in the local or national economy. These lenders are so sure of themselves that they will fall over each other to grant us non-recourse loans for up to 90% of the cost of each of our properties."

After we talked more about deal-making and Section 1031 tax-free exchanges, Michael pulled out his wallet. He unfolded a First Chicago Bank check that had his name printed in the upper left corner. He wrote the date, January 15, 1981, on the top line, my name on the second line, a dollar sign on the line for the amount, and then he signed the check and put down his pen.

"Deal!" Michael said, looking at his watch. I saw it was 7:15. "Now we have 15 minutes left to figure out how much money I'm going to pay you in annual salary and how much money I'm going to give you right now with this check as my good faith deposit. I need you to resign from Citibank tomorrow morning and, in less than two weeks, be working with me in Chicago. You're going to sell my equity interests in five shopping centers for $100 million or more, and then we'll invest the $100 million through tax-free exchanges in the same kind of real estate deals you've been doing for Citibank clients, like the Parkdale Mall in Beaumont."

He went on to explain that he would give me this good faith check now for $100,000 and start me out at a salary of $100,000 a year. This was a big deal to me at the time because, even with my new promotion to VP, I was making only $39,000 a year at Citibank—the equivalent of $120,000 in 2020. By 2020 standards, my new $100,000 salary in 1981 would be worth about $300,000. *Not bad for a 27-year-old former bank vice president!*

The deal that Michael proposed to me seemed fair; he explained that at any time during our first year if we couldn't agree on anything, I could quit, keep the $100,000 good faith deposit plus the salary I had earned up until that date, and forfeit the 2% profit interest I had earned in each deal. But if I stayed at least 12 months,

I could leave by returning the $100,000 good faith deposit and keep my 2% profit interest in each deal.

From where I was sitting, there was no downside to this deal. If things worked out as well as Michael was suggesting, I'd be making millions, not hundreds of thousands of dollars. And if they didn't work out, I'd make a minimum of a $100,000 annual salary paid monthly on top of keeping the $100,000 good faith deposit—almost $200,000 in cash for up to 364 days of work.

"It's a deal," I said, not even thinking about negotiating. I watched as he wrote the $100,000 amount on the check and handed it to me. Then he paid our bar tab and headed to LaGuardia so he could fly home to Chicago to help put his newborn baby girl to bed. I watched him walk to one of the Lincoln Town Cars outside.

The next morning, I got a phone call from Michael's controller, Phil.

"I understand you and Michael met last night, and he wrote you a check drawn on First Chicago Bank, is that correct?"

"Yes …" I answered cautiously, worrying that maybe there was a problem with the deal. After all, it *had* sounded almost too good to be true.

"Can you give me the number on the check?" he asked. "I have to record this check, and we'll start working on a legal contract. Can you tell me what details you discussed?"

I explained our agreement that I would make $100,000 in salary, keep the $100,000 good faith deposit for a year, earn 2% of the profit from the reinvestment of the $100 million in equity, and I said that Michael wanted me to relocate to Chicago.

"I can be in Chicago," I said, "but I should work in Dallas. Dallas is where the hot deals are right now, and I know the important developers there because I've covered the state for Citibank."

Phil said he was sure that my basing myself in Dallas wouldn't be a problem as long as I would fly up to The Standard Club in Chicago for investment committee meetings on the first Monday of every month. He said he was going to start working on the contract, and he told me to go ahead and cash my check for $100,000.

I went downstairs to talk to my Citibank branch manager and asked if I could get the funds cleared that day. My branch manager said he knew the manager at Michael's bank in Chicago and would call him—I should have the funds cleared by noon.

At noon I was still waiting for the check to clear First Chicago Bank—I wanted the funds safely in my account before I made any irreversible career moves. I got a call from my Citibank branch manager a little after noon, telling me there was a problem in Chicago but that he was optimistic the funds would still clear that day. It was a tense two more hours before I got another call at 2:00 p.m. saying the funds were mine. I ran right into my boss's office and resigned.

I should have done a lot more due diligence on Michael, his finances, and his business ethics. But I was afraid if I didn't take his offer that I might be out of a career. Two weeks earlier, on January 2, 1981, my boss Stephen Furnary, had told me that he and the other senior executives in the Real Estate Equities Department were planning to leave Citibank and set up their own shop in March, and they were not going to take me with them. I was heartbroken, and now, I had a way out of my predicament.

I spent the next two weeks flying back and forth to Texas, housecleaning at Citibank, and reassuring my Texas developer clients that someone competent would take over my pending deals. I had obligatory exit interviews at Citibank where trained counselors asked me about my bosses and how Citibank could have done a better job keeping me on board.

I was pleasantly surprised to discover that I had accumulated three and a half months of paid vacation by not taking all of my obligatory Citibank four-weeks-a-year vacation time. This meant that my last day of work would be January 30, but I'd be paid through May 15. Actually, I'd taken lots of time off during my five years at Citibank, but the bank had recorded most of my vacations as business trips since I'd never checked out entirely when I was on vacation.

Although I didn't technically begin working for Michael until Monday, February 2, 1981, I began calling every commercial real estate broker, lawyer, and developer I knew in Texas, explaining I had $100 million I needed to invest right away. I couldn't believe my good fortune. I had $100 million to work with and knew that I could turn it into a lot more.

My First Deal with Michael

I left Citibank and moved to Dallas, Texas, where commercial real estate was booming. I never actually did "move"—I kept my apartment in New York City for the next 20 years, teaching one day a week at NYU. On Monday, January 19, 1981, I checked into the Plaza of the Americas hotel in downtown Dallas and began working on deals for Michael, even though I didn't go on Michael's payroll until February 2. Four weeks later, I was still living out of a suitcase at the hotel, chasing deals all over Texas and flying to New York City every Sunday evening to have dinner with my mother and teach at NYU on Mondays.

Every few weeks I would fly to Chicago for an investment review meeting with Michael's business associates. I especially enjoyed these trips to Chicago, which was then the world's capital for outstanding innovative architecture. In New York City, success in commercial real estate was largely dependent on location, but in Chicago, success was largely dependent on design. In 1974, Chicago's Sears Tower passed New York's World Trade Center as the tallest building in the Western Hemisphere, and it remained the tallest building in the western hemisphere until One World Trade Center was built in 2013.

As much as I enjoyed Chicago, I also enjoyed the investment review meetings. Michael knew many important real estate developers in Chicago—people like Sam Zell, Marshall Bennett, and others—who had played a major role in developing the Chicago skyline, and who sometimes attended our meetings.

As mentioned in *Chapter 16: Teaching at New York University* (page 191), one of these flights to Chicago in 1981 proved extremely embarrassing.

I had settled into my first-class seat and was sipping a glass of champagne when Michael boarded the plane and walked past me on his way to coach. I wasn't sure if he had recognized me, and

Guide to Flying on Other People's Money

To the Editor:

Your editorial on corporate employees vacationing at the expense of stockholders ("Flying High for Free, More or Less," Oct. 23) reminded me of how I learned always to fly discount.

I spent the first five years of my business career at Citibank learning to fly first class everywhere at stockholders' expense. One month after leaving Citibank to become president of a private $100 million company, I found myself embarrassingly booked first class for $459 on a flight with my multimillionaire chairman who had a $99 advance-purchase discount ticket.

Several weeks later, I received a call from his controller explaining that they were eliminating from my budget the $30,000 I had itemized for my (first-class) flights, raising my immediate compensation by the same amount and modifying my employment agreement so that I paid for all my corporate flights. The explanation was, "Michael doesn't mind you flying first class but wants to be sure that you're spending his money the same way you'd spend your own."

Douglas Florian

I have always flown at the lowest discount fare since and derive significant satisfaction when I see a neighboring passenger's ticket at several times my cost. One of my banking friends in mergers and acquisition investment tells me that if not for the junior executives flying first class, he would lose his best source of leads on which inefficient companies are ripe for a corporate takeover and restructuring.

PAUL ZANE PILZER
Dallas, Oct. 23, 1985

This Opinion piece in the ***New York Times*** explains what happened when I found myself embarrassingly booked in first class on a business flight while my boss was in coach.

when we landed I had to quickly run to a waiting Lincoln Town Car which took me to my hotel.

Later that week I got a call from Phil who told me that Michael was changing my compensation plan. Henceforth, he said, I would pay for my own flights and would be reimbursed as if I had flown first-class. Even if I flew coach, I would be reimbursed for a first-class ticket, and would be allowed to keep the difference. As Phil explained it, and as I later wrote in an opinion piece in the ***New York Times***, "Michael doesn't mind you flying first-class but he wants to be sure that you're spending his money the same way you'd spend your own."[16]

My first deal for Michael, which I negotiated in February, was similar to the preferred equity investment kind of deals I'd been structuring for clients of Citibank. A Houston developer owned an office building he claimed was worth $18 million with a $12 million first mortgage. My guess was that the developer had built the entire building for $12 million because he'd had no other visible source of cash. After expensing as much of the construction as he could get away with and taking $2 million in depreciation, I figured that the developer had an $8 million taxable basis in the property. This meant that if the developer sold the entire property for $18 million, he'd have only $6 million in cash proceeds after the $12 million mortgage and a taxable gain of $10 million on which he'd have to pay almost $4 million in federal and state income taxes, netting the developer just $2 million after-tax to share with his investors.

I met with the developer, explained the numbers, explaining that I agreed that his building was worth $18 million. I told him we were ready to buy a 50% preferred interest in the $6 million of equity of his existing partnership for $3 million. The $3 million could be structured as a tax-free distribution to the developer, netting the developer and his investors $3 million after-tax. Moreover, to sweeten the deal, I'd let him charge our new partnership an extra

16. Pilzer, P. Z. "Guide to Flying on Other People's Money." Opinion. ***New York Times***. October 29, 1985. Section A, 29.

$100,000 a year in building management fees which he wouldn't have to share with his investors.

Of course, what I didn't highlight to the developer was that our $3 million 50% preferred equity investment was *preferred*, meaning that we'd be entitled to the *first $3 million* in proceeds above the mortgage, then he'd be entitled to the *next $3 million*. We'd split the rest 50/50. The developer would bear 100% of the first $3 million in losses if the property declined in value. It probably wouldn't have mattered if I had told him this because the developer, like others I'd met in Texas, would have stopped listening the minute I talked about anything in Texas declining in value—the notion back then was that everything only goes up in Texas, especially commercial real estate.

We shook hands on the deal, and I began working on the legal documents, which I wanted to be perfect and to serve as a template for hundreds of similar deals to come. I contacted Jenkins and Gilchrist (J&G) to represent us. They were a prestigious law firm in Dallas that I had often used when I worked at Citibank. Simon, the associate who had worked on my deals at Citibank, was pleased. He had just been promoted to junior partner, and I was the first new client he was bringing into the firm.

Procedurally, he should have asked me for a retainer of at least $50,000, but it never came up because his firm knew me from Citibank and recognized Michael's and his father-in-law's names.

Simon and I worked day and night to finish the legal documents, and we were ready to close on Friday, February 20, 1981. Back in Chicago, Phil was managing the sale of the first of Michael's shopping center equity interests, and we had to do a tax-free exchange on the same date. We signed all the documents that Friday afternoon and told the developer that we would wire his title company the $3 million on February 23 by 10 a.m.

I was ecstatic! I'd closed my first deal in less than three weeks, and I'd already lined up almost $100 million in similar deals for the next few months.

I made the last flight out that Friday night to Miami, Florida, where I had rented a studio apartment at The Cricket Club for the winter. I arrived in Miami just in time to get to my midnight dinner reservation at The Forge, the most prestigious nightclub and restaurant in Miami since the 1920s. I picked up the entire tab for my friends at The Forge that night and for most of the weekend at The Cricket Club. Then I flew back to Dallas on Sunday night to get back to work on my next deal.

The House of Cards Begins to Fall

It was noon Monday, February 23, 1981, when I heard from Simon, my lawyer at J&G. Simon had gotten calls all morning from the developer's attorney saying that the $3 million wire had not arrived at the title company. I told Simon I'd get right back to him, and I immediately called Phil in Chicago. Phil said he'd get right back to me that day but never did, and I kept calling Simon all afternoon to tell him I couldn't reach anyone in Chicago. I even placed three unreturned calls to Michael.

The next day, there were already two messages from Simon when I arrived at my Dallas office at 7:30 a.m. Simon had gotten calls at home from the developer's attorney, demanding the wire instructions and tracking number from Michael's bank, Northern Trust Corporation. Simon asked me for the tracking number on the wire, the same wire we told them we'd sent on Friday, February 20. I was embarrassed that, in my haste to make the last flight out to Miami on Friday afternoon, I had forgotten to obtain the tracking info from Phil in Chicago and send it to the developer and my lawyer. Throughout the day, I made frantic calls to Phil and Michael in Chicago. None of them were returned.

Finally, Phil called me back at my Dallas hotel late Tuesday night. "Hi Paul," he began. "First, I want to assure you that everything will be OK. Michael's good for the money, but we need to exchange the developer's Houston equity interest simultaneously with our shopping center equity interest, and this may take us a few days. Plus, we've had a problem with Michael's bank, the Northern; they are demanding that we pay down Michael's line of credit. They even showed up at the title company trying to seize our cash proceeds from the shopping center equity interest. But don't worry, we're on top of this, and tomorrow I will fax you new wiring instructions from First Bank Chicago, Michael's new bank." I was stunned: Phil and Michael had lied to me last Friday when they told me they had wired the money, and then I had lied to the developer, to the developer's counsel, and even to Simon, my lawyer. There were no wiring instructions from Friday because the wire had not been sent.

The next morning, Wednesday, February 23, was more of the same. I got a call from our lawyer, Simon, right after he got a call from the developer's counsel asking for the tracking number on the new wire transfer. This type of back and forth went on throughout the day until I reached out again to Phil in Chicago at 7:00 p.m. I demanded to know what was going on. Phil told me it was "above my (his) pay grade" and "you need to talk to Michael about it." But of course, Michael wasn't available.

My $100,000 "Good Faith" Deposit

This went on for two more days until Friday, February 25, when I got a call from Simon, my attorney at J&G, that he needed to see me ASAP. I told him to come right over.

"Paul, I'm in big trouble," Simon said, looking glum as he walked into my office. "You're technically a new client. I should have collected from you a retainer of at least $50,000 for legal fees before I agreed to represent you. Now you've piled up a $70,000 bill, and my partners are breathing down my neck."

Simon explained that he hadn't charged me any retainer because he knew and trusted me, and now he was afraid of losing his job.

"They might fire me!" he said, his voice trembling. "I don't know what I'm going to do. My wife is six months pregnant, and she is freaking out!"

I was as alarmed as he was. The developer was owed $3 million, Simon's law firm was out $70,000, and my reputation was on the line. Yet, Michael was nowhere to be found.

I still had the $100,000 in my Citibank personal bank account that Michael had given me as a good faith deposit last month when he hired me, so I pulled out my checkbook and wrote Simon's law firm a check for $70,000, marking it "Retainer." So much for

Michael's $100,000 "good faith" deposit.

That left the $3 million we owed to the developer, and I lived through another week of lies and misrepresentations from Michael until we wired the $3 million to the developer on Friday, March 6, two weeks late, without even an apology or explanation.

On Monday, March 9, 1981, Michael flew to Dallas to meet with me and review our next batch of deals as if nothing had happened. I picked him up at the airport and told him what havoc I had been through as we drove to my office in Dallas. He was silent—I could tell he didn't care.

I didn't realize it back then, or even for the next year, but Michael was headed toward bankruptcy and was leveraged to the hilt. As a result, every time he had a closing or had money in a bank, one of his banks would find out and jump on it. When he did finally wire the $3 million on Friday, March 6, I insisted that he pay me back the $70,000 I had paid to Simon's law firm. He said he would pay me "tomorrow," but it took him months to do it. Each time I brought up the $70,000, he would say, "Don't you trust me?" or "You're in a lot more trouble if I'm not good for the $70,000."

Sadly, he was correct. I couldn't tell anyone what was going on with my boss's finances. If I did, no one would want to do business with us. Everyone thought I was working for one of the richest families in the world and that I had $100 million, which I needed to invest for them that year.

Over the next few months, I experienced this same situation over and over with Michael. I'd make deals, but there always seemed to be a problem when it came to wiring funds. I had a great reputation from my days at Citibank, so people didn't ask me for a large, non-refundable down payment when I entered into a contract. But the stress of seeing how long it would take Michael to follow through tore me up every time.

In November 1981, our first deal from February, the Houston office building, received an unsolicited offer to sell for $22 million, $4 million more than we had valued it for when we purchased our 50% preferred equity interest. We'd get our $3 million back plus $2 million in profit, with our $2 million profit going 98% to Michael and 2% ($40,000) to me.

Michael was overjoyed at making a $2 million cash profit in nine months on a $3 million investment. He flew to Texas to see me. Over dinner, I told him I couldn't continue living like this. It wasn't how I did business; I couldn't go through weeks of waiting for developers to get paid. My reputation was on the line, and I didn't want to risk it any more than I already had.

"Don't worry about it, Paul," Michael said, downplaying my concerns. "Every deal is like this. It just takes a while."

I knew I had to get out of there, but Michael wasn't listening to my concerns; he already had another plan.

The Idea for a New Business

"What we need to do," Michael said, during a meeting in my car, "is show investors how smart we are to acquire these preferred equity interests for, say, $3 million, and then turn around and sell the same interests the same year for, say, $5 million. We'll set up a new entity here in Texas for our new business, one that the Chicago banks who are chasing me don't know about. You see all those buildings?"

He pointed out the window, motioning to a pair of gleaming new buildings in downtown Dallas. One was the First National Bank of Dallas; the other was the First City Bank of Dallas. "What I need you to do," he said, "is go make us appointments to visit these bankers and show them what we're doing. They'll lend us the money for the rest of our deals. Then you'll go and find the deals in Texas."

Up until that moment, it had never occurred to me that anyone could line up preferred real estate equity interests in partnerships, walk into a commercial bank, and borrow up to $100 million to buy them without putting any money down. But Michael was totally confident that we could do this and wanted me to do it for our new business. This went against everything I had learned about making loans at Citibank.

Citibank had taught me to ask the following question each time I wanted to make a loan: *What would happen if everyone connected with the borrower or developer, including me (the lender), died in a plane crash?* How could we (Citibank) give back to the proverbial little old lady who trusted us with her life savings her money when she came into the branch to pay for her grandson's college education? In other words, lenders don't make much money, typically only a few percentage points between the rates on deposits and loans, but we need to make sure we never lose any of the money we loan and that our collateral will turn into cash through (just) the passage of over time.

However, despite my conservative training as a banker, at that moment, I knew that Michael was right; borrowing 100% on my deals was absolutely something I could do. But I wasn't going to do it for him. I was going to do it for myself.

Despite my problems with Michael, he had more confidence in me than I had in myself. In taking advantage of the credibility I had developed, Michael gave me the confidence to ask for 100% financing on my deals.

I stayed until the end of my contract—two more months. Then I resigned graciously on February 2, 1982, paying Michael back my $100,000 "good faith" deposit, thus keeping my 2% profit interests in our deals. Our first deal, the Houston office building, did sell for $22 million, earning me $40,000. When I left Michael, I thought the rest of my 2% profit interests would soon be worth up to $2 million. But the rest of our deals were seized over the next few years by the Chicago banks, wiping out my 2% profit interest along with Michael's investments.

Chapter 19 - Learnings

1. To incent me to leave Citibank in 1981 when my undisclosed salary was $39,000, Michael wrote me a check for a $100,000 signing bonus and gave me an annual salary of the same amount. In retrospect, should I have negotiated for more? What would you have done if this were you?

2. Days after I became a vice president at Citibank, I left to work with Michael, who wound up effectively bankrupt, his assets seized. Did I have an obligation to stay at Citibank after being promoted to vice president?

3. When I worked with Michael, we kept misrepresenting our situation to developers due to Michael's monetary problems. What would have been a better way to handle this circumstance that would still have resulted in our deals taking place? What would you have done, or have you done, if or when your employer was going broke?

4. By the time I was done working for Michael, my profits from the experience had dwindled down to $0, and I was out my job at Citibank. But the learning experience was priceless! Why or why not would it have been worth it to pursue legal action against Michael?

5. In essence, Michael promoted me into working for him under false pretenses. But he firmly believed his own lies that he had endless money coming in for our deals. Ultimately, he greatly increased my self-confidence, allowing me to start my own business—asking banks for 100% or more financing on each deal. In hindsight, should I be angry or grateful to Michael for hiring me out of Citibank?

BECOMING AN ENTREPRENEUR

PAUL ZANE PILZER

PART III

ENTREPRENEURSHIP (1981-PRESENT)

BECOMING AN ENTREPRENEUR

PAUL ZANE PILZER

CHAPTER 20

MY FIRST $10 MILLION DEAL

What I learned in class about Regulatory Accounting Principles (RAP) for financial institutions at age 22 led to me doing lucrative sale/leaseback transactions for banks and S&Ls caught in the Savings and Loan Crisis of the 1980s, and to my exposing the crisis in my first book, Other People's Money: The Inside Story of the S&L Crisis *(Simon & Schuster, 1989).*

During my last semester at Wharton, I took an advanced accounting course called Financial Reporting with someone I'll call "Professor Johnson." He was a partner in the Philadelphia office of Coopers & Lybrand, which today is PricewaterhouseCoopers or PwC. It was one of the Big Eight accounting firms that dominated the profession back then, and Professor Johnson taught only one accounting course a year at Wharton in the spring semester.

One evening at Wharton, I attended an on-campus MBA candidate recruiting event for Coopers & Lybrand, where the speaker told us it takes eight to ten years to make partner at the accounting firm, and partners earned $100,000 to $300,000 a year (that's about $400,000 to $1.2 million a year today). The next day after class, I asked Professor Johnson why he was teaching and earning a part-time professor's salary while taking time away from his lucrative accounting practice. He explained that there was a shortage of people qualified to teach accounting and all the big accounting firms were making a contribution by giving almost every executive paid time off to teach at colleges throughout the nation.

That was the second most important thing I learned from Professor Johnson—once you join a profession, you have to keep putting back into your field. Although I didn't know it then, this second learning would inspire me three years later to seek a part-time position teaching real estate finance at NYU in 1979 while I was still working full-time at Citibank.

Learning to Love Accounting

At Wharton, in January 1976, the first and most important thing I learned from Professor Johnson was to love accounting and, specifically, financial reporting. Professor Johnson saw accounting as a magnificent order of checks and balances for running a business and as a language for comparing financial items between different entities, where everything fits together once you've learned about all the pieces and how they work.

Professor Johnson taught me that the beauty of accounting, and especially public accounting, was that everyone plays by the same rules, which are all based on GAAP, which I mentioned in *Chapter 17: Doing Windfall Deals at Citibank* (page 221). These standards are set for businesses by an independent non-profit organization called the Financial Accounting Standards Board (FASB). In using these standards, businesses can measure their performance, set goals, and improve society using the same yardstick to compare and improve themselves. FASB was only three years old in 1976, having been established on July 1, 1973. As I later learned, Professor Johnson was one of the CPAs who served on the initial board of FASB.

Equally important as teaching me about the rules of accounting (GAAP, FASB, etc.), Professor Johnson taught me where the rules come from. I also learned that while FASB applied to profit-making businesses, other independent accounting organizations similar to FASB used GAAP to set uniform accounting standards for their industries, such as the Federal Accounting Standards Advisory Board (FASAB) for U.S. government agencies and Regulatory Account Principles (RAP) for Savings and Loan Associations. When it came to serving on these agencies, the keyword was "independent." People who served on these rule-making boards needed to be experts in their specific fields, but these same people needed to also be independent so they would not be unduly influenced by the needs of their own firms or clients.

Zane May Interests, 1982-1989

In March 1982, at 28 years old, I was living in Dallas and decided I needed a partner with credibility and a big wallet, even though I believed that I could put together real estate deals without putting any of my, or their, money at risk. I went to see the richest man I knew, billionaire Sid Bass of Fort Worth, who at that time was the largest stockholder of Disney. Michael, my former boss, had introduced me to Sid the year before, offering my expertise in structuring tax-free exchanges for Sid and his family. I secretly hoped Sid would want to become my partner, but I didn't want to ask him directly and put him on the spot.

Over lunch in Fort Worth, Sid said, "Paul, you don't need someone with just money, like Michael, that will drive you crazy. You need someone with an intellect like yours, drive, education, money, of course, and most importantly, experience—experience that someone your age just hasn't had the time to accumulate."

Sid said he could only think of one person in Texas qualified to be my partner, Alan M. May, who lived in Dallas. Sid knew Alan through his business success (Alan had co-founded and sold Steak & Ale Restaurants) and through his philanthropic work (he'd served on numerous boards, including the Dallas Museum of Art and Boston Museum of Fine Arts).

Sid introduced us in April 1982, and it was love at first sight. Alan, 19 years my senior, was my intellectual match and our personalities were a perfect complement. He had graduated from MIT in 1957, where he wrote a thesis that was years ahead of its time: "Using a Computer to Predict the Stock Market." A few years later, when he was earning his MBA from NYU at night while working for Bankers Trust, he was required to read and critique his own thesis from MIT. Just like his former boss at Bankers Trust, Alan wore a belt and a pair of suspenders and enjoyed pointing out the merits of having both.

In May 1982, though we had started acting like partners from the moment we'd met, Alan and I were not technically partnered. Alan came by my office at 3131 Turtle Creek Boulevard every day, as it was only two blocks from his home. Most days, we invited real estate brokers, developers, and investment bankers to meet with us to discuss opportunities. Alan had a much larger personal balance sheet than I did, and we made a handshake agreement that we'd split any deal we did together 50/50 as long as it didn't require our personal guarantees. However, if we had to sign any obligations, he would be compensated for risking much more money than me due to his larger net worth.

State Federal Savings and Loan Association

On Monday morning, May 24, 1982, I told my secretary, Karen, to book a flight for me from Dallas to New York for the next day—I was going home to see my mom and then looking forward to spending an extended Memorial Day weekend in the Hamptons. Karen booked the flight but also reminded me that Alan had scheduled a meeting later that morning for the two of us with Herbert Marcus, a commercial real estate broker.

Herbert was the grandnephew of Stanley Marcus, who I'd met through the Dallas art world a few months earlier. Herb also knew me through my friendship with Menashe Kadishman.

"Here's the deal," Herbert told us. "State Federal Savings and Loan Association is one of the leading S&Ls in Oklahoma, with hundreds of thousands of depositors, and they just finished moving into their brand-new headquarters building in downtown Tulsa. They spent $10 million to build their new building, and now they are in serious trouble. Financially, they can't afford to stay in the building, and operationally, they can't afford to leave the building since they need the space to run the S&L. To make matters worse, if they have to move, re-tenant, and sell the building, it's probably only worth $6 to $7 million to a third party. And to make matters even worse than that, they've lost so much money that, when their books close for the month this Monday, [June 1], their 'surplus' (equity) will be $1 million below the minimum threshold to remain open. The feds could come knocking on the door any moment and shut them down!"

"Hold on a minute," I interrupted Herbert. "Who's the owner or decision-maker for the S&L, and can you get us a meeting with him tomorrow? We'd like to fly there and meet with them first thing in the morning."

Herbert, looking annoyed by my interruption, explained that State Federal was a mutual association, which meant that technically there weren't any stockholders or owners, just a board of directors who managed it for the benefit of the members (the depositors and borrowers). Each of the directors was a prominent Tulsa businessperson who would be in serious trouble if the S&L went out of business or if they went out of business without having enough money to pay off all its depositors. The latter would not only cause them financial hardships, but Herbert whispered loudly, "They could face potential criminal charges for negligence!" The chairman of the board and CEO was 71 years old and had very little banking experience. He had been in his position less than five months and was formerly the editor-in-chief of the ***Tulsa World*** newspaper, where he had worked for 50 years.

I asked Herbert to set up a meeting with the CEO the next morning in his office at the S&L in Tulsa. He arranged a meeting for 10:00 a.m. and we booked the first Southwest Airlines flight from Dallas to Tulsa for Tuesday, May 25.

I could already feel something good was going to come of all this.

I told Karen to cancel my trip to New York.

Meeting with State Federal Savings and Loan Association

The next morning, Alan, Herbert, and I got on the 7:00 a.m. Southwest Airlines flight to Tulsa. Neither of us carried any bags since we expected to return that same day. The airline was always enjoyable to fly on back then because it had pretty girls as flight attendants—in hot pants and tight t-shirts, no less—who made flying a fun experience. Southwest Airlines was started by Herb Kelleher, whom I had met through Citibank and NYU and gotten to know better during my first year in Dallas. In fact, Herb was one of the first people I called when I arrived in Dallas in 1981.

Our plane arrived in Tulsa in less than an hour, so while Alan and Herbert picked up the rental car, I phoned Karen and asked her to call ahead to let State Federal know we'd be arriving early. The CEO and CFO were waiting for us in their conference room when we arrived more than an hour ahead of schedule.

After everyone went around the table and introduced themselves, I asked the CEO questions about his former career at the ***Tulsa World*** newspaper and how he had transitioned to State Federal. He lit up whenever we talked about his newspaper days but was out of his element when we discussed the S&L. The CFO, who had been with the S&L for more than 20 years, kept our meeting on track, bringing the conversation back to why we were there when needed.

The CFO explained that they had located other office space to move to, just outside of downtown, and now needed to sell their building for $10 million as soon as possible. The CEO jumped in, saying, "*We're hoping* to sell it for $10 million," indicating that they were ready to make a deal and implying that they were willing to sell it for much less, probably $7 or $8 million. Nobody brought up the elephant in the room: the S&L was about to record a $1 million loss for just the month of May, which on June 1 would bring their "surplus" (equity) below the minimum amount required by their regulators to remain open.

Our Proposal to State Federal Savings and Loan Association

After about two hours of small talk, mostly about the economy in downtown Tulsa and the features of the building, I reached into my briefcase and pulled out a yellow pad with pages of notes I had written the night before. Then I addressed the group.

"How much is the building carried for on your books under Generally Accepted Accounting Principles?"

"$6.8 million," replied the CFO.

"Then here's what I recommend we do," I said. "First, we are ready to purchase your building, this week if you wish, for $10 million. This will give you an immediate profit of $3.2 million on your books, which will add to your surplus." The CEO interrupted me to point out that they needed at least 30 days to move out.

"Second," I continued, "You don't have to move out. We'd like you to lease back the entire building from us for the next 30 years. If you ever don't need all the space, you can sublet whatever you wish."

Everyone leaned in toward the table. Even Alan and Herbert were rapt.

"Third, we're going to put $1 million down now on the purchase of the building, and you're going to give us a $9 million first mortgage at 16% interest, with 12% paid currently and 4% accrued until the end of the mortgage." That got their attention—the highest interest rate home mortgage they had ever made was less than 12%!

"And finally, although we trust you and you trust us, you never know what could happen over the long term. So, we're going to cross-collateralize each other so no one can default: if we ever miss a monthly payment on the $9 million mortgage, the same amount will automatically be deducted from the payment you owe us on the 30-year lease, and vice-versa. If you ever miss a lease payment on the 30-year lease, that amount will be automatically deducted from our payment on the $9 million mortgage."

I could tell it all sounded good for them, so good that it might not be true. As I paused for questions, Alan kept motioning to me that he'd like to see me outside the room, but I ignored him until I could answer all their questions.

How S&Ls Keep Three Sets of Books—Cash, GAAP, and RAP

The CFO went first. "This all sounds good, but we are a regulated entity. What do we have to clear, and with whom, to be sure we can enter into this transaction? And how will it be recorded on our books?"

I was hoping someone was going to ask that!

"Great question," I replied. "As an S&L, you have three sets of financial statements prepared under three different sets of accounting principles. The first set is simply cash accounting principles—how much cash is in your vault and teller windows and is available to you in instant credit if you need more cash for operations.

"The second set of principles is GAAP accounting, Generally Accepted Accounting Principles, which are the same principles that apply to businesses and the principles your accountants follow to produce your monthly reports to your members. In the case of this transaction, you are governed by ***FASB 66: Accounting for Sales***, ***FASB 17***, and ***FASB 13: Accounting for Leases***. Under FASB 66, you have to take in a least 10% of the purchase price to record a sale—anything less than 10% would be considered an option to purchase versus a sale of the building. Under FASB 13 and 17, your lease cannot be considered a capital lease, which roughly means your lease rate and terms cannot be higher than a reasonable market rate lease, and the present value of the lease payments cannot exceed the current market value of the building." I took a breath to assess the men around the table. Their eyes were still glued to me, so I continued.

"Here are the rules we need to follow to structure the lease, so it is not capitalized."

I opened my briefcase and took out three dark blue booklets published by the Financial Accounting Standards Board, approximately 50 pages each. They were titled ***FASB 13: Accounting for Leases***, ***FASB 17: Accounting for Leases***, and ***FASB 66: Accounting for Sales of Real Estate***. I thought about how proud Professor

Johnson would've been if he could've seen me as I continued.

"The third set of financial statements is sometimes the most important for a financial institution. These are financial statements prepared under something new called Regulatory Accounting Principles, or RAP. RAP are principles promulgated by your primary regulator, the Federal Home Loan Bank Board (FHLBB), to ensure that the entities they regulate stay solvent."

I explained that the day before, in anticipation of our meeting, I had phoned the office of the chairman of the Dallas Federal Home Loan Bank Board, which was their chief regulatory agency, and spoken to the chief accountant.

"I didn't disclose your name," I told them, "but he assured me that under current FHLBB RAP, the transaction we are contemplating here would allow an S&L to record an increase in surplus (equity) equal to the amount the building is sold for ($10 million) less its book value ($6.8 million), regardless of any GAAP rules that made the lease a capital lease. The FHLBB makes its own rules for the S&Ls they regulate, not the FASB. The chief accountant is available to speak to you to verify what I just said."

"That's crazy," the CFO jumped in. I could tell by the way he narrowed his eyes at me that he thought I was wet behind the ears. "How can a regulatory agency like the FHLBB be allowed to make up its own accounting principles? That's like hiring a fox to watch the hen house!"

"I agree," I told the CFO, hoping he would calm down, "but I don't make the rules, and neither do you. We just follow them."

What I didn't tell the CFO and CEO was the main reason I'd

been on the phone with the Chairman's Office of the Dallas FHLBB. I had recently been nominated by a powerful U.S. Senator to join their board and hopefully, eventually, become its chairperson.

Closing the Deal

Alan, who had been waiting patiently to let me finish, asked if we could all take a break. The CEO and CFO left the conference room.

"Paul, are you crazy?" he started in as soon as we were out of earshot. "This S&L is insolvent, they are going bankrupt!"

Although I convinced Alan otherwise at the time, he was correct that the S&L was going bankrupt—it was closed by the feds eight years later on February 16, 1990. The building and assets were sold in 1990 to a banking group owned by the Sam Walton family, a family that would ten years later play an important role in my career as an author and later as an entrepreneur. By 1999, 13,000 other S&Ls (out of 14,000 in the U.S.) had been similarly closed or merged out of existence.

"Listen," I told Alan, "the success or failure of this deal is in the details, not the structure. I plan to set the lease rate high enough so that we will receive enough money every month to pay the 12% current interest rate on the mortgage, plus yield us a 40% cash rate of return, at $400,000 a year, on our $1 million equity investment—enough to fully get our $1 million back in two and a half years and enjoy a $400,000 annual cash flow for the next twenty-seven-and-a-half years! At a 40% cash-on-cash rate of return, the S&L only has to remain solvent for 30 more months for us to get back our investment."

"Don't you dare think of getting us our money back like that," Alan said. "This deal is worth much more for its tax benefits than it is for its cash flow. I've been dying to find a safe deal like this to try my hand at syndication!" His consternation had turned to excitement, and while I didn't fully understand what Alan meant back then about syndicating tax benefits, he was correct, and I was eager to learn.

The CFO and CEO said they would do the transaction as we described, but only if we could close in 72 hours before Friday, May 28, the start of Memorial Day weekend. We agreed that both parties would start writing the closing documents and work around the clock just as soon as the three of us had time to go to Walmart to purchase fresh underwear, pajamas, toothbrushes, and toothpaste.

We then called my lawyer, Simon, from J&G in Dallas, to fly in with his associates to help us out, but we were more than halfway done on Tuesday by the time they arrived 24 hours later.

I have many fond memories of the next 48 hours that it actually took us to close. We worked day and night, each taking sleep breaks at a nearby Holiday Inn. We rented only one room with two beds and a cot, which was more than we needed since at least one of us was always waking up when the other was going to bed. Back at the conference room where we assembled the documents, our critical shortage was secretaries to type on State Federal's new IBM Displaywriter word processor. Fortunately, as a former journalist, the CEO knew how to use the Displaywriter and typed about 100 words per minute, and so did I. So, we could go all night when the S&L's support staff wasn't available.

To allow the CEO and CFO to save face, we never told them we knew about their surplus problem or that, without our transaction, they could be shut down after June 1.

We closed on Thursday, May 28, in the morning and ran to the courthouse to record our closing documents, one and one-half days before their Friday, May 29 deadline.

Roberto Polo—The "Tony" Investment Banker

Just before our actual closing that Thursday morning, I realized that I didn't personally have available my half of the $1 million down payment in my checking account, nor did I have any blank checks. Frankly, I never expected we could actually close that fast. I phoned my former colleague, Roberto Polo, in New York, who had just left Citibank and started his own commingled foreign investor fund and explained the entire State Federal building deal, including how Alan and I were expected to fund $1 million by the next day.

"Roberto, I need $500,000 today, and I'll pay you back at a 20% interest rate within 30 days. Can you help me?"

"Yes, of course, Paul. For you, anything. But I also have heard good things about your partner Alan through the art world, and I'd like to meet him. Are you both available to come to dinner at my home in New York this Sunday? Plus, $500,000 is kind of small for my new fund. Could I lend you both the full $1 million you need? My fund already has $20 million in excess cash, and Citibank isn't paying us anything near 20% interest. Just tell me now where to wire the money."

"Deal!" I replied. "I'll be right back."

I put Roberto on hold and explained to Alan, who had been sitting in the room with me, what was happening. He was pleased at not having to come up with his share of our $1 million down payment on a few hours' notice. And he told me to tell Roberto that he was looking forward to meeting for dinner in New York that Sunday.

Before I hopped back on the phone with Roberto, I asked Alan, "Do you have an account where Roberto can wire the money?" Alan opened his wallet and took out a worn check folded into thirds. I picked up the phone to talk to Roberto again, and Alan watched intensely as I read aloud to Roberto the bank routing and account numbers off his check. Alan told me afterward he was impressed that I had a relationship where someone would send me seven figures without any documentation and trust me to record it later.

On Thursday morning, on the flight back to Dallas, Alan sat next to me and outlined his plans and the next steps for our new partnership, starting with him picking up half the rent for my office retroactively to April when we first met. While I was exhausted and thoroughly pleased with what we had accomplished, Alan seemed to be just getting started.

We landed in Dallas at Love Field and drove together to DFW Airport, where I was booked on the first flight to New York. I surprised my mom by calling to tell her I was coming home for Memorial Day weekend after all.

Alan noticed that the $1 million had already arrived in his checking account, and he asked me who was "that Roberto Polo guy on the phone from New York." I explained how during my last two years at Citibank, my job was to locate real estate preferred equity deals in the U.S., and Roberto's job, before he'd left Citibank, was to locate foreign trust clients who wanted to invest in my deals. To get our deals closed, we regularly had to trust each other's word, moving tens and sometimes hundreds of millions of dollars in and out of our customer's accounts and documenting the transactions later, even if it meant staying up all night.

"But . . ." Alan said, "don't you realize that you're both no longer working for Citibank? You're on your own, and neither of you has the resources of Citibank to back you up."

"I guess so," I replied. "But trust knows no boundaries when it comes to working, or no longer working, for an organization like Citibank. You either always do what you promise to do, or you don't. We've learned to only promise to do what we can deliver." I shrugged. "Anyway, Roberto is looking forward to our dinner in New York City this Sunday to discuss art, repayment of our loan, and how we can do more business together."

A 1982 U.S. Regulation Creates a $50 Billion Business

I first met Roberto in my second year at Citibank, where he was a legend—rumor had it that his wife was the daughter of the King of Spain, although she turned out to be a niece. For almost ten years, Roberto headed the department in Citibank's Investment Management Group (IMG) that managed tens of billions of dollars for Citibank's wealthiest clients, especially those in Latin America. These clients were sometimes more concerned about the secrecy of their transactions than their actual financial returns. They had to be since sometimes, a new political regime would claim malfeasance by the family of the prior regime and seek to seize their assets.

On May 1, 1982, a new U.S. regulation took effect requiring U.S.-based banks to report to the federal government all financial transactions over $10,000, even transactions on behalf of non-U.S. citizens or non-residents. Suddenly, thousands of wealthy clients felt they could no longer trust Citibank to maintain their privacy. To continue serving his clients, Roberto Polo and many of his Citibank employees set up their own investment management shop at 400 Park Avenue, diagonally across the street from the Citibank headquarters. A Citibank officer later told me that Citibank clients with $50 billion in assets followed them across the street.

Certain non-resident employees, including Roberto himself, had to reside outside the U.S. at least 183 days a year to maintain their U.S. non-resident status. If they were declared U.S. residents, their client's transactions would be subject to the new U.S. reporting regulations.

Dinner in New York with Roberto Polo

Alan and I went to dinner on Sunday at Roberto's spacious apartment on upper Park Avenue in New York City. Roberto insisted on us not repaying the $1 million loan in 30 days, and we agreed to pay it off over five years at a 16% interest rate. This effectively added $1 million to our cash profit from the State Federal Building deal.

At dinner that evening with Roberto, Alan noticed the great works of art hanging on the walls, some of which I knew had been purchased anonymously at major auctions. When Alan complimented Roberto on some of the pieces, Roberto said, "Oh, it's not my art! I purchase and help my clients choose the works. They ask me to keep it on my walls and in my name since the insurance for personal art kept at home is a small fraction of what the insurance would cost if it were stored in a vault or commercial space."

To this day, I have never understood what happened to Roberto over the next few years.

On May 27, 1988, I read in the ***New York Times***[17] about Roberto getting arrested for using his client's money to buy art in his name—which is exactly what I believe he was doing. Legitimately. When I later spoke to Roberto about this, he explained that a disgruntled former client had claimed that he never authorized Roberto to buy art for his account.*

***Readers who are interested in more details of this story should read "The Fall of Roberto Polo" by Dominick Dunne in the October 1988 issue of *Vanity Fair*. But readers should also know that I disagree with the few details of this story of which I have personal knowledge.**

The Syndication of The State Federal Office Building

Alan and I flew back from New York to Dallas together from LaGuardia Airport on Monday, May 31. It had now only been one week since Herbert Marcus had come to see us about State Federal, but what a week! We met at the airport gate, and I could tell by

17. Vogel, C. 1988. "Financier's Absence Deepens $130 Million Mystery." ***New York Times***, May 27, 1988.

Alan's restlessness that he had something exciting to tell me.

"Paul," Alan enthused as we boarded the plane, "while you think that the value of the transaction we just completed is in the real estate, there's more value—value we can harvest today—in the tax benefits!"

As we settled into our seats, he explained that the U.S. marginal tax rate for federal income taxes alone was 70%, and it would decline to 50% that year (1982), thanks to the 1981 Economic Recovery Tax Act signed by President Reagan. At a 50% federal marginal tax rate, plus another 16% for state and city tax, the marginal income tax rate for a high net worth individual in New York or California was roughly 67%, or two-thirds, 66 cents on every extra dollar they earned.

"But," he continued, "that also means for every extra dollar they lose, whether they lose it in cash or in a non-cash method due to depreciation and accrued interest, they get back 66 cents in reduced income taxes. The deal you structured in Tulsa generates $600,000 a year in non-cash tax deductions, mostly from depreciation of the building and accrued interest on the first mortgage. That means, during the first five years alone, an investor who is allocated these non-cash $3 million in losses saves $2 million, or 66%, in income taxes that they would have to pay on their other income."

Alan explained that we could structure a deal where an investor gives us $2.2 million of equity to become a 50% limited partner in our Tulsa building—$2.2 million which we would earn personally as fees paid to both of us. In return, the investor would get $5.2 million in tax losses over the first five years. This $5.2 million in tax losses would save the investor 66%, or $3.432 million, in income taxes on their other income—all for their $2.2 million investment. That meant a 156% immediate cash return for the investor in what's known as a 2.36-to-1 write-off tax deal.

"For every $1 the investor invests," Alan went on, "they get $2.36 in tax losses, worth 66% or $1.56 in immediate cash tax savings. And this return is in *addition* to whatever they make with us on the real estate, where we split the building ownership 50/50."

"Wow," I remarked. Alan had spoken so fast that I could barely follow what he'd said. "How do we find the investor who needs to shelter at least $5.2 million in ordinary income?"

"We don't," said Alan. "We break the $2.2 million investment into 30 units and sell each one for $75,000 (1/30 of $2.2 million) to individuals who each need to shelter at least $173,333 (1/30 of $5.2 million) in ordinary income. Security firms on Wall Street will line up to locate the 30 investors for us, especially for a deal as good as this one. I've already spoken to Tony Monk of Lepercq, de Neuflize & Co., a firm on Wall Street I've invested with in these types of deals, and Tony says they will commit to selling this entire offering for us by August 1, provided we can finish the prospectus describing the offering by July 1."

"Who's going to write the prospectus, hire a Big Eight accounting firm, get the law firm to issue a clean opinion on the tax benefits, and all the other items required to do the syndication?" I asked.

"That's my job," Alan said with a big, reassuring smile. "You did a great job in Tulsa negotiating and closing the real estate part of this deal, but now it's my turn to take over with the syndication.

Besides, your time, and especially your ability to locate deals like the one we just did in Tulsa, is too valuable! There are 14,000 S&Ls throughout the United States, most of them are in trouble, and all of them need to improve their surplus (equity) by selling us their headquarters building and leasing it back like we did in Tulsa. And when we are done with the S&Ls, there are 9,000 commercial banks in the U.S. in almost the same situation."

Alan was serious. While I was ready to hang out in the Hamptons for the summer and rest on my laurels—after all, we had just made a $3 million profit from a single deal—Alan saw that we were only embarking on our potential.

He gave me a list of tasks he needed over the next week, along with a PERT (Program Evaluation Review Technique)[18] Chart of all the things we needed to do together to be ready to sell units by August 1.

A PERT Chart is a project management tool used to graphically represent a complex timeline. It was developed in 1957 by the U.S. Navy to manage production of the Polaris Nuclear Submarine—I hadn't seen a PERT chart since Wharton and didn't ever expect to see one again, let alone need one in my work.

Borrowing Credibility from Our Vendors

One of my tasks was to create a 30-year projection, month by month, of the financials for the syndication, assuming different rates of inflation. This meant creating a 480-column spreadsheet for each inflation rate assumption. I loved that assignment since I

18. ***Wikipedia***. 2021. "Program Evaluation and Review Technique."

got to use my new Apple II computer with VisiCalc software, the first spreadsheet program ever produced for a personal computer. In 1981, VisiCalc was the application that turned the personal computer from a hobbyist's toy into a serious business tool. I completed this task in about six hours.

About a month later, when we were completing the prospectus, one of the partners from the Big Eight accounting firm we were using, Peat Marwick (now called KPMG), came by my office to discuss my projections. The accountant asked for my work papers, saying he had to verify my projections. I was absolutely shocked: Not only didn't he trust my computer, but he planned to have a team of junior associates using ordinary calculators check the math on each line item 480 times—that would take weeks or possibly months!

I went to Alan's office and closed the door, my frustration simmering below the surface. I told Alan that he had to stop them—besides being an incredible waste of time, at $75/hour, this might cost us, personally, $50,000 or more! Alan waved a hand at me and told me to relax. He had already negotiated a $25,000 fixed price for Peat Marwick to check the spreadsheet projections, by hand, with calculators, and he admonished me never again to question a bill or work estimate from one of our legal or accounting firms without checking with him first.

"Paul," he explained, "when one of these firms puts our 50-hour-old projections on their 100-year-old letterhead, 'our projections' become 'their projections' in the eyes of our investors. We are, in effect, renting for pennies the name and reputation of billion-dollar professional firms to get them to opine that our numbers are correct."

Alan finished our prospectus the next month, and our offering became legally available to investors on Monday, August 2, 1982, for a selling period of 90 days. We would have to refund everyone who subscribed unless all 30 of the $75,000 units were sold by October 30.

By the end of that week, we'd received subscription forms with checks for 45 of our 30 available units from more than 40 different investors—we had 50% oversold. The first subscription came from Herb Kelleher of Southwest Airlines.

Alan's Insatiable Appetite for Art

The following Wednesday, Alan called me from New York to tell me we had collected all our money and he'd be bringing our original subscription documents home to Dallas on Friday for safekeeping. I suggested that we have dinner Friday in Dallas to celebrate! Alan hesitated and then replied, "That might work … I expect I'll get back to Dallas from London in time for dinner on Friday. How's your deal flow going on new sale/leasebacks like State Federal?"

As I updated Alan on the status of our pending deals, I wondered: *What is Alan doing in London, and who goes to London for just one day?* But Alan wasn't volunteering any extra information.

What I learned, later on, was that Alan had an insatiable appetite in the 1980s for legal Egyptian antiquities—antiquities that are typically purchased with a phone call or a handshake, and often by putting down one-third to one-half of the purchase price with the

ZANE ALAN ASSOCIATES, LTD.

A Limited Partnership Formed to Acquire

State Federal Building
Tulsa, Oklahoma

Lepercq, de Neuflize & Co.
Incorporated

Zane Alan Associates, Ltd. This 300-page prospectus was our first syndication of the equity and tax benefits in a property on Wall Street, and the beginning of Zane May Interests.

seller trusting you for the balance. No wonder Alan was relentless in wanting us to do more sale/leasebacks despite his long resume of accomplishments; he needed more money to buy more art!

On this particular trip to London, Alan purchased, on the installment plan, The Head of Amum from the 25th Dynasty, excavated in 1898 from South Karnak by Margaret Benson, the daughter of the Archbishop of Canterbury and the first woman to legally excavate in Egypt. To this day, Alan refuses to tell me what he paid for this piece, except to admit that when he sold it years later, it represented a "high price." Today, it is probably worth around $10 million.

Over the next ten years, Alan and I purchased 65 more properties and did sale/leasebacks and syndications with financial institutions nationwide. One of them, the sale/leaseback of the Thanksgiving Tower in downtown Dallas, got written about in the *New York Times* on June 13, 1985—my mother phoned to tell me how proud she was reading about it, although she had absolutely no idea what I had accomplished.

How We Got Paid to Advertise Our Sale/Leaseback Business

Sale/leasebacks in real estate in the 1980s were hot, and everyone wanted a piece of the action. Fortune 500 companies, CEOs, CFOs, accountants, lawyers, appraisers, and investment bankers—these professionals needed to learn about sale/leasebacks to advise their boards or corporate clients on how to structure them, or their clients might go elsewhere.

I became a contributing editor of ***Real Estate Review*** (New York University, 1979) and a contributing editor of ***The Real Estate Finance Journal*** (Wharton Business School, 1981). Starting In the 1980s, I wrote 35 technical academic articles on commercial real estate investing, including how to structure sale/leasebacks and tax-advantaged equity syndications.[19]

In January 1983, I started getting calls from continuing education providers wishing to hire me to speak on sale/leasebacks and tax-advantaged equity syndications at their upcoming educational conferences. In virtually every state, every two years, lawyers,

---

19. Pilzer, P. Z. 2016. "Real Estate Articles, Books, Courses." ***PaulZanePilzer.com***, June 13, 2016. http://paulzanepilzer.com/realestate-htm.

accountants, real estate brokers, and most financial professionals are required to take about 12 hours of state-approved CE (continuing education) accredited courses to renew their licenses.

One day I walked into Alan's office and said, "Look at this. This company from Seattle, The Northwest Center for Real Estate Education, is offering to pay me $10,000 to give a one-hour presentation on sale/leasebacks and another $10,000 for a presentation on equity tax benefits in syndications of sale/leasebacks."

Alan immediately stood up.

"Not a chance," he said. "Do you think I'm going to let you give away our trade secrets to the competition?"

I didn't see it that way.

I explained to Alan that each time we put together a new deal structure to offer accredited, high net worth investors the opportunity to invest with us, even though the SEC limited us to 35 investors per syndication, we printed about 250 offering memorandums.

"Where do you think the other 215 copies of the offering memorandums end up? I'll tell you where—they end up hidden in the drawers of the desks of our would-be competitors, the other lawyers, and other accountants. In other words, the people we should be worrying about as would-be competition are already doing whatever they need to do to find out what we're doing on their own. I bet some of our investors may have even bought a unit in part just to get to see our legal documents. My speaking at a conference isn't going to tell them something they don't know. They have already figured it out. If anything, my speaking is going to promote our business and bring us more companies who want to do

To scale our sale/leaseback business, we needed access to *Fortune 500* CFOs, investment bankers, and corporate tax attorneys. We created this two-day conference that we ran six times a year for $595/participant that soon attracted more than 1,000 paid attendees a year.

A major corporate finance decision for the 1980's is whether a company should own or lease its commercial real estate. The transaction whereby a company sells and continues to utilize its office or production facilities is called a Corporate Sale/Leaseback. This complex form of transaction usually involves at least the following highly sophisticated players:

1. Corporate Owner/User
2. Investment Banker
3. Real Estate Broker
4. Equity Component Packager
5. Debt Component Packager
6. Equity Purchaser
7. Debt Purchaser
8. Public Accountant
9. Tax Accountant
10. Real Estate Counsel
11. Tax Counsel

All of these parties must work in absolute synchronization to close a corporate sale/leaseback. However, the benefits to all of the parties involved are worth the effort. The corporate owner/user retains control and identity while raising off-balance-sheet capital at 300-400 basis points below its normal cost of funds. The debt purchaser obtains both the credit of the corporate owner and the credit of the real estate at yields typically slightly above the return expected on the credit of the corporate owner alone. The equity purchaser obtains a long-term inflation hedge and immediate tax relief. Moreover, he is usually never out of pocket actual cash due to a staged-funding multiple write-off transaction.

THIS CONFERENCE IS DESIGNED FOR BOTH THE NEWCOMER TO THE FIELD AND THE MOST SOPHISTICATED SALE/LEASEBACK SPECIALIST. The newcomer will learn the basics of the overall transaction and the specialist will learn the roles and utility curves of the other parties involved. The Conference will focus on explaining the economic, legal, financial reporting and tax issues that arise in negotiating and closing a corporate sale/leaseback. The speaker presentations will address first the overall transaction and then the roles of the individual Players.

The course handbook will contain detailed speaker outlines, sample transactions, vital clauses, checklists, and other written materials intended to facilitate the sale/leaseback process and serve as a reference guide on future transactions.

New York University
School of Continuing Education
The Real Estate Institute

CONFERENCE FACULTY

The faculty listed below is among the most experienced individuals and firms in the sale/leaseback business. It is estimated that these individuals and the firms they represent are responsible annually for over 50% of the credit corporate sale/leasebacks in the United States today.

RICHARD H. ADER, Executive Vice President, INTEGRATED RESOURCES, INC., Director of Integrated's Real Estate Investment Banking Division. Responsible for the acquisition of more than $4.0 billion of net leased real estate.

A. GEORGE KALLOP, Senior Vice President, SHEARSON/AMERICAN EXPRESS INC. Manages Realty Finance Group which specializes in structuring/marketing of sale/leaseback limited partnerships, income property syndications, major property sales and mortgage financings. Shearson presently markets over $500 million of real estate each year through limited partnership offerings.

ROBERT L. KINNEY, President, MELLON FINANCIAL SERVICES. Formerly Director and General Manager of Merrill Lynch Hubbard's Real Estate Investment Management Group. Represents corporate and public pension fund clients with assets of $450 million invested in real estate.

ANTONY E. MONK, Managing Director, LEPERCQ, DE NEUFLIZE & CO., Inc. Heads sale/leaseback tax-oriented real estate group that has negotiated and arranged approximately $1.0 billion of transactions on approximately 90 properties.

ROBERT NAU and NICK ADAMSON, Vice Presidents, SALOMON BROTHERS, INC. Nau manages Real Estate Sale/Leaseback Group which has arranged over $500 million in transactions during the past two years.

PAUL ZANE PILZER, Managing Partner, ZANE MAY INTERESTS and Adjunct Associate Professor of Finance, New York University. General Partner in over $80 million of real estate transactions specializing in sale/leasebacks. Numerous awards for teaching excellence.

PATRICK S. TOTMAN, Senior Vice President, Finance, SAFEWAY STORES, INC. Responsible for all corporate finance activities. Has completed over $500 million of sale/leaseback and mortgage transactions since 1980.

ALAN VITULI, C.P.A., Senior Vice President, SMITH BARNEY, HARRIS UPHAM & CO., formerly Senior Tax Partner and Director of Mergers and Acquisition Services, Coopers & Lybrand. Author on numerous articles on real estate investing including credit leasing.

SETH ZACHARY, Esq., Tax Partner, FINLEY, KUMBLE, WAGNER, HEINE, UNDERBERG, MANLEY & CASEY. Specialist in tax law representing numerous developers, syndicators, joint ventures, and partnerships.

CORPORATE SALE/LEASEBACKS IN REAL ESTATE

DAY ONE

8:30am-9:30am
SPEAKERS:
Conference Moderator:
Mr. Paul Zane Pilzer,
Zane May Interests
Mr. Antony Monk,
Lepercq, de Neuflize & Co., Inc.

1. INTRODUCTION— THE EVOLUTION OF AND RATIONALE FOR THE CORPORATE SALE/LEASEBACK
- Historical Perspective
- Business Rationale for the Transaction
- Types of Players Involved and their Roles:
  - Corporate Owner/User
  - Investment Banker
  - Real Estate Broker
  - Equity Component Packager
  - Debt Component Packager
  - Equity Purchaser
  - Debt Purchaser
  - Public Accountant
  - Tax Accountant
  - Real Estate Counsel
  - Tax Counsel

9:30am-10:30am
SPEAKER:
Mr. Richard Ader,
Integrated Resources

2. TOPIC: THE BUSINESS RATIONALE FOR THE CORPORATE SELLER/LESSEE
- Reducing the Cost of Long-term funds by 300-400 basis points
- Stepping up the Asset Value
- Off-balance Sheet Financing
- Other Benefits

1030am-10:45am
BREAK Coffee and Refreshments

10:45am-11:45am
SPEAKER:
Mr. Antony Monk

3. TOPIC: THE BUSINESS RATIONALE FOR THE PURCHASER/LESSOR
- Economic Incentives
- Tax Incentives
- Inflation Protection
- Availability of Funds at Corporate Rates versus Real Estate Rates

11:45am-1:00pm
LUNCH

1:00pm-2:00pm
SPEAKERS:
Mr. Robert Nau,
Mr. Nick Adamson,
Salomon Brothers, Inc.

4. TOPIC: STRUCTURING AND PLACING THE DEBT COMPONENT OF A (CREDIT) CORPORATE SALE/LEASEBACK
- Structuring the Debt
- Absorbing the Interest Rate Risk
- Placing the Debt Offering
- Providing a Secondary Market

2:00pm-3:00pm
SPEAKER:
A. George Kallop,
Shearson/American Express Inc.

5. TOPIC: STRUCTURING AND PLACING (MARKETING) THE EQUITY COMPONENT IN A CORPORATE SALE/LEASEBACK
- Protecting the Equity Investor
- Components of the Offering Memorandum
- Preliminary Marketing Efforts
- Placing the Equity Offering

3:00pm-4:00pm
SPEAKER:
Mr. Patrick S. Torman,
Safeway Stores, Inc.

6. TOPIC: NEGOTIATING THE SALE/LEASEBACK FROM THE VIEWPOINT OF THE SELLER/LESSEE
- Criteria for Selecting an Underwriter
- Negotiating Critical Elements of the Deal
- Retaining Financial Incentives and Flexibility in the Lease Agreement
- Structuring the Risk/Reward Relationship
- Checklists and Considerations
- Pitfalls to Avoid

4:00pm-4:30pm
SPEAKERS:
ALL FACULTY MEMBERS

7. PANEL: QUESTIONS, DISCUSSION, AND WORKSHOP

4:30pm-5:30pm
COCKTAIL RECEPTION
COURTESY OF LAWYERS TITLE INSURANCE COMPANY

DAY TWO

8:30am-9:30am
SPEAKER:
Mr. Alan Vituli,
Smith Barney, Harris Upham & Co.

8. TOPIC: FINANCIAL REPORTING CONSIDERATIONS OF SALE/LEASEBACKS FOR THE SELLER/LESSEE AND THE PURCHASER/LESSOR
- Avoiding the Capitalized Lease
- Lessee Ownership in Lessor Company
- Sale/Leaseback Profit Recognition
- Lessor Financial Reporting Objectives
- Comparison with Tax Results

9:30am-10:30am
SPEAKERS:
Mr. Seth Zachary,
Finley, Kumble, Wagner, Heine, Underberg, Manley & Casey
Mr. Alan Vituli

9. TOPIC: STRUCTURING THE TAX AND LEGAL ELEMENTS OF THE SALE/LEASEBACK TRANSACTION
- Protecting the Syndicator and the Individual Investor
- Assigning the Lease
- Enforceability Problems and Their Remedies
- Repurchase and Termination Agreements
- Special Securities Considerations

10:30am-10:45am
BREAK Coffee and Refreshments

10:45am-11:45am
SPEAKERS
Mr. Seth Zachary,
Mr. Alan Vituli

10. TOPIC: STRUCTURING THE TAX AND LEGAL ELEMENTS OF THE SALE/LEASEBACK TRANSACTION (CONTINUED)
- Tax versus Financial Reporting for the Seller/Lessee
- Accruing Liabilities for Both Parties
- The Quality of the Purchaser/Lessor's Tax Deductions

11:45am-1:00pm
LUNCH

1:00pm-2:00pm
SPEAKER:
Mr. Paul Zane Pilzer

11. TOPIC: FINANCIAL INSTITUTION SALE/LEASEBACKS—CASE STUDY AND DISCUSSION
- Actual Case Study led by the Syndicator of a recent Transaction where the Seller/Lessee was a Financial Institution who also supplied the Debt Component
- Special Considerations for Commercial Banks and Savings and Loans
- Regulatory Issues

2:00pm-3:00pm
SPEAKER:
Mr. Robert L. Kinney,
Mellon Financial Services

12. TOPIC: THE REAL ESTATE (NON-CREDIT) SALE/LEASEBACK Purchasing Sale/Leasebacks for Property Appreciation
- Introduction
- Some Examples of Recent Transactions
- Business Rationale
- The Objectives of the Purchaser/Lessor
- Objectives of the Seller/Tenant
- Questions and Answers

3:00pm-4:00pm
MODERATORS:
Mr. Paul Zane Pilzer,
Mr. Seth Zachary

13. TOPIC: WORKSHOP DISCUSSION AND CASE STUDIES OF SITUATIONS AND CREATIVE SOLUTIONS
- How to Accelerate the Recognition of Capital Gain
- How to Annually Recognize or Retain Property Appreciation
- Improving the Tax Benefits for the Purchaser

ACCREDITATION & CERTIFICATION

Participants who complete the entire Conference will receive two Continuing Education credits in Finance from New York University's School of Continuing Education. A Certificate of Completion and Accreditation (suitable for framing) will be available from New York University for a slight additional processing fee.

REGISTRATION INFORMATION

REGISTRATIONS may be made by returning the registration form with your check or credit card information. Please make checks payable to: THE NEW YORK CENTER FOR REAL ESTATE EDUCATION. For immediate registration call the NEW YORK CENTER office (214) 880-0297. Confirmation will be mailed upon receipt of your tuition. Registration will be strictly limited at each location and registrations will be accepted in the order received, based upon receipt of full tuition.

REGISTRATION FEE is $595 per person and includes tuition, course materials, refreshments, cocktail reception, and luncheons. Additional course materials $200 per set. The fee for groups of three or more registering simultaneously is $545 per person.

CANCELLATION AND REFUND POLICY: A refund (less $75.00) will be made to any person who cancels the registration in writing prior to seven business days before the course beginning date. In the event the individual withdraws after this date, the amount charged to the individual for registration, tuition fees, and preparation of course materials shall be $150.00. The date of cancellation shall be the date written notice is received by NEW YORK CENTER. No refunds will be made after the start of the conference.

TIME SCHEDULE: Program registration begins at 8:00 a.m. the first day of the program. Program hours are 8:30 a.m. to 4:30 p.m.

TAX DEDUCTION: All expenses of continuing education (including registration fees, travel, meals and lodging) taken to maintain and improve professional skills are tax deductible (Treas.Reg.1-162-5 Coughlin v. Commissioner.203F2d307). TAPE RECORDING of NEW YORK UNIVERSITY programs is not permitted.

EXTRA BROCHURES: Because we use multiple mailing lists, there may be occasional duplication. Please circulate any extra brochures you may receive. Thank you.

HOTEL ACCOMMODATIONS

NEW YORK CENTER does not arrange hotel accommodations. However, each of the hotels where this course is scheduled will hold a block of rooms up to three weeks before your course starts. To receive priority treatment (including discounts off room rates) when you make your reservations, contact the hotel directly and state that you are attending the NEW YORK UNIVERSITY SALE/LEASEBACK CONFERENCE.

Contact: HOUSTON — THE WESTIN OAKS — The Galleria, Houston Texas 77210, (713) 623-4300 WASHINGTON, D.C. — THE SHOREHAM HOTEL, 2500 Calvert St. N.W., Washington, D.C. 20008, (202) 234-0700

(Please cut on dotted line and return entire form with address label attached.)

REGISTRATION FORM

Mail to: **NEW YORK CENTER FOR REAL ESTATE EDUCATION**

750 N. St. Paul St., Suite 1110, Dallas, Texas, 75201 OR FOR PHONE REGISTRATIONS CALL 214-880-0297

☐ Please register me for CORPORATE SALE/LEASEBACKS IN REAL ESTATE ☐ HOUSTON on November 8-9

☐ WASHINGTON, D.C. on December 7-8 ☐ This confirms telephone registrations made earlier.

NAME ______________________ OCCUPATION ______________________

NAME PREFERRED ON BADGE ______________________ FIRM NAME ______________________

FIRM ADDRESS ______________________ CITY & STATE ______________ ZIP ________

BUS. PHONE ______________________ HOME PHONE ______________________

☐ Check enclosed made payable to the NEW YORK CENTER in the amount of $ ________ ☐ Please bill me later ☐ Please bill my Company

REGISTRATIONS CANNOT BE GUARANTEED UNTIL FINAL PAYMENT HAS BEEN RECEIVED. ATTENDANCE IS STRICTLY LIMITED AT EACH LOCATION. PLEASE REGISTER EARLY TO INSURE YOUR ADMISSION AND PREFERRED LOCATION.

CORPORATE SALE/LEASEBACKS IN REAL ESTATE

New York University
A private university in the public service
School of Continuing Education
The Real Estate Institute
11 West 42 Street
New York, N.Y. 10036

Non-Profit Org.
U.S. Postage
PAID
Englewood, N.J.
Permit No. 449

New York University is an affirmative action/equal opportunity institution.

a sale/leaseback, either directly with us or indirectly through their financial professionals."

"Are you positive any potential would-be competition has already figured us out?" Alan asked.

"Absolutely, I replied. "If your product is any good, your competition always figures out how to copy it—even though they may not do so because it's patented or cheaper to license it from you. What I want to do is get our name out there as the premier firm when it comes to structuring sale/leasebacks and tax-advantaged equity syndications."

"Okay," Alan replied, the hesitancy still in his voice. "But instead of you speaking for someone else, we should run our own CE-approved educational conferences. There are probably thousands of people we could charge $600 a head to hear you speak. And this way, we'll control the environment and get more free promotion for Zane May Interests."

That was in January 1983. The next day, Alan had me to call my superiors at NYU and ask if we could "borrow" their accreditation license for their Accounting and Law CE courses in all 50 states. They agreed, provided they got to approve the content of the courses, the amount of CE credit for each course, and that they would receive a royalty of 15% of gross revenues. Looking back, I believe the royalty we paid to NYU over the decade exceeded $1 million.

Later that afternoon, even before we had put together a draft of our agreement with NYU, Alan formed the New York Center for Real Estate Education, a non-profit corporation that allowed us to mail brochures advertising our conferences for the non-profit U.S.

postage rate of $0.04 each versus the regular postage rate of $0.29 each. Postage is sometimes the biggest expense in a mail-order business because, depending on your mailing list, you typically have to mail one million solicitations to get 5,000 affirmative responses. That first year alone, we mailed out one million brochures at a postage cost of $40,000 versus $290,000—what a difference!

That same week Alan rented out hotel ballrooms for four two-day conferences in New York, Washington, D.C., Houston, and Los Angeles (see our New York Center for Real Estate Education brochure). I went to work lining up "faculty" from the nation's largest law firms, accounting firms, investment banks, and CFO-type organizations. Everyone wanted to speak for NYU, and, of course, typically wanted 10-100 of their clients and partners to attend, hear the speakers, and mingle. We limited each conference to 300 paid attendees (1,200 total), and our gross revenues exceeded $600,000 in 1983—in 1984, revenue exceeded $1 million (1,800 attendees).

This extra revenue covered most of our corporate overhead for the next eight years and took the pressure off us to get a deal done to pay the rent. Plus, it was lots and lots of fun and encouraged me to keep up with the latest IRS, SEC, and other regulations regarding sale/leasebacks and equity syndications.

Our company was featured in ***Financial Enterprise: The Magazine of GE Capital*** (Fall 1989), with pictures of me with my homes and cars and Alan with his art. One particular photo that stands out from that era and that appeared on the cover of the ***Dallas Life Magazine*** (Dallas 1984) was of me sitting cross-legged on my

Checker Cab alongside my Rolls-Royce. To the outside world, I appeared to be the spendthrift, young millionaire accumulating mansions and cars. In reality, it was my conservative older partner who had an insatiable appetite for more money so he could invest it, wisely, I might add, in his art.

***** POSTSCRIPT *****

How Alan Got Me a Butler

A few months after the State Federal deal, when Alan and I were working intensely on a pipeline of promising deals, Alan asked me to join him on a conference call scheduled for 8:00 p.m. I told him I couldn't do it. I had worked late every night for two weeks and hadn't had time to get to my dry cleaners before they closed at 7:00 p.m.; I was running out of shirts and suits. Back then, like most businessmen, I wore a suit and tie, with a freshly laundered shirt, every day to work.

Alan threw his hands in the air and exclaimed, "This is crazy! You are brilliant enough to find us a million-dollar deal every month, yet you're wasting time picking up your own laundry. Here, give me your laundry ticket." Alan held his hand out, and I gave him my ticket. He then called his butler at home to come and get it, with instructions to pick up my laundry and bring it to the office.

The next week Alan and his wife, Marcia, helped me hire my own butler—which led to me hiring a driver, chef, maid, and a second chef (for my ski house) over the next two years. Soon, a full-time staff of six people was taking care of me and my homes in New

To the outside world, I appeared to be the spendthrift, young millionaire accumulating mansions and cars. In reality, it was my conservative older partner who had an insatiable appetite for more money so he could invest it, wisely, I might add, in his art.

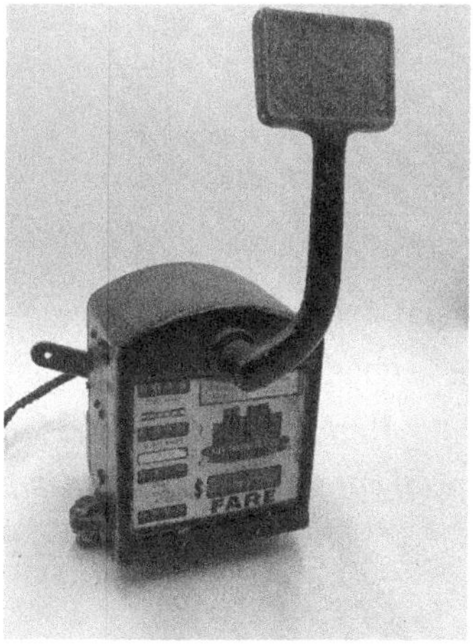

I purchased a 1982 Taxi (with the meter) to use as a "casual limousine" when Checker Cab Company announced they were going out of business.

GE Capital started out helping GE customers finance large GE purchases—like power plants and aircraft engines. They became so good at financing that they expanded to financing all types of purchases whether or not they were GE items. GE Capital in Fall 1989 featured my partner Alan and me in ***Financial Enterprise: The Magazine of GE Capital.***

& real estate

by William Summers

Texas real estate has swallowed up many a smart businessman, but not Alan May or Paul Zane Pilzer. Seven years ago, May and Pilzer found just what they needed to overcome that tough market. Each other.

At a time when a sagging economy has driven many competitors out of business, Pilzer and May have shown an eclectic touch. They've consistently bought the right property in the right market at the right time. Since forming Zane May Interests in 1982, Pilzer, 35, and May, 54, have acquired office buildings, shopping centers and industrial space totaling 7.5 million square feet.

Accomplished businessmen long before they met, Pilzer and May form a team that has all the ingredients to achieve unusual success.

"I'm the accelerator," says Pilzer. "Alan is the brake."

Pilzer knows how to accelerate. A whirl of energy, he travels the globe as businessman, professor, author and public policy activist.

"My mission is to make sure I'm always on the cutting edge of the business world," Pilzer says.

May, meanwhile, controls the reins from day to day, managing Zane May's 55 employees. A careful strategist, he looks at about five deals a day, but completes two a year.

May's resume had plenty of sparkle before he met Pilzer in 1981. As a student in MIT's Sloan School, he wrote a thesis on predicting the stock market by computer. A few years later, while in night school studying for his MBA at New York University, he learned that NYU had reprinted his thesis.

"I was required to read my own bachelor's thesis to get my MBA," he says.

May was already managing $500 million of the Bankers Trust pension investment portfolio when he received his MBA. At his boss's suggestion, he stayed clear of commodity-based equities and invested entirely in blue chips. It's an approach he still appreciates today.

"I worked for a man who wore a belt and suspenders," May says. "To this day, I still wear a belt and suspenders."

After a brief stint in the Army, May returned to Bankers Trust as a loan officer in the petroleum division. The youngest loan officer in the company's history at age 23, May used

ite books, collect art and much more

William Summers is a staff writer for Financial Enterprise.

his background in engineering and his numerical ability to be one of the first cash-flow lenders of his time.

May rose to assistant vice president before leaving to be vice president of finance for Elcor Corp. in Midland, Texas. He then moved to Steak & Ale Restaurants as chief financial officer, where his job was to expand the company beyond four restaurants and $3 million in annual sales. May began by buying back the company's joint ventures in franchises to prepare for a public offering. But he found that investment bankers could not be bothered with a company so small, and they refused to take the company public.

Determined to succeed, May sent those bankers a four-color annual report in which he forecast $11 million in sales for the following year. When the company met that goal, Steak & Ale was taken public in the smallest initial public offering ever done by Goldman, Sachs & Company.

May led an expansion that pushed sales over $100 million in 1976. What's more, Steak & Ale achieved the highest return on sales of any publicly owned food chain.

May and his associates sold the company to Pillsbury in 1976. May did not want to move to Minneapolis, so he left to manage his own assets and consult for a number of Fortune 500 companies. Among other projects, he helped turn around the W.R. Grace restaurant group, and he advised the Hunt family on several mergers and acquisitions.

Pilzer, meanwhile, was doing all he could to redefine the term "wunderkind." He got off slowly at Lehigh, posting a 1.8 grade-point average in his first semester. He then convinced officials that to stay focused he needed to take an unusually heavy workload. He took up to 10 courses a semester to earn his journalism degree in less than three years. After running his own business for one year, he enrolled at the Wharton School, where he got his MBA in 16 months at age 22.

"I have low blood pressure," Pilzer says. "I'll fall asleep if I sit still."

Paul Zane Pilzer relaxes by listening to his self-playing 1920 Steinway piano.

Pilzer then joined Citicorp on the personal staff of now Chairman John Reed. He was making a good living, but he wanted to try something on his own. That summer, Pilzer rented a house in Westhampton, kept one room for himself, and rented the others. He took in enough cash to pay for his room and pocket $1,000. Soon he was building several beach homes. He'd work all day in the city, hop a train to Westhampton to supervise construction, and return to work the next morning. For the next few years he owned and rented enough homes to generate a six-figure income.

By day, Pilzer was carving a name as one of Citicorp's sharpest young bankers. As a junior vice president at 25, he would consistently beat out his older rivals.

One afternoon one of those rivals traveled from Chicago to Pilzer's office. "You Pilzer?"

"Yes."

"I'm tired of losing to you. I want you to work for me."

Alan May's art collection has come a long way since he paid $2 for a Manet on his honeymoon.

"You can't possibly hire me away from here," Pilzer told him.

In the next 45 minutes, the man said he wanted Pilzer to invest $100 million for him before the end of the year. He offered a compensation package so generous that Pilzer could not refuse.

Even so, Pilzer's decision to leave Citicorp after five years was not an easy one.

"John Reed pushed me hard. He taught me that most highly successful people are often underachievers. They run the race only well enough to be number one. They settle for being the best, rather than pushing themselves as hard as they can."

Pilzer took that philosophy to Dallas to start the company that would become Zane May Interests. He soon found that many Texans shared his view of the world.

"I began to think of myself as a Texan who happened to be born in Brooklyn," he says. "In New York, I always felt embarrassed about my financial success. Texans wanted to learn how I'd made it so that they could too."

In 1981, Pilzer and May were introduced by investor Sid Bass. They worked together on the syndication of an office building in Tulsa in 1982 and became partners later that year. Their core strategy is to buy income-producing property for less than 50 percent of what it would cost to build that same property.

May and Pilzer make the most of their time away from the business. May has collected art ever since he paid $2 for a Manet print on his honeymoon. Today his Dallas home could pass for an art gallery. His affiliations in the art world range from New York's Metropolitan Museum of Art to the Boston Museum of Fine Arts.

Thirty times a year, May travels to New York to take courses in Egyptian art history at NYU's Institute of Fine Art. His library holds a striking display of Egyptian artifacts. On one pedestal sits the Divine Head of Anna, which dates to 700 B.C. It was discovered in 1896 by the Archbishop of Canterbury's daughter, the first woman legally to excavate in Egypt. May's library holds 1,800 books on Egyptology.

Pilzer, too, still has a link to Manhattan. For 10 years he has been an adjunct professor of finance at NYU, flying to campus once a week in the fall to teach graduate and undergraduate courses.

"I try to teach my students how to learn," Pilzer says. "They see that the beginning of true knowledge is first identifying how little you know, and then developing a game plan for how to get it."

Pilzer is also an accomplished author. His first book, "Other People's Money," addresses the savings-and-loan crisis and is being published by Simon & Schuster this fall.

Pilzer does much of his writing at his Utah home, where he spends his winters.

"I'll ski for two hours and write for 18. Sometimes I go five days without thinking about shaving."

Pilzer has advised members of the Reagan and Bush administrations. He says a long-range goal is to be appointed secretary of education or chairman of the Federal Reserve.

For now, though, Paul Zane Pilzer and Alan May work together to make their real estate work harder.

"We're like brothers," Pilzer says. "Ours is a partnership built on trust."

To this day the two men have not signed a formal partnership agreement. ■

Reprinted from: ***Financial Enterprise*** *The Magazine of GE Capital* ***Fall 1989***

York, Dallas, Los Angeles, and Park City, Utah.

As my net worth increased and my dinner parties got later and louder, I ended up buying the homes on both sides of my primary home in Dallas and connecting them, making almost 14,000 square feet altogether with 12 parking places. I'd always loved working on cars, and I now had a dozen places to park my toys. In 1982, I bought a nine-passenger 1981 Yellow Checker Cab with 119,000 miles on it as an actual New York City cab, with a mechanical meter, and I shelled out $6,500 each for two almost-new 1983 convertible Jeep CJ7s to use as guest cars.

Growing up, my father had taught me to give thanks to God and reward myself whenever something exceptional happened, like getting accepted into Wharton or making a particularly good sale of bedspreads to Macy's. He meant a reward like a new tie, so I'd always be reminded to be grateful when I wore it.

Two years later, in late 1983, I was working on three big deals with Alan, and I promised to reward myself with my first really expensive new car if one of these big deals closed. I went car shopping and narrowed down my choices to a $119,000 1984 Rolls-Royce Silver Spur, a $45,000 1983 Ferrari 308 GTS, a $25,000 1984 Jaguar XJ, and a $35,000 eight-passenger 1983 Mercedes limo.

All three of our real estate deals closed back-to-back since they each had to close by December 31 for tax and reporting purposes, so I didn't have the time to be buying cars, but when the dust settled on January 2, 1984, I was ready to pick my reward.

At 29 years old, I had an extra $1 million I didn't need in my bank account, plus no personal debt.

I phoned the Rolls-Royce dealer first to tell him I had decided not to buy the Silver Spur and was surprised the same car I wanted was still available. Not only was it available, but by the time I got off the phone, the salesperson had lowered the price from $119,000 to $67,000 if I agreed to take the title within twenty-four hours. Deal!

The Rolls was symbolic because when I left Citibank in January 1981, my former secretary Pat gave me a small red toy Rolls-Royce. She had written on the box, "I hope that one day you will drive a real Rolls-Royce."

A similar conversation surrounding price took place with the Ferrari dealer. Despite being told that there was a waiting list and Ferraris always sold above MSRP, I ended up purchasing the Ferrari for $39,000—15% off! By the end of the day, I had purchased all four cars I'd had my eye on for $160,000. It was like getting the Jaguar XJ and the Mercedes limo for free compared to what I'd been ready to pay that morning for just the Rolls and the Ferrari. Now that's what I call consumer surplus!

I now had eight cars, a six-person personal staff, three connected homes in Dallas, which gave me lots of wall space for art (including a large Basquiat, who stayed at my house when he visited Dallas) and lots of toys, among them a 15-foot-long LGB toy train running outside on 2,000 feet of track.

The first time my mother came to visit me in Dallas she arrived late at night. As she entered the main house, she noticed the two large identical staircases on each side of the living room.

"Paul," she said, "which stairs do I take to your house?"

I enjoyed telling her that they were both my staircases leading to

When I left Citibank in 1981, my department gave me a farewell party. My secretary gave me this metal toy Rolls Royce as a desk ornament. She wrote on the box, "I hope one day you will drive a real Rolls-Royce."

the same place.

One day a former high school classmate came to visit for the weekend, and I overheard him commenting about my lifestyle to his father on the phone.

"Hi Dad, I'm staying this weekend at Paul Pilzer's house in Dallas. Paul made a lot of money after college, but coming from Brooklyn, Paul had no idea how to live with money because he never knew anyone rich, except Richie Rich from the comics. Staying in this house is like living in a Richie Rich comic strip."

The nickname stuck—he called me Richie Rich whenever he visited, especially when we went out in the Rolls-Royce.

Alpha Particules (1984), measuring 86" x 68", is a painting by Jean-Michel Basquiat (1960-1988). Basquiat sometimes joined me in SoHo after my NYU class on Monday nights and stayed at my home when he visited Dallas. I was disappointed and angry after he overdosed in 1988 that I ordered my staff to remove everything related to Basquiat from my home. I purchased this painting in 1984 for $14,000 and sold it at Christie's for $300,000 in 1989—it sold again in 2017 for $4 million!

BECOMING AN ENTREPRENEUR

PAUL ZANE PILZER

ADDITION D

A Brief History of the S&L Industry 1933-1990
(Adapted and updated from Other People's Money,
Simon & Schuster, 1989)

The first S&Ls, later called thrifts, started in the early 19th Century in England, accepting deposits from consumers saving for a rainy day and making home mortgages and other loans to entities that benefited these same consumers, like hospitals and public schools. However, they didn't take off in the U.S. until the early 20th Century, when millions of new American immigrants started deferring the current consumption of their wages (i.e., "saving") to bring family members over to the New World. Once these family members arrived, they would start saving to purchase a home or college education for their children. They also needed home mortgages.

By 1982, the U.S. had more than 14,000 S&Ls, compared to 9,000 commercial banks. Today, there are less than 1,000 S&Ls left in the U.S., and financially they are virtually identical to commercial banks.

Until 1982, S&Ls were highly regulated by the federal government to keep them out of trouble, or so everyone thought. Banking Regulation Q, passed in 1933, guaranteed S&L depositors 100% insurance of their interest and principal and mandated the maximum interest rate S&Ls could pay their depositors (about 5.75% in 1980). Other regulations and usury ceilings mandated the maximum interest rate they could charge on home mortgages (about 4-9% from 1950 to 1980). Together, these rules virtually guaranteed that S&Ls couldn't go broke.

Then, in the late 1970s and early 1980s, interest rates rose to double digits (15-20%), the highest rates ever. New technology allowed consumers to purchase Certificates of Deposit (CDs) from S&Ls, insurance companies, and other financial institutions located anywhere, through their local stockbroker or by U.S. mail. Just like in the run-on-the-bank scene in the movie ***It's a Wonderful Life***, depositors earning 5.75% on their savings accounts went to their local S&L, asking to earn 15-20% interest on their savings or they'd go elsewhere. At first, there was nothing an S&L could do but watch depositors withdraw their savings and leave. Regulation Q prohibited them from paying depositors more than 5.75% until 1980, when the federal government said S&Ls could pay whatever they needed to, even 15-20% in interest, to keep depositors in place.

The S&Ls and the federal government had no choice: after the first few depositors withdrew their money, there was no cash left in the S&Ls, which had invested their depositors' savings mostly in fixed-rate 30-year mortgages earning 4-9% interest. The S&Ls were between a rock and a hard place. If they didn't raise depositor's interest rates to 15-20%, they would go out of business overnight when depositors demanded to take out their savings; but if they did raise depositor's interest rates, they would be assured a slow death, earning only 4-9% in interest on their home mortgage loans but paying out 15-20% in interest to depositors on their savings.

Looking back, it's hard to believe the S&Ls and our nation

didn't see what was happening, but everyone simply assumed that interest rates were so high they would have to come crashing down. In reality, it took almost a decade for interest rates to come back to single digits in the late 1980s.

BECOMING AN ENTREPRENEUR

PAUL ZANE PILZER

Chapter 20 - Learnings

1. FASB (Financial Accounting Standards Board) measures a business's financial performance on a universal scale. In your industry, is there such a board or agency that allows you to quantify your performance using universal standards? Who governs how your organization's performance is measured?

2. I found it quite beneficial to partner with Alan May, who was older, had a similar intellect, and more years of business experience—but he needed me because he wasn't in the commercial real estate industry. In your business, or in a business you would like to start, have you entered into a partnership with another person? What qualities would you seek in a partner?

3. Roberto Polo loaned Alan May and me $1 million without a written agreement in place. What kind of trouble might Roberto be in today if he executed a transaction like that?

4. Roberto purchased art for his clients in his name using their money and kept the art on the walls in his home to reduce insurance costs. He was later charged and jailed for using a client's money without their permission to purchase art. Why would what Roberto did be construed as a crime—try not to cheat and read the fascinating ***New York Times*** or ***Vanity Fair*** articles!

5. When we closed on the State Federal Office Building deal, I still thought of it as a single deal, while Alan saw it as a series of recurring deals that we would scale into a multi-decade business. How do you determine the difference between a single big transaction and a new scalable, potentially lifelong business?

BECOMING AN ENTREPRENEUR

PAUL ZANE PILZER

CHAPTER 21

MEMPHIS: MY FIRST $100 MILLION DEAL

At age 29, I acquired an industrial property for $31 million from the world's largest owner of commercial real estate (Prudential), hired the world's largest owner/manager of industrial real estate to run it (Trammell Crow), financed it for $36 million with the world's largest commercial real estate lender (GE Capital), and sold it ten years later for $73 million to a respected pension fund (Alaska Permanent Fund).

The Roman philosopher Seneca defined luck as "what happens when preparation meets opportunity." That was certainly true of our new company. Alan and I had only met each other in March of that year, and we had already acquired a $10 million building from an S&L, borrowing $9 million from the same S&L who leased back the entire building for 30 years. We then raised $3 million in equity, immediate profit to us, by selling tax-oriented investors a 50% equity interest in the building whereby they received a 150% annual return for five years in tax benefits alone. And, most importantly, we had established relationships with our vendors, appraisers, accounting firms, law firms, private equity firms, investment advisors, and more who wanted to help us sell more syndicated equity investments in commercial real estate. We called our new company Zane May Interests.

In December 1982, right after Christmas, we sat down over lunch at our booth in The Palm Restaurant in downtown Dallas to plan the upcoming year. I say "our booth" because we had eaten there so often in the past five months that the restaurant had painted life-size caricatures of each of us on the walls behind the built-in benches on the booth where we sat. These caricatures stayed on those walls for 35 years until the restaurant closed in 2017.

Over lunch, I explained that while we had a growing pipeline of sale/leaseback deals with financial institutions, I foresaw an equally lucrative opportunity to acquire multi- and single-tenant industrial buildings, particularly older properties. Unlike office and retail buildings where the tenants and customers demanded shiny new premises that constantly needed upgrading, the boxes and pallets stored in industrial warehouses didn't care what the premises looked like or how old they were. Industrial tenants cared mostly about location and transportation arteries, and the older a property was, the more likely that it already had the best located industrial spurs (rail lines), truck roads, and loading docks. Moreover, due to new CERCLA (Superfund) environmental rules, industrial buildings could be purchased for a fraction (typically 50% or less) of the replacement cost, even after paying the costs to clean them up.

"It makes sense," Alan said. "Who do you know that owns large portfolios of industrial buildings in the United States?"

"Brian J. Strum," I told him. "Well, not Brian himself, but his employer, Prudential. Brian is the vice president of Real Estate Investments for Prudential Insurance Company. He and I go back four years. We planned charity events for The Real Estate Board of New York where he represented Prudential, and I represented Citibank."

Prudential Insurance Company

Prudential (formerly Prudential Insurance Company) is the largest owner of commercial real estate in the world. That was true in the early 1980s and it's still true today. The company, which started in New Jersey in 1875, provides insurance, investment management, and other financial products to retail and institutional customers. It has total assets of approximately $4 trillion, which is a staggering amount of money to think about.

Consider for a moment a pile of cash totaling $1 million. A billion dollars is 1,000 piles of one million dollars. And a trillion dollars is one million piles of one million dollars. Prudential had four million piles of one million dollars to invest.[21]

Prudential originally started as a burial insurance company because in the 1800s there were a lot of ways to die. U.S. life expectancy rose from about 40 years in 1800 to about 50 years in 1900 to 80 or more years today.[22] In the 19th Century, disease was rampant, accidents were common, and death was almost a daily fact of life. People wanted to know that if they died, their family would have enough money to bury them, and they wouldn't end up in the Potter's field—a literal field where the bodies of the unknown

21. Tretina, K. 2001. "Prudential Life Insurance Review." ***Investopedia***.

22. Bastian B, Tejada Vera B, Arias E, et al. 2020. ***Mortality trends** in the United States, 1900–2018*. National Center for Health Statistics. 2020.

or impoverished were buried. That led to the creation of burial insurance societies, which caught on because people were concerned about what would happen to their bodies when they died. Before long, burial insurance turned into life insurance.

I'm going to share a secret about life insurance that people usually don't talk about. Life insurance isn't life insurance! It's death insurance. It's designed to make sure that when you die, there's going to be money for your spouse or kids to have a funeral, bury you, live in the same house, and go to college.

But life insurance sounds a lot more appealing than burial or death insurance, which is what life insurance is, insurance against death.

Prudential became the largest owner of real estate because it became the largest issuer of life insurance—it currently has about $4 trillion of issued life insurance. They did this by earning people's trust. The name 'Prudential' tells you they're going to be prudent with your money. And their symbol is the rock of Gibraltar. It doesn't get any more solid than that!

Real estate investing was a perfect match for Prudential's obligations to its policyholders; the return on real estate generally matches inflation and the nation's economic growth. Policyholders needed to know that their loved ones would have enough to financially survive their demise. What else could Prudential do with billions in annual revenue from life insurance premiums that don't need to be paid back for 25 years or more?

To grow, life insurance companies need to demonstrate their ability to make profits over the long term on a consistent basis for their policyholders, potential policyholders, and stockholders. In an ideal world, Prudential would purchase good real estate investments, appraise them each year, and tell policyholders how much more their property investments were worth than when they had purchased them. Ideally, a life insurance company would go through each of their real estate assets annually, analyzing which properties had more, or less, the potential upside, as well as dispose of assets they didn't feel had as much upside potential as others.

MAI = Made as Instructed

But the world of investing in commercial real estate is far from ideal, particularly when it comes to figuring out the value of a property without actually selling it. The Appraisal Institute (and its predecessor organizations, 1932-1935) created the designation MAI (Member, Appraisal Institute) to signify that an appraiser was of sound moral character and couldn't be bought off by a potential borrower seeking financing. But by the 1970s, when I entered the world of real estate finance, MAI generally stood for made as instructed.

One of the first things I learned as a real estate lender and borrower was how to hire the "right" appraiser. This typically meant lining up at least three appraisers when you needed to hire one for an appraisal and letting them know, without ever saying so, the minimum amount they had to appraise a particular property for if they wanted this appraisal assignment or ever wanted more of your business.

GAAP Accounting Determines Sales for Financial Institutions

The only real way an organization like Prudential could demonstrate its ability to profitably acquire and sell commercial real estate was to do exactly that. Except that's not so simple for a large organization like Prudential, which today is publicly owned, because it is subject to Generally Accepted Accounting Principles (GAAP).

In early 1978, I learned how GAAP regulations determine profits for financial institutions. I was helping my boss at Citibank prepare for a special meeting to determine what our profits *would be* reported as for the prior quarter, and thus for the last full year. Our 1977 profits would ultimately determine our stock price, executive bonuses, and the amount the bank would pay in federal and state income taxes. Up until then, I naively thought that our profit for a given quarter was locked in at the end of the quarter based on our actual revenue less expenses. That's when I learned that one of the largest expenses on our income statement was something called "loan loss reserves," the amount a lending officer allocates to each loan or pool of loans based on the expected interest and principal that probably won't be collected from the pool.

Of course, no one knows in advance how much won't be collected on an outstanding loan, the banker has to guess. And the cumulative amount of all those guesses, say $200 million on a $20 billion portfolio of loans, allows the bank to deduct $200 million from the earnings they pay a percentage of in income taxes and that they report to stockholders.

What surprised me in preparing for that meeting was that there seemed to be an unwritten target amount of earnings that senior bank management wanted us to achieve, retroactively, weeks or months *after* the quarter had already passed. We could achieve this amount retroactively for the prior year by setting the amount of loan loss reserves in the current year on each loan.

Of course, an argument could have been made that the longer Citibank waited in determining what *probably* wouldn't be collected, the more accurate the number would be because the loan officer would have better information with the passage of time. But our stockholders and regulators needed to know as close as possible to the end of each quarter and each year.

Over time, the system will eventually catch up with its own mistakes: $100 million or so in understated earnings due to excess loan loss reserves in a present quarter will one day be recaptured as $100 million in extra profits if the loans are collected in amounts in excess of their expectations.

But in the C-suite where I worked, the bank seemed most concerned with reporting almost fictional stable, growing earnings from quarter to quarter with no surprises—Wall Street doesn't like surprises!

REO—The Assets Nobody Wants

REO stands for "real estate owned," which, to an investor like you or me, sounds like a good thing. But REO to a financial institution means property that the institution has acquired through an unsuccessful sale at a foreclosure.

Commercial banks and insurance companies are not supposed to make mistakes. Mistakes make their depositors, policyholders, and regulators nervous. When they hold a loan on a property, the amount of the loan should be a low enough percentage of the property value so that, if they have to foreclose on the property, there are bidders ready to purchase it at an amount greater than the amount of their loan (including unpaid interest). This is considered a successful foreclosure because the financial institution gets back all its money from the winning foreclosure bidder, with any excess funds going to the original borrower.

An unsuccessful foreclosure occurs when nobody wants to pay the foreclosure price; the lender that "bids" the amount of its loan plus unpaid interest is the highest bidder, and the financial institution takes title to the property as REO. The relative amount of REO that a financial institution has on its books is a good indicator of how well or poorly it has been managed.

Let's say a borrower is purchasing a new property for $1 million, and a bank or insurance company lends them $750,000 at a 10% interest rate. The new asset, the loan created for the lender, would be valued at par ($750,000) and earn the lender $75,000 (10%) a year in interest. Now assume the borrower goes bust, and the lender posts the property for foreclosure sale for $825,000 – $750,000 principal plus $75,000 in unpaid interest and expenses. There is probably no bidder willing to buy the loan and foreclose on the property for $825,000 or anything close to that amount—otherwise, the same bidder probably would have made a deal with the borrower and the property would have avoided foreclosure in the first place.

Once the lender forecloses, its problems have just begun. Its $750,000 REO asset is no longer paying it $75,000 a year in interest. Now it costs the lender $75,000-150,000 a year. As the new owner of the property, the lender (now owner) probably has to start paying out about $75,000 a year in real estate taxes, utilities, and tenant improvements—the income from their asset has gone down $150,000 a year. But the lender's biggest problem is yet to come: from its own accountants.

Strict GAAP and RAP (Regulatory Accounting Principles) rules govern how much (or how little) the lender must acquire the foreclosed property (the REO) for on their books, and it is sometimes as low as 50% of the original principal of the loan or $375,000. A lender might protest to its accountants and regulators that this now-REO property is worth more than $375,000 because it was once worth $1 million. The response of the accountants and regulators will almost always be: "Prove it by selling this piece of REO for more than $375,000. Until you do, you're taking a write-down of $375,000 on this asset which will go against your earnings this year!"

No wonder lenders don't like REO!

Depreciation

"Depreciation expense" is an accounting term that means a reduction in the value of an asset due to usage, age, obsolescence, etc. It is applied for income tax purposes under schedules set by the IRS and for financial reporting purposes by the Financial Accounting Standards Board (FASB). Depreciation is applied to machinery and buildings but not to land. For U.S. taxpaying real estate investors, it's the ultimate tax shelter.

Buildings used to decline in value prior to 1900 because they were made of wood and got weaker every year. Over the past 100 years or so, most buildings have gone up every year in value, but the IRS still allows taxpayers a deduction for this fictional depreciation. For financial reporting purposes, particularly for public entities, it's a distortion of the truth—businesses are charged depreciation expense on their income statement for the decreasing value of their buildings when the value of their buildings is actually increasing. The U.S. government and the FASB prefer the same schedules to be applied equally to all taxpayers and companies; accounting rules are not meant to be accurate as much as they are meant to be a uniform basis for comparison.

For example, if you purchase an apartment building on leased land for $10 million where your investment earns you 6% or $600,000 a year, instead of paying income taxes on $600,000 a year in actual income, you would be allowed a tax deduction for depreciation expense as if the building had declined in value linearly over 27.5 years—about 3.63% or $363,636 a year. This makes your annual taxable income only $236,363 versus $600,000. Why? Because the IRS says so.

Similarly, if you were a large company subject to GAAP and owned this property, not only would you get this same tax deduction courtesy of the IRS, you would also be forced to take a write-down of this building's value on your balance sheet of the same $363,636 a year. After ten years, you would have reduced the "cost" or "basis" of this building on your books by $3,636,363, by twice this amount or $7,272,727 after 20 years, and by $10 million to $0 after 27.5

years. If you sold the building for no profit, at your original cost, $10 million, you would be required to report on your financial statements a profit of $3,636,363 after ten years, $7,272,727 after 20 years, and $10 million after 27.5 years.

How Prudential Systematically Manages GAAP Profits

Let's say the Prudential real estate department in 1982 earned $200 million in profit from sales of real estate investments, including $100 million in profit from REO sales. Prudential senior management in 1983 would likely expect the real estate department to improve by 5% in 1983, earning $210 million in profit from sales, including $105 million from REO sales. Here's how Prudential's real estate department would go about achieving this goal.

The real estate department would create a list of each investment property Prudential owned that they might want to sell, an estimate of what it could be sold for (i.e. its market value), and the value of the property on Prudential's books (its GAAP value or GAAP basis), which is the amount Prudential paid for the property including improvements but less accumulated depreciation.

In most cases, the largest determinant of GAAP profit for a company like Prudential is not how much more they can sell a property for versus how much they paid for it—it's how long they have owned it. If they've owned it for 27.5 years, their GAAP profit is 100% of the sales price since, after 27.5 years of depreciation, their GAAP basis would be $0.

In early 1983 Prudential would have created a list of the properties they would be willing to sell that year, ranked by each property's expected GAAP profit from a sale. Then the real estate department would go to work selling a combination of properties to generate the desired, say, $210 million in GAAP profit, including $105 million in REO disposal. Large real estate investments are so complex that it is difficult to be sure whether a specific asset can be sold at all in a given year, let alone at a specific price. That's why Prudential probably would have created a 200% larger list of properties capable of generating the desired $210 million profit so as not to put their real estate department under pressure to sell any specific asset at a specific price.

But despite Prudential's desire not to put their employees under pressure to sell any specific property in 1983, I knew from my experience at Citibank that Prudential probably had a list of certain properties which had to be sold that year because they: 1) had the potential to produce an enormous GAAP profit from a sale, 2) had environmental issues that Prudential didn't want to deal with, or 3) were REO.

Near the top of that list was a large portfolio of 33 industrial buildings meeting all three of these criteria, a portfolio we came to collectively call "Memphis."

Memphis—GAAP Profit, Asbestos, and REO All in the Same Asset

After my lunch with Alan May in December of 1982, we returned to our office, and I phoned Brian Strum at Prudential in Newark, New Jersey. I was afraid he wouldn't take my call or even remember me—when you leave a large, powerful organization like Citibank and go out on your own, you never know how the people you used to work with are going to treat you. It had been almost two years since I had left Citibank and spoken to Brian. I reached his secretary first, and she remembered me. She and I discussed the annual Real Estate Board of New York (REBNY) dinner, and she expressed that she and the rest of the team missed working on it with me. Then she put me on hold for a few minutes, came back on the line, and transferred my call.

"Paul," Brian said enthusiastically, "I hear you're killing it down in Texas and making lots of money! What's up?"

I was happy he remembered me and explained that I had a new partner, that our firm had a big appetite for older industrial properties at low prices per square foot. "What have you got for me?" I asked.

"Your timing is perfect," Brian answered. "We are just finishing this week our book of all the properties we'd like to sell in 1983, encompassing retail, office, and industrial. I'll see that you get one of the first copies. But in addition to seeing the entire portfolio, I'd like to introduce you to John McClaren, our head of REO. He's Irish but, like you, born in Brooklyn. I think you two will get along well."

I thanked Brian for the referral, wrote down John's contact information on a yellow sticky note, and typed out a letter of introduction to John on my new IBM PC with dual floppy disk drives, one disk for the word processing operating system and one for my data. Then I walked out of my office and handed the floppy data disk to my secretary along with John's contact info and told her to get the letter out overnight via FedEx to John, copying Brian. Next, I typed out a separate letter to Brian thanking him for introducing me to John.

The following week, right after New Year's Day, I received a call from John McClaren. John asked me how I knew Brian. I dropped every name I knew at Prudential in my reply. Then I queried John for almost an hour about his career at Prudential, asking what he'd done before being put in charge of domestic REO, what his departmental objectives were for 1983, and what properties he felt we should look at right away. John was responsible for dozens of REO properties owned by Prudential, not because Prudential was a bad lender, but because they were so huge with thousands of major real estate investments throughout the nation.

The first deal John mentioned was Memphis. As he described the property, I asked all sorts of accounting and technical questions about how Prudential had acquired it. Surprisingly, he answered all of them without hesitation. At one point, he had a person from Prudential's finance department join us on the call to answer my accounting questions directly. I could tell someone, probably Brian, had said good things about me before our call.

Prudential told me that the property known as "Memphis" consisted of 33 industrial warehouse buildings totaling 3.3 million square feet, and that it sprawled over hundreds of acres east of the Memphis International Airport. Prudential had lent $12 million on this portfolio in the 1960s and foreclosed on it during the recession of 1973-1974. They took the property on their books as REO for $6 million, a 50% write-down, and then depreciated it 36% over

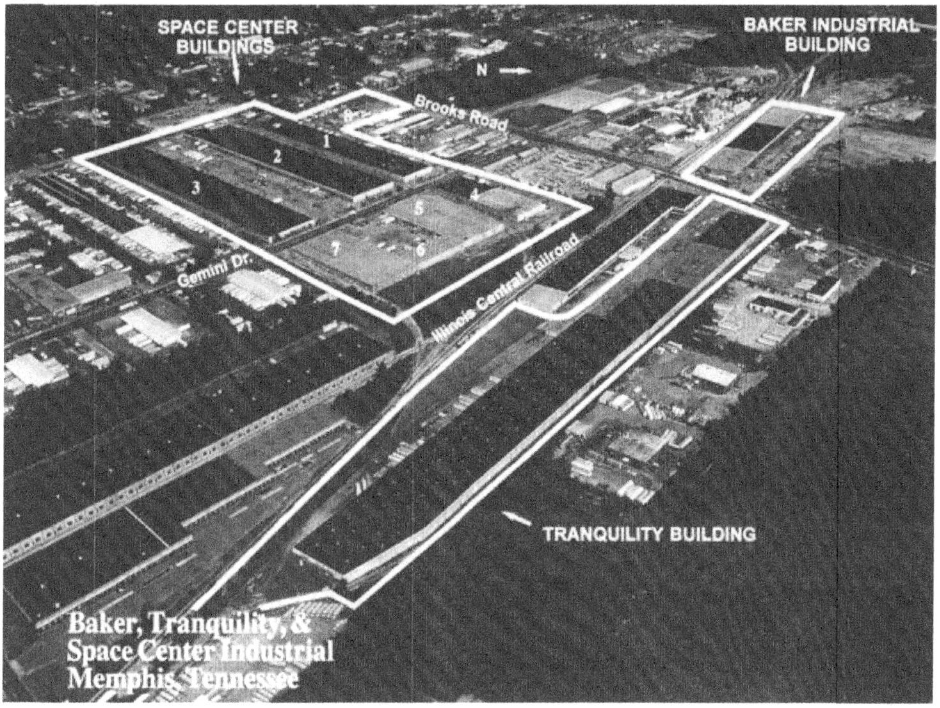

"Memphis" consisted of 33 industrial warehouse buildings, totaling 3.3 million feet, sprawled over hundreds of acres east of the Memphis International Airport. Prudential had foreclosed on it during the recession of 1973-1974 and carried it on their books as REO for $3.84 million.

the next ten years. This meant that in 1983 Prudential carried this property on its books for $3.84 million, and anything they received from a sale above this price would be GAAP profit. To me, these numbers meant that each dollar John sold Memphis for above $3.84 million would make him a hero at Prudential.

Then John mentioned the price he wanted for Memphis, which I wrote down in my notes as the "asking price"—$13.63 per square foot, or $45 million! I knew from the other deals we were chasing that a fair price for a 20+ year-old industrial portfolio like this would be $10-12 per square foot or $33-36 million, nowhere near the $45 million Prudential was asking.

But instead of being annoyed, I was elated. In that first phone call, I knew two things for sure:

1. The ridiculously high $45 million asking price would scare away other potential buyers from working on the deal because they wouldn't want to waste their time or insult Prudential with a low offer.
2. Before the end of 1983, Prudential was going to sell this Memphis property at any price, even $30 million, because with a $3.84 million GAAP basis, they couldn't turn down the potential to book $26-41 million or more in GAAP profit, especially profit coming from the successful elimination of REO.

Two days later, a box arrived from Prudential. It weighed 40 pounds and contained detailed descriptions of each of the 33 buildings and lease summaries for 700 tenants. I assigned our two deal-makers, Richard Jaffe and Bob Petrucello, to summarize the leases and told them to schedule at least one trip to Memphis every month for the next six months.

The property was in a rough area of Memphis, at the intersection of Interstate 240 and Interstate 55, near Elvis Presley's birthplace. The buildings were not institutional quality; no "institution" (major insurance company or bank) would want to own buildings that looked like these at any price; they had been built just after World

33 Warehouse Industrial Properties Memphis, TN (4 of 4)

Creating Demand

- Federal Express Deal
- Medical Labs
- Bloomingdale's Warehouse
- Made Tenants into Leasing Agents by Recruiting their Suppliers and Customers

The Memphis buildings were old, dirty, rundown, and probably had asbestos. In contrast, I liked the property even before I saw it because the buildings were virtually 100% leased—which meant there was lots of potential upside from increasing rents. The 100% occupancy figure told me the rent was underpriced.

War II and were dirty, rundown, and probably had asbestos and other environmental issues. Institutional investors wanted to own gorgeous, shiny new real estate properties that they could show off to their financial investors—not rundown buildings in bad parts of town.

In contrast, I liked the property even before I saw it because the buildings were virtually 100% leased and generating $3.3 million in cash flow, which meant there was lots of potential upside from increasing rents. How did I know right away there was an upside?

The 100% occupancy figure told me the rent was underpriced.

In general, real estate rents should be priced so that the property operates at around 95% occupancy. This way, you will always have space available for new tenants and space for existing tenants whose businesses are growing and who desperately need to expand. With most properties, you can receive more total rent from 95% of the building than from 100% of the building.

Suppose you own a 100,000-square-foot building. Would you rather rent 100,000 square feet at $1 per square foot yielding $100,000/year? Or rent only 95,000 square feet at $1.06 per square foot, a higher-yielding $101,000/year, and have 5,000 more square feet available for new or expanding tenants?

Most of all, I loved this deal because of something going on three miles away on the other side of the Memphis Airport runways.

As we looked at the deal over the next few months, I realized the maximum price at which we could purchase this property would be $10-12 a square foot, equating to $33-36 million for the 3.3 million square feet. I instructed Robert and Bob never to share this information with Prudential but to keep inundating Prudential every week with due diligence requests for more lease information, operating history, pictures, etc. Alan and I started visiting Memphis and talking to tenants, which signaled to Prudential that we were interested. We developed a friendly relationship at multiple levels in our respective organizations; Robert and Bob got to know John's associates, and I got to know John McClaren—they'd fly in to meet us in Dallas, and we'd fly to New York (technically to Newark) to meet with them.

At this time, we also started talking to them about 12 more properties, including a portfolio of six shopping centers in Sun City, Arizona, that we purchased from them in 1985. But throughout 1983, each time we met, Memphis was our top priority.

Like a fly fisherman with a line too weak to bring in the fish all at once, I was taking my time to make this deal. We were traveling back and forth so much that Alan got concerned we were spending too much time and money on something that might not happen.

"How do you know no one else is going to buy these buildings?" he asked one day, a tinge of concern in his voice. I had to laugh.

"Alan," I assured him, "these buildings are such dogs that people in Nashville, 200 miles away, can hear them barking. No institution whose employees hang around with the white glove people at Prudential is going to want these. But they have even greater potential because of something that's three miles away."

I opened my briefcase and took out some aerial photographs, which had a dotted line showing the border of the Memphis properties on the east side of the airport, and the border of something labeled "other industrial properties" on the west side of the airport. Then I explained that one of the greatest assets of this property wasn't even on the property itself. It was something so new that Prudential didn't even show it on their descriptions of the area.

Federal Express

Today, everyone knows the name Federal Express, which renamed itself FedEx in 2000—how could you not know a company with 425,000 employees! It's consistently ranked among the ten most

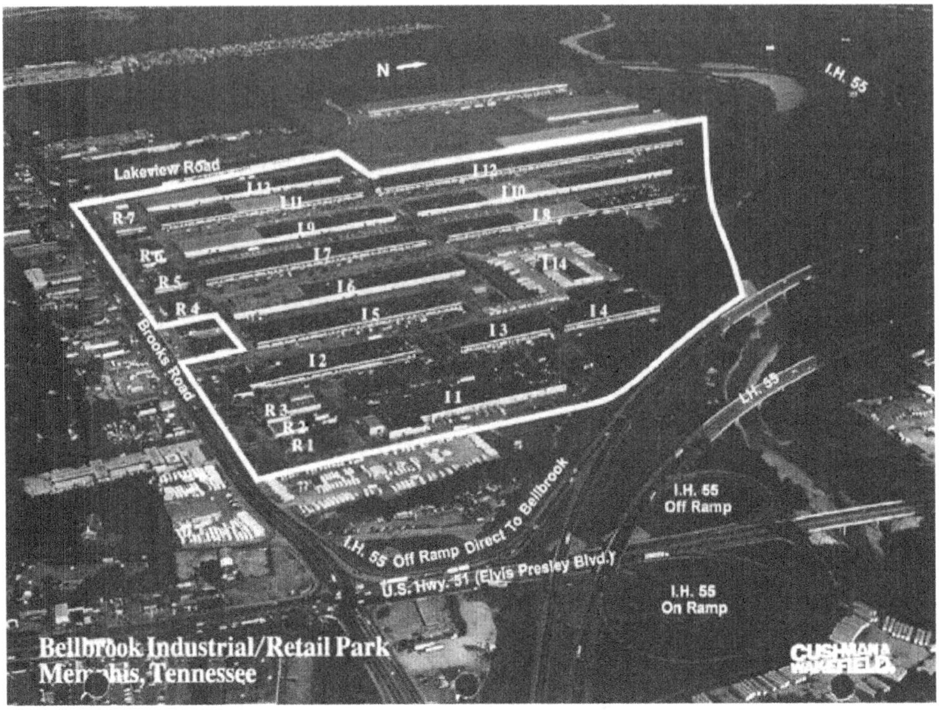

The Bellbrook Industrial Park (1984), which we called "Memphis," was located adjacent to the airport and the new area that was going to become the worldwide headquarters for FedEx.

admired firms in the world, with annual sales exceeding $70 billion and annual profits in excess of $6 billion!

But back in early 1983, FedEx wasn't even a billion dollar company, let alone a $70 billion company. It was another freight shipper with "potential" that had only been around ten years.

The idea for the company was developed by Fred Smith while he was a student at Yale University. FedEx's doors officially opened in 1971, and by that time, they had already accomplished some important innovations, like the Drop Box in 1974, the overnight letter in 1980, and SuperTracker, a handheld scanner that allowed package tracking in real-time, in 1986.

Nevertheless, I thought FedEx was going to take off, especially by shifting from shipping mostly documents to mostly products. Irrespective of the growth potential of FedEx, it was not yet a major asset to the Memphis property.

The Seller Gets Anxious

I had never in my life seen a property with a GAAP book value of $3.84 million and an asking price of $45 million—a potential $41.16 million or 90% profit. Prudential probably hadn't seen this much profit potential from one deal either, and they were anxious not to let it get away. Every few weeks, John or his associates would ask me or my associates when we were going to make a formal offer. They were dying to know our price.

We continually ducked the question and made up excuses as to why we didn't know the final price yet. One day we told them we didn't know the final price because we were going to add their property to a separate 400,000-square-foot industrial property nearby—a property we purchased the following year. I knew that telling them we were nowhere near $45 million could bury the deal at any time unless we were the only potential buyer left standing who could close in the 1983 calendar year.

Throughout most of 1983, Prudential was eager to pin down a price, but each time they brought up the subject of pricing, I'd deflect the question.

"Oh, it's going to take us a little more time to figure out the price," I'd tell them excitedly. "We love the property and want to buy it, but I have to go through each of the buildings carefully.

We don't want to move too fast and have to renege on or lower our offer."

Negotiating the Price

By Labor Day, the property still sat unsold. Two other potential buyers had come and gone and John was getting antsy; he was under serious pressure to get this REO property off their books and to book tens of millions in GAAP profit. He called and got straight to the point, which I took to mean he was not hanging up without an answer. "When are you guys going to submit your offer?"

"John, look, I don't want to insult you," I began. "So, I'm going to have to go away ..."

"No, no, no!" he said. "Give me an offer."

"John, you already told me you've got people ready to buy it for close to your asking price, so I don't want to insult you with my offer. Go sell it to them!"

I knew he was bluffing, which to me was the same as threatening. My father taught me never to threaten because once you've promised conditionally to do something and don't do it, you've lost credibility. Success in business comes from building relationships with people with whom you can do more business, but once you lose credibility, they are done with you.

John had been telling me for months that he had buyers ready to pay close to the asking price, but if that was the case, he would have already made a deal.

"Look, we put a lot of time into this deal," I told him. "I personally know many of your tenants, and I know your buildings. I like this project, but we, like you, are ultimately responsible to our investors, and we can't buy it for $45 million."

"Who said anything about $45 million?" he said. "I'm ready to sell it to you for $40 million. Let's talk terms."

We negotiated back and forth until I told him, "I can't do the $40 million because my lenders won't back me. So, unless you give me a purchase money loan, I can't do this deal."

He wasn't expecting that.

"What would a purchase money loan deal look like?" he wanted to know.

I switched from "me" to "we" so our conversation would be less adversarial.

"You sell Memphis to us for $40 million, closing by the end of 1983. We put down $4 million, 10%, enough for Prudential to book $36.16 million in GAAP profit under FASB 66, Accounting for Sales of Real Estate. Prudential grants us a $36 million purchase money loan at 6% interest, amortizing over a 30-year schedule—that's a $2.59 million annual payment, or a 7.195 constant on the initial loan principal."

I could tell by the questions he asked that I had John's attention, especially when I said "$36.16 million in GAAP profit."

During the next three weeks, the two of us and our lawyers went back and forth on the terms of the $36 million purchase money loan while the Prudential real estate lending group visited the property and did their due diligence to grant us the loan. The lending group was handling this as a new independent loan request for $36 million, 80% of the $45 million value originally claimed by John McClaren's

REO group. We signed a formal loan application in early October and put down a 1% ($360,000) good faith loan application fee. It took two more weeks, until the middle of October, for Prudential's real estate lending group to approve the $36 million loan.

Meanwhile, Alan and I were busy lining up the $4 million in tax-advantaged equity that we would need to close. We actually lined up twice that amount, $8 million, because the deal was so good that almost every potential equity investor we contacted wanted a piece. The property would produce $3.3 million in net income before a mortgage payment of $2.59 million a year, which meant our deal could receive up to $710,000 in annual cash flow, a 9% cash-on-cash return on our investor's $8 million investment, plus 50% of the property appreciation.

Prudential sent us a signed loan commitment around October 17 which said "subject to final corporate committee approval" on the last page, but John told us to ignore that language. He had never seen the corporate committee not accept the recommendation of the real estate lending group. Everyone on both sides went to work, reviewing leases, appraising each of the 33 buildings, ordering engineering reports, etc. We were set to close on Halloween.

Then, three days before closing, on a Friday afternoon, John called me. I suspected he wanted to talk about something big, and I took the call in our conference room with my team on a speakerphone.

"Hi, Paul. This is not a good week for me. The corporate committee just rejected approving the $36 million purchase money loan on Memphis," he said on our speakerphone.

"On what grounds?" I wanted to know.

"They don't think the property is worth $45 million, despite the 33 appraisals we've both obtained to the contrary. In fact, the chair of the committee told me and the real estate lending group that he doesn't think the property is worth even $30 million."

"But you already own this property!" I told him. "If they don't think it's worth $30 million, then they should take my $4 million now and foreclose on the $36 million purchase money loan later!" I was starting to panic.

"Yes," John said. I could hear his frustration. "But the logic doesn't work that way. In fact, the corporate committee doesn't want the Prudential lending department to make a loan on this property for any amount! They don't seem to understand that if they don't approve the loan, Prudential is still going to be stuck owning the property as REO!"

"But John, we've spent a fortune on lawyers, accountants, engineers, and appraisers. Alan and I have hundreds of thousands of dollars invested in underwriting!" Now my stomach was turning.

"Paul, I feel terrible for you and for what we've done to you and your investors. I was told by my superiors, all the way up to Brian Strum, that they would sell it for $40 million with a 90% purchase money loan. I did exactly what they told me. I'm fed up."

I'd noticed that many of the "we's" in John's sentences had turned to "they's."

We had reached a turning point.

When a leader treats his loyal followers badly, they, and sometimes even his own army, will turn on him. This same thing sometimes happens in business with employees, even with senior executives, when their superiors do not support them. And this had just happened with John. He had enjoyed meeting me, Alan, Robert, and Bob; we had become friends as we tried to put this deal together. And now he felt he had been lied to. He was told to sell it for $40 million with a $36 million purchase money loan, and there we were, ready to close, but they had reneged on the deal they'd told him to get done.

"So, where do we go from here?" I asked. "It sounds like your company doesn't want to own these 33 buildings. And we do."

"I'm authorized to sell it to you for all cash. Are you prepared to purchase on an all-cash basis? And still, close this year?"

"John, we can't come up with $40 million all cash. The reason we could pay $40 million was the $36 million low-interest-rate purchase money loan."

"Who said anything about $40 million?" he asked.

"I told you, John, I cannot buy it for $40 million without the purchase money loan!"

"Stop talking about the amount," he said. "Listen to my words. I'm authorized to sell it to you for all cash."

"At what price?"

"What price do you think?" he asked. "Make us an offer."

"$36 million," I said.

"What? I can't hear you, Paul. It must be a bad connection."

I repeated my offer, and he again said he couldn't hear me.

"$36 million," I repeated sheepishly for the third time. I was gulping because I knew that price would be a tough amount for

Alan and me to raise on this deal, but doable if we gave away most of the equity ownership to our investors.

"What?" he yelled. "I still can't hear you? My connection must be getting worse."

Bob Petrucello leaned over the conference table and hit the mute button on our speakerphone.

"He's on our side, Paul! He's telling us to go way below $36 million."

"$30 million!" I shouted out declaratively once the mute button had been punched again.

"Ohhhh, $30 million, now I hear you," John said. "That's too low, but we're getting closer."

We continued "negotiating" this way until we finally settled on $31.2 million, all cash, closing by December 31. Alan, Robert, Bob, and I were elated; it was as if we had just found $4.8 million in equity for free! Now, all we had to do was raise $31.2 million in cash in the two months left of 1983.

GE Capital—The Origins of Commercial Paper

To close quickly on an opportunistic deal like Memphis, we needed a lender who was as smart or smarter than we were, one who acted more like a partner than a lender, and one to whom we would probably have to give a piece of the action. There was one lender at the top of our list: Gary Wendt, then the head of real estate lending at GE Capital.

General Electric was originally formed in 1892 after acquiring all the assets of Thomas Edison's Edison General Electric Company.

In addition to manufacturing everything electric from light bulbs to kitchen appliances to televisions, GE was a leading manufacturer of many products which cost tens of millions of dollars each. They made products from electrical power stations to airplane engines to wastewater treatment plants. Not only did GE design and sell these expensive products, they became expert in helping their customers pay for them. In fact, GE got so good at helping its customers finance GE products that it branched out into helping these same customers finance anything they wanted to buy. Then, GE started issuing its own commercial paper, raising capital to lend directly to the most creditworthy companies in the world. In 1979, GE surpassed Citibank as the world's largest lender to major corporations. At Citibank in the 1970s, we called GE "the bank without a regulator" as GE beat us out on deal after deal. In 2014, GE Capital had 35,000 employees and about $500 billion in assets.[23]

Legend says GE got into the direct lending business when its treasurer was waiting in a buffet lunch line on a hot summer day. The story goes that it was July 8, 1974, at the Metropolitan Club on Fifth Avenue and 60th Street in New York.

Before I go on, I need you to know that the prime rate is the rate at which banks traditionally lend money to their most creditworthy or "prime" customers. This was typically done on an unsecured basis with a simple paper IOU note that came to be known as "commercial paper." The prime rate in the 1970s (and decades earlier) was set every week in a morning meeting by a committee at Citibank, then called First National City Bank (FNCB). The committee typically

23. ***Wikipedia***. "GE Capital."

announced the new rate by noon, and other U.S. banks followed suit. FNCB formally changed its name to Citibank in 1976.

The recession of 1973-1974 was brutal on interest rates—the prime rate started out at 6% in 1973 and nearly doubled by June 1974. This wreaked havoc on the budgets of the nation's largest corporations. As the second half of 1974 began, everyone was anticipating a significant decline in interest rates, led by the committee at FNCB. The bank's cost of funds and all other indicators pointed toward a major reduction in the prime rate—the question was by how much.

But then, on the morning of July 8, 1974, in what was popularly described as "greed not need," FNCB decided to increase the prime rate to 12% instead of lowering it as expected. This drove many corporate treasurers to expletives about FNCB since their companies had budgeted for the opposite. One of these expletive-issuing executives was the treasurer of IBM, who was standing on a food buffet line at the Metropolitan Club. Coincidentally, standing next to him was the treasurer of General Electric. Back then, both of these companies were worth more and had a better credit rating than FNCB.

"How much paper do you have outstanding now at Citibank?" the treasurer of GE asked the treasurer of IBM. Citibank was the popular nickname then for FNCB.

"We owe Citibank about $100 million right now, and we're growing so fast that I'm not able to pay them off until the middle of next year. But my board is breathing down my neck to pay off this obligation, which now is going to cost us 12% in interest."

"Then why don't you stop by my office after lunch," the GE

executive replied, "We have more than that amount on deposit at Citibank, earning only 2% interest. I'll lend you $100 million for six months at, oh let's split the difference, 7%, and you'll use the money to pay off your 12% interest rate commercial paper at Citibank. You'll save $5 million in reduced interest over the next 12 months, and I'll earn $5 million in extra interest on our extra cash now at Citibank."

To add insult to injury, not only did GE lend IBM $100 million that afternoon, they used the same commercial paper documents that Citibank (FNCB) had used, simply replacing the name FNCB with GE.

The transaction worked out well for both parties, but particularly for GE, which found the lending business so profitable that it started its own lending division called GE Capital. GE Capital expanded to issuing its own commercial paper and making loans to all types of organizations whether or not they were financing the purchase of GE products. GE Capital surpassed Citibank five years later in 1979, as the nation's largest commercial lender, and was the world's largest private lender with more than $600 billion in assets by 2008.[24]

24. Sadly, after 15 years of virtually taking over the commercial lending business from Citibank and others, GE Capital got into enormous trouble in The Great Recession from which it still has not fully recovered as of this writing in 2021. GE Capital peaked at $600 billion in assets in 2008 (see Gryta, Thomas, and Ted Mann. "The Long Shadow of GE Capital Looms Over GE." ***Wall Street Journa***l, March 26, 2018.

Hansen, S. 2021. "The Rise and Fall of General Electric (GE)." ***Investopedia***.

Wikipedia. "GE Capital."

Aircraft Engines to Aircraft Financing 2014: 35,000 employees, 40 countries, $499 billion in assets. "GE only wanted to be a bank if it didn't have to play by

Our Deal with GE Capital

It was Friday afternoon, October 28, 1983, when we made our deal with Prudential, and now we had only 64 days to line up $36 million to close by December 31. The money we needed was as follows:

Financing Needed to Close Memphis, Nov-Dec 1983

	$31.2 million	Cash Purchase Price to Seller
	$2.0 million	Reserves for Repairs, TI & Environmental
	$1.5 million	Lender's Fees
	$1.0 million	Walking-Around Money (working capital)
+	$0.3 million	Misc. Closing Expenses
	$36.0 million	Total Financial Proceeds from Lender

I knew we had to reach Gary Wendt, the head of Real Estate Lending at GE Capital, right away. I phoned the two people in the world I knew who could get to Gary, structure a deal by the next morning, a Saturday, and have him call in his people to start working over the weekend: real estate investment bankers Jeffrey Juster and David Wallenstein.

The next day, on Saturday afternoon, Jeffrey phoned to tell me that he had just spoken with Gary. I was pleased that Jeffrey had the kind of relationship that allowed him to move this fast, and I thought to myself, *I probably can't get Gary Wendt to return my*

the same rules that other banks do," said Matt O'Brien of the ***Washington Post***. O'Brien, M. 2019. "Financial Reform Is Working, Kind of: GE Doesn't Want to Be a Bank Anymore." ***Washington Post***, April 26, 2019.

phone call, let alone over a weekend.

Jeffrey told me that GE knew the property and was interested in lending us the money, but GE Capital had three additional concerns in addition to us passing normal due diligence items:

1. Time in Business: As such a new company, Zane May Interests might not pass GE's underwriting standards.
2. Management Experience: Zane May Interests had little or no experience managing industrial properties anywhere, let alone in Tennessee.
3. Cash Flow Management: GE would require a "lockbox bank account" where all tenant rents would be sent to a bank account controlled by GE.

Assuming we could pass muster on these three major items, he said GE would be prepared to close the deal by the end of the year under the following terms.

"Take it or leave it."

Financing Quote from GE Capital

- Loan Amount: $36 million (up to 80-90% of MAI appraisal)
- Term: 10 years
- $1 million limited personal liability
- Full personal liability if borrower filed bankruptcy
- Closing by December 31, 1983
- 10% Equity Kicker paid on value above $40 million at the time of sale or refinance

- 8% Loan Constant Payment ($2.88 million)
- All unpaid interest to accrue and/or be paid down from cash flow

We took it, and I began working on GE's additional concerns.

Trammell Crow Gets Us Credibility

The most prominent owner/manager of industrial property in the United States at the time was Trammell Crow Company, founded in 1948 by Trammell Crow. the *Wall Street Journal* in 1986 called the Trammell Crow organization "the largest landlord in the United States."[25]

I knew Trammell personally through my political activities. Trammell later became national chairman of the Republican Party, and he served as chairman of Pilzer for Congress when I ran for office eight years later.

On Monday morning, October 31, 1983, I called Trammell's office, and his secretary told me to come right over—his office was across the street from mine in Dallas. We were joined by Don Williams, the CEO, who I had never met before. I didn't know it then, but Don's family was about to become significant in my life. Don's son Brandon worked for me from 1989-1990 as my summer intern and my full-time researcher when I wrote ***Unlimited Wealth***, and in 2001, I hired Don's son Bryce to be the CEO of Extend Health, a company I started in 1999 with Anthony Meyer that we

25. The ***Wall Street Journal*** in 1986 called Crow the "largest landlord in the United States." Martin, D. "Trammell Crow, Innovative Developer, Dies at 94." ***New York Times***, January 16, 2009.

sold in 2009 for $418 million to Towers Watson[26].

I began my Halloween meeting with Trammell and Don by explaining the Memphis deal, focusing on the fact that properly leased, similar industrial properties could be worth $22 per square foot, and we were coming in at $11 per square foot. I also shared some of my ideas for improving the property.

Don explained to me that the Crow organization managed industrial properties in Memphis for at least ten different owners. I expressed my desire to have their top operating people in Memphis focus on leasing our property and give priority to our property versus another Crow-managed property when making space recommendations to tenants. Don explained that the Trammell Crow organization would always bring a tenant to the best-suited and best-priced location for the tenant, regardless of who owned the building. But he did leave the door open that we could give his employees financial incentives, provided they were supervised by the local Crow partner, Charlie Brindell, who ran all of the Memphis area for the Crow organization. Don then dialed Charlie on the speakerphone, electronically adding him to our meeting.

With all the decision-makers present, we were able to work out the terms of a management and leasing deal in that first meeting. We signed a letter of understanding that afternoon which stated the following:

1. Trammell Crow in Memphis would manage all 33

26. Brandon Williams was important to me when I ran for Congress, and in 2022 he was elected to Congress representing New York's 22nd District.

buildings for Zane May Interests at their full standard price, 4% of revenues, plus leasing commissions.

2. Zane May Interests would keep their employees on-site and be allowed to spiff Trammell Crow leasing agents for bringing them tenants, on top of what their agents already earned from Trammell Crow.
3. Partners and selected employees of the Trammell Crow organization in Memphis (not nationally) would receive a 10% profits interest in cash flow and sales/refinance profits from our property. (I told them the profits interest alone should be worth $3 million! As you'll see in a moment, Charlie and his partners later earned $2.94 million from this 10% profits interest.)

Even through the phone line, I could feel Charlie Brindell's approval of the last point. I was confident none of the other ten owners he managed property for in Memphis had granted the equivalent of equity ownership to him or his employees.

Our meeting ended and I ran back to my office to call Jeffrey Juster with the good news. Jeffrey told me that making Trammell Crow our partner would clinch getting our loan approved by GE Capital. He wanted to call Gary Wendt at GE with the news right away. Jeffrey also noted that both GE and Trammel Crow would be grateful to us for introducing them to each other.

Everything went surprisingly smoothly over the next six weeks. We closed on the purchase with Prudential and the financing with GE Capital, in the middle of December.

Over the next decade, I became great friends with Charlie Brindell and his family and occasionally stayed in their home when I visited Memphis. Once I went with him to drop his daughter off at the prestigious St. Anne Elementary School and got to meet with the headmaster. I let Charlie and his local Trammell Crow partners use my 1981 ski house in Park City, Utah, and in 1988 they purchased this ski house from me.

Memphis Operations

Richard Jaffe was in charge of leasing all Zane May Interests properties, and he rented a two-bedroom apartment in Memphis at our expense so he and Bob Petrucello could conveniently visit often and be on site. Their main job was to make sure our property got attention from the Trammell Crow leasing team.

"I want to see lots of dinner receipts and credit card bills from you guys having dinner with Trammell Crow agents every month," I told my team. "These guys like to eat, so take them out to dinner, often. If anybody in Memphis can lease this property at twice the current rents, they can, as long as you two keep us in front of them."

The property wasn't going to get leased on its good looks, and we knew it. So, we developed a compelling story that made people want to give it a look.

The centerpiece of our story was that Memphis is in the dead center of the U.S., less than 12 hours' drive time from more than 50% of the U.S. population. It's no wonder FedEx chose to place its world headquarters there. Our story was that if you wanted to do business all over the U.S., Memphis was the place to be.

Partnering with FedEx

Back in the 1970s, before email and companies like DocuSign, if you wanted to quickly send a legal document needing a signature, you went to FedEx to have it delivered overnight and sent back the same way the next day. At that time, most of FedEx's business was delivering envelopes, not packages.

The FedEx motto was "In by 5:00 p.m., delivered the next morning by 10:00 a.m." But what they actually did was pick up your package by 5:00 p.m., fly or drive it to Memphis by midnight, sort it (based on where it was going) by 2:00 a.m., and then fly or drive it to its destination for delivery by 10:00 a.m. the next day, the second day, or sometimes the third day (at a lower price).

FedEx chose Memphis as the place to do business because it could reach half the country by inexpensive driving, not expensive flying, even though everyone associated FedEx with overnight air freight. It was a genius business model for the time.

Our Memphis property was located a few miles from FedEx world headquarters—we were actually closer than FedEx was to the Memphis airport. In 1983, companies like DHL and UPS were retooling their operations to compete, so FedEx knew it had to up its game and lower the cost of its product. During the first week in 1984, I called FedEx to set up a meeting with Don Harrington, their head of business development. Don responded immediately once I told his office that we were the new owners of most of the industrial space near their headquarters. We agreed to meet later that month in Memphis at his office.

"If I get my tenants to start using FedEx, can they get a discount?"

I wanted to know.

"Well, I tell you what I'll do for you, Mr. Pilzer," Don replied. "We can give them a discount of 10%."

"That's not what I meant by a discount. I want them to get a 50% discount," I said.

"How do you expect us to stay in business if we give your tenants 50% off?"

"Because my tenants will do 50% of the work," I said.

FedEx had staging areas and bins all over their Memphis campus that were designated by where the packages and envelopes were headed. When the FedEx envelopes and packages arrived in Memphis by midnight, FedEx would sort them to the designated area based on where they were going—to ship out via air or truck by 2:00 a.m.

"My tenants are going to bring you their packages, all pre-labeled, directly to the staging area or bin where you want them. They will tie into your computer system, so you'll know what's coming when you schedule your transport planes and trucks."

Don was interested but expressed that FedEx was already doing this for its major customers—giving them an on-site terminal to label and presort their outgoing packages even before they left their shipper's address. He liked the idea of offering this benefit to smaller customers already in Memphis, with pricing based on volume. But he wouldn't commit to any discounted pricing below 10%. He did agree to give our tenants a most favored nation's clause, which meant that they would be guaranteed to receive the lowest price anyone else received based on their volume. I could tell Harrington saw the potential of having a customer with an on-site label printer located within walking distance from a FedEx departure point, but I could also see that nothing big was going to happen while we dealt in hypotheticals; I had to come back to him with a significant customer. And I had just the right customer in mind.

Bloomingdale's

In 1984, Bloomingdale's was the hottest retailer in New York City, primarily due to one person, Marvin Traub, who joined in 1969 and was the CEO from 1978 to 1988. Marvin made the name Bloomingdale's synonymous with luxury and retail excitement. And while doing so, Marvin turned Bloomingdale's from a sleepy regional department store chain to a nationally known brand, even though Bloomingdale's had no stores outside of the New York City metropolitan area.

In 1974, I graduated from college and worked for my father's business, Pilzer Brothers, Inc. We made curtains and bedspreads, and over 90% of our sales were to one retailer: Macy's. All my life, it seemed crazy to me to have all our eggs in one basket. In the summer of 1974, I called on Macy's main rival, Bloomingdale's. The curtain and bedspread buyer there was Margaret Traub. After my first meeting with her, I ran to tell my father that Margaret was the daughter of President Traub.

In just a few months, we were doing a brisk business with Bloomingdale's. At age 20 I was featured in an article highlighting Bloomingdale's called "Affinity to Furniture" in ***Home Furnishings***

Daily on November 27, 1974.[27] As a vendor, I had the pleasure of socializing with Marvin at store events, and I kept handling the Bloomingdale's account during my time at Wharton until I started working at Citibank in 1976. Separately, in the 1990s, Marvin Traub bought a ski house two miles away from mine in Park City, Utah.

Bloomingdale's, like most retailers back then, produced an annual Christmas catalog plus several additional seasonal catalogs that were sent to their national mailing lists. Customers ordered by telephone, and product would be pulled from the store shelves and sent UPS ground with a 5-10 day delivery time.

In 1984, right after my meeting with FedEx, I called on Marvin to share with him my vision.

"Marvin, think of this: you stock your bestselling mail-order items in Memphis, not New York, and offer the following to your customers: 'Order by 10:00 p.m. with delivery the next morning by 10:00 a.m., anywhere in the U.S., for a flat $10.'" ($10 was about half the normal $20 delivery charge). Today, this is commonplace with Amazon's next and same day delivery, but this was decades ahead of its time in 1984.

Marvin referred me to the head of the catalog division at Bloomingdale's—they tried a modified version of my proposal in 1986. Although it took two years to implement and never achieved great volume for us in terms of actually leasing space in Memphis, it became a signature story in our marketing pitch to new prospective tenants: "Your customer's customer can order by 10:00 p.m. and get

---

27. Levine, A. "Behind the Curtain." ***Home Furnishings Daily***, November 27, 1974.

HOME FURNISHINGS DAILY, WEDNESDAY, NOVEMBER 27, 1974

home textiles/curtains/draperies linens/domestics/bath

behind the curtain

by Al Levine

Affinity to Furniture

"FOUR WEEKS AFTER 'HERCULON' CAME OUT of Larry Schnuer's mouth, olefin sleepcovers were on sale at Bloomingdale's."

This is the way that Paul Pilzer, youthful vice-president for sales of Pilzer Bros., recounts the start of the company's growing program on Herculon sleepcovers.

The Bloomingdale divisional merchandise manager for home furnishings came to Pilzer Bros. to ask what it could do with high-quality Herculon sleepcovers.

"Larry, with his knowledge of the furniture market, recognized that the success of Herculon in upholstered furniture can be tied in with sleepcovers," Paul says.

The initial reaction to the speedily launched Pilzer Herculon sleepcovers earlier this season bolsters Paul's view both that sleepcovers are a big growth area and that olefin can play an important part in this growth.

OLEFIN, A BIG FACTOR in the furniture market, is a natural for sleepcovers, Paul says.

"The sleepcover market is furniture. A lot of people are using it as an inexpensive convertible, so upholstery types of fabrics are logical for sleepcover usage.

The company, he points out, has been successful with upholstery types of fabrics, including rayon/acetates, and linen/cotton with Scotchgard.

"We anticipate a big market for Herculon and all upholstery fabrics."

Other stores from Gimbels, New York, to Macy's, San Francisco, have picked up olefin sleepcovers, Paul reports.

At Gimbels, he points out that the furniture background of Richard Swed, buyer of sleepcovers and decorative pillows, was an asset in working on olefin styling.

"He was formerly a furniture buyer, and was experienced with Herculon upholstery."

BLOOMINGDALE'S RECENTLY INCLUDED CHALET, a broad plaid in Herculon, in its promotion of quilted sleepcovers keyed to the holiday season. Four-way fitted Chalet covers to fit Hollywoods (39x-75x20), Hi-risers (34/75x22), Studios (34x75x18), were priced for the sale at $48, with wedge covers at $15 and pillow shams at $12.

Sleepcovers and blinds are in the same department at Bloomingdale's, so it was a natural thing for Ralph Vacarro to have shades made to go with the Herculon sleepcover program, Paul points out.

For Pilzer Bros., which does about 50 per cent of its business on bedspreads and draperies, the balance on sleepcovers, the move into Herculon involved a major capital investment in new machines and cutting tools, Paul observes.

Paul notes that sleepcovers are growing not only in the conventional areas like Los Angeles and Chicago, but "also elsewhere around the country."

"The big growth is in the 39x75x20 Hollywoods," he reports.

"The studio look is desired all over," he sums up. "It's right for the 1970s life style."

PAUL AND HIS BROTHER LEONARD graduated from Lehigh University last June and were both on their way to graduate school. Paul was heading for Wharton Business School, and Paul for law school.

But the good response on the Herculons played a part in their decision to defer graduate study.

"I may go to Wharton, but I enjoy what I'm doing," says Paul. Leonard is vice-president, production.

Elias, their father, is president of the company, and runs the factory at 102 Madison Avenue.

Elias founded the company with three brothers in 1920: Morris, Max, and Manny. Pilzers are very much active in the drapery/bedspread/sleepcover market.

Max's son, Paul, is president of Silver-Pilzer, which manufactures bedspreads for Montgomery Ward and J.C. Penney Co.

Morris's son, Steve, is vice-president of Star Bedspread Co. Max's brother-in-law, Stanley Mandel, operates Stanley Studio.

I joined my father's bedspread business after college in May 1974 and was initially successful at sales. I learned a lot but left abruptly in January 1975 to attend Wharton Graduate Business School for my MBA.

delivery by 10:00 a.m. the next morning."

Most of all, Bloomingdale's got us the attention of FedEx, who was excited to be doing business with Bloomingdale's. This led to our next deal for our tenants: capitalizing on the benefits of locating your business next to FedEx in Memphis.

Medical Laboratories

I was touring our property one day when I noticed a tenant unpacking FedEx boxes filled with sealed test tubes. Richard Jaffe told me they contained blood and urine samples from all over the U.S. It turned out that this tenant functioned as the back-office laboratory for thousands of doctors offices and medical analysis clinics. Doctors nationwide would take individual patient blood and urine samples throughout the day, say, on Monday, deliver them by 5:00 p.m. to their local FedEx drop-off location, and FedEx would deliver them to our tenant the next morning, Tuesday, by 10:00 a.m. Our tenant would start their analyses at 11:00 a.m. and typically finish their work by Tuesday afternoon, delivering their reports to doctors in the evening for them to deliver the results to anxious patients the next day, Wednesday.

We walked in and met the general manager of the medical lab. He had no idea that FedEx shipped almost all of their packages to Memphis to be sorted on the way to their final destination. Or that we could get him 10% or more off FedEx rates that he could mark back up to his customers. Or that we could get all his incoming packages delivered to his Memphis facility by 2:00 a.m. instead of by 10:00 a.m. at a lower price.

This last benefit, the 2:00 a.m. delivery, got his attention. First, he could (and eventually did) double his volume with almost no increase in fixed costs by running a complete eight-hour shift from 2:00 a.m. to 10:00 a.m. Second, with an overnight shift, he could beat out his competition by delivering his reports to doctors and clinics the next morning instead of the next evening and charge more for one-day service even though it might actually cost him less. But third, and most importantly, his medical supplier customers could beat out *their* competition by offering anxious patients next morning results instead of two-day results. Think of a doctor being able to take a patient's blood sample in Los Angeles at 4:00 p.m., have it analyzed in Memphis at 2:00 a.m., and have the results faxed back to the doctor by 3:00 a.m.

As his business expanded, in great part due to ongoing customized solutions from FedEx's customer service department, the success of this tenant became one of our signature stories in attracting new leasing prospects to Memphis. Our local Trammell Crow property managers taught Trammell Crow leasing agents nationally the benefits of opening a 24-hour medical lab and other facilities in Memphis.

Making Our Customers into Salespeople

The traditional image of a landlord is someone who immediately contacts you when your rent is late but never seems to have time to help you grow your business. This was far from the case for us in Memphis. We took time to study each tenant's business and determine how we could help them improve their model. One day, I read a report showing that one of our tenants had gone from occupying 50,000 feet of space to 100,000 in just one year. I told Richard Jaffe to schedule a meeting with this tenant during my next visit to Memphis.

When we met, I was surprised to learn that this tenant's sole business was making and distributing penny nails. Penny nails came in many different sizes, and this tenant would buy pre-cut rolls of steel and put them into a machine that would crank out 700 nails a minute. But because there are so many different sizes, he was always making the nails to order rather than using downtimes to produce nails for inventory.

The economy in the 1990s was booming, and people were building new homes. Each new home needed about 30,000 nails, and contractors in pickup trucks were lined up to pick up their orders—they couldn't start building their homes until they got their nails.

"It sounds like you're doing great," I said to my nail-making tenant. "You've gone from occupying 50,000 square feet to 100,000 in just one year, and at this rate, you'll need 50,000 more square feet next year. And we've got a 90,000 square foot space adjacent to you that's becoming available next year."

"I doubt I'll take it!" he said. "My bottleneck is Bubba (yes, that was his name), this guy in Birmingham, Alabama, who sells me my cut steel. He meets my prices but then doesn't deliver the steel when he promises. I've got pickup trucks lined up to buy my nails every day, ready to buy twice the volume I make now, but I can't make my nails fast enough because we're always running out of steel. Last year I had to go down to Alabama and yell at Bubba to keep up his production and to make sure he didn't ship my steel to someone else offering him a higher price. And he treats me like this even though I'm his biggest customer!"

"Well, let's solve that problem right now," I said, with a big smile on my face. "You and I are going to go to Birmingham to see him together. We're going to convince Bubba to move to Memphis and take that vacant 90,000 feet in the space right next to yours, and he's going to make his steel rolls right here next to your premises. By drawing on his finished inventory next door, you'll be able to double your sales without increasing the size of your leased space or carrying more inventory."

The following month Robert, a Trammell Crow leasing specialist, my Memphis nail-maker tenant, and I drove the three hours from Memphis to Birmingham. I scheduled the trip to coordinate with a site inspection of some more industrial buildings we were considering purchasing. When we met, Bubba told me about his family and how much his daughters loved the Christian school they attended in Birmingham. I used that as the opportunity to start talking about St. Anne's in Memphis—the school I had visited with Charlie Brindell when I stayed in his home. Bubba couldn't believe that a Jewish professor from New York University knew all about St. Anne's, adding, "If my kids could get into a school like that, my wife would move to Memphis in a heartbeat."

It took us almost two years, but eventually, Bubba took the vacant 90,000 square feet next door. He didn't move his family, but opened a second location occupying the entire space we had available. The move was incredibly beneficial for everyone. We got a new 90,000-square-foot tenant, and now I had two large tenants in a symbiotic relationship locked together when it came time for renewing their leases; the nail maker wasn't going to leave because his biggest supplier was right next door, and his steel supplier wasn't going to leave because his biggest customer was next door. And we made sure that their lease expiration dates were staggered years apart, lest some new developer ever tried to steal both of them.

Over the next ten years, our Zane May Interests team combined with the Trammell Crow leasing guys, tried this same approach with every one of our larger tenants. I would walk in as their landlord and find out what they did, where they got their raw materials, and where they shipped their finished product. Then I'd ask them to go with us to meet with their biggest customers and their biggest suppliers to see if we could move any of them to our Memphis project. Most of the potential deals we chased didn't work, but the process proved incredibly lucrative for Trammell Crow, who almost always got at least one new tenant prospect out of each meeting.

I've always loved stories of how businesspeople began their businesses and stories of how they love serving their customers. Over the next decade, I probably visited 50 businesses in Memphis. Several of their stories, and what I learned from them, showed up in my books ***Unlimited Wealth*** (Crown Publishers, 1990) and ***God Wants You to Be Rich*** (Simon & Schuster, 1993/1995/2006).

In short order, we purchased another 400,000 square feet adjacent to our 3.3 million square feet, giving us 3.7 million square feet of space in one place to lease.

Over the next decade, we drove our 100% initial occupancy on the original space at $1.01 per square foot to 95% occupancy at nearly twice that rate, $2 per square foot, so we could always accommodate tenants who needed facilities near their customers and suppliers. This virtually doubled our net operating income on just the original space from $3.3 million in 1983 to $6.5 million in 1993, allowing us to sell the original property in 1993 for $73 million to the prestigious Alaska Permanent Fund.

Everyone made out well from our Memphis deal. GE received the prime interest rate on $36 million for ten years, about $33 million in interest, plus a $3.2 million 10% equity kicker. Charlie Brindell and his Trammell Crow partners made top-dollar leasing commissions and personally received a $3.28 million equity bonus. And Zane May Interests and our investors made $26.46 million on a purely sweat equity investment.

1993 Sales Proceeds from Memphis

	$73 million	Sales Price
-	$1 million	Sales Commission & Closing Expenses
-	$36 million	Loan Balance
-	$3.2 million	GE Equity Kicker (10% over $40 million)
=	$32.8 million	Total Equity After Sales Price
-	$3.2 million	10% Profits Interest to Trammell Crow
=	$29.6 million	Profit to Zane May Interests employees, investors, and partners

BECOMING AN ENTREPRENEUR

PAUL ZANE PILZER

Chapter 21 - Learnings

1. Don't be in a hurry to buy any business asset without first understanding how the seller will record the transaction on their books. Slow down and be methodical in your approach, like you'd be with a fish on a thin line that you don't want to break while you bring it in.

2. Every large organization has rules, scheduled meetings, and procedures to follow for everything—especially for the disposition of assets. Are you comfortable enough with your knowledge of accounting to be able to ask the right questions of a potential asset seller?

3. Could any part of my team taking Trammel's team out to dinner to get them to bring tenants to the Memphis property be construed as a conflict of interest? Or is this a normal business practice? What do you think about business entertaining?

4. We married up the nail maker and their steel supplier to forge a symbiotic relationship that would persevere for years. Where in your business can you partner up your suppliers and customers to create a similar dynamic?

5. Were we mostly lucky to buy and sell the Memphis property at optimal times, or did our preparation create the value, fulfilling Seneca's adage that "luck is what happens when preparation meets opportunity?" What's more important in your career today—luck or preparation?

BECOMING AN ENTREPRENEUR

PAUL ZANE PILZER

CHAPTER 22

OTHER PEOPLE'S MONEY

Entrepreneurs and authors must be on the "cutting edge" (black ink) versus the "bleeding edge" (red ink) of new products, ideas, and trends.

In January 1975, I became upset when my professor explained, *"Economics is the study of scarcity. There is a limited supply out there of scarce resources land, fresh water, oil, labor, and other raw materials. How we distribute our scarce resources for maximum efficiency, whether it be capitalism, communism, socialism, or any other 'ism' you call it, is the science of economics."*

This belief in scarcity contradicted my religion. As I explained in *Chapter 10: My First Macroeconomics Class* (page 117), I couldn't accept that God would have created a world of scarcity where the only way to get ahead was by taking from someone else. This was when I began working on what I thought would be my first book, ***Unlimited Wealth***, to contradict conventional economic theories based on scarcity. But my life had other plans—my career at Citibank, as an entrepreneur, and in Washington took me on a 15-year detour. ***Unlimited Wealth*** became my second book and was published in 1990. My first book was destined to be about S&Ls.

Becoming an Expert in Savings and Loans Associations

As I shared earlier in *Chapter 4: God Loves Savers* (page 45), the first contact I had with a savings and loan association was at age three, or perhaps earlier. I would swing on my father's arm on deposit day as we entered the Bowery Savings Bank in the Empire State Building, where he would make regular deposits to the custodian savings accounts he had established for his children's education.

My next contact with an S&L was at age 14 with Flushing Federal Savings Bank (technically a mutual savings bank, similar to an S&L), in Manhasset, New York, where I made regular deposits from my paycheck, dreaming of and saving for my first car. (See *Chapter 1: Discovering Passion*, page 1)

I could go on and on, but suffice to say that like most people growing up in the United States, savings & loans (and mutual savings banks) were part of my American experience. Ever since the 1946 movie ***It's a Wonderful Life***, S&Ls were associated with deferring gratification and taking positive action (i.e., "saving") for something good for yourself and/or your family.

My first contact with the S&L industry as an adult was at Citibank in 1976, when I became the bank's expert on NOW accounts and S&Ls (see *Chapter 15: My Career at Citibank Takes Off*, page 175).

As I explained in detail in Chapter 20: My First $10 Million Deal (page 291), all this knowledge of the S&L industry led to making my first $10 million deal in May 1982 with the State Federal Savings and Loan Association. More similar deals with S&Ls around the nation followed.

The Garn-St. Germain Depository Institutions Act of 1982

A few months after the State Federal deal on October 15, 1982, the U.S. Congress passed the Garn-St. Germain Depository Institutions Act of 1982 (the "Act"), the worst financial legislation ever passed in the history of the United States. The Act made legal most of the bad practices that the S&L's primary regulator, the Federal Home Loan Bank Board (FHLBB) engaged in, and added many more. It cost the federal government $300 billion in the 1980s, the equivalent of about $900 billion today. Of course, this was before the COVID-19 pandemic—today, trillion-dollar, not just billion-dollar, government bailouts have become commonplace.

First, prior to this Act, S&Ls were required to have a minimum of 3% surplus (equity). That meant that for every $100 million of insured deposits they took from consumers, an S&L would have to have $3 million of their owner's money at risk. But, at the time the Act was passed, more than 75% of the S&Ls couldn't meet this requirement and were in danger of being shut down. Incredibly, the Act simply lowered the threshold minimum surplus requirement from 3% to 2%, boasting that now only 25% (versus formerly 75%) of the S&Ls were at risk of being shut down for falling below their minimum equity capital requirement.

Second, prior to this Act, S&Ls were illiquid. Depositors could ask for their deposited money back at any time, but S&Ls didn't have the money because they had invested it in long-term 30-year home mortgages. They could sell their mortgages in a secondary market in home mortgages, except a typical $100,000 30-year fixed-rate home mortgage made in 1975 at 8% interest was worth less than

$60,000 in 1982 in the secondary market because market interest rates had risen from 8% to 18%. Incredibly, using the FHLBB's power to make their own accounting rules under Regulatory Accounting Principles (RAP), the Act instructed S&Ls to liquidate their existing 30-year mortgages in the secondary market and not recognize their losses. Instead, they were allowed to amortize their losses over the average remaining life of the sold mortgages, locking in their losses forever with no way out even when interest rates fell back to normal levels. This meant an S&L that 12 years earlier had made a $100,000 30-year home mortgage at an 8% rate could sell this mortgage for $60,000 and not record or report their $40,000 loss. Instead, the S&L would amortize the $40,000 loss over an 18-year period at $2,222 per year.

Third, and this was the worst part, prior to the Act, S&Ls were highly restricted in where they could invest their depositors' money. Basically, they were limited to safe home mortgages, municipal bonds, and treasury securities. Incredibly, the Act gave the S&Ls permission to invest their depositors' money in stocks, junk bonds, vacant land deals, casinos, other S&Ls, you name it! This was consciously designed to allow S&Ls that liquidated their home mortgages at a loss, or that fell below their minimum capital requirement, the opportunity to gamble with their remaining assets and win back their losses!

But this last major part of the Act had a much more sinister application.

Suppose you were an investor with $100 million to invest in real estate, vacant land, bonds, or stocks. Now, instead of investing your own money in these items, you'd put just $2 million of your money into a newly chartered S&L of which you owned 100% and get $98 million of "brokered deposits" overnight by simply paying a few basis points more than the market interest rate. Your depositors didn't care since the federal government insured them for 100% of their capital and interest at the rate you promised them.

If your $100 million of investments increased in value to $150 million, you would be allowed to take $50 million out of your S&L as dividends, leaving your S&L with your original $2 million in equity and $98 million in deposits. But if your $100 million in investments decreased in value to $50 million, you could simply walk away, losing only your $2 million in equity and dumping your $48 million in losses on the federal government, which had to pay off your depositors' $98 million.

If you're following what I wrote, you are probably asking, "Why wouldn't I take $4 million and form two $100 million S&Ls with $2 million each in equity, and bet them against each other on, say, whether or not interest rates will rise?" Whether interest rates rise or fall, one S&L will win $20 million to $50 million, and one S&L will lose this same amount, but you can't lose since you have only $2 million per S&L at risk. Incredibly, this is exactly what many of our leading politicians and their families did with their own funds, only they typically put up $20 million to $200 million in equity (2%) to get $1 to $10 billion in deposits per S&L.

How I Almost Became an S&L Criminal

I was in Washington, D.C., on October 15, 1982, when the legislation

On November 18, 1985, I testified before Congress. My speech was titled "Taking Uncle Sam for a $200 Billion Ride." Here I am in the White House, being congratulated by Vice President and Mrs. Bush, while my mother, Miriam Pilzer, smiles with pride.

passed. I phoned my partner back in Dallas and said, "Alan, you won't believe this. President Reagan is about to sign the Act. When he does, we'd be fools to continue buying property and putting our own money at risk. We need to buy some existing S&Ls, and charter our own new, clean S&Ls called De Novo S&Ls." Alan agreed it was an opportunity we should look into.

Over the next two years, Alan and I looked at several S&Ls to purchase, and three times we hired specialty law firms to help us charter a new, empty, clean De Novo S&L. But each time we got close to a deal, Alan got cold feet. I remember arguing with him, "Look, Alan, we've analyzed this S&L opportunity from every angle and paid the best law firms in the country who have given it a clean bill of health. What's wrong?"

"What's wrong," said my wise and more experienced partner, "is the obscene amount of money that's going to be made by these S&L

After I testified before the U.S. Congress in 1985 on ***Other People's Money***, the artist Richard Shaffer painted my portrait in 1988 and titled it ***J'Accuse*** as a tribute to Édouard Manet's portrait of the writer Émile Zola in ***Portrait of Émile Zola*** from 1868.

On the left is me in Paris at the Musee d'Orsay in 1988, standing in front of Édouard Manet's ***Portrait of Émile Zola***

entrepreneurs at the expense of the American public. But tomorrow, according to your research, that same amount of money is going to be lost by the federal government. Eventually, this is all going to blow up, and someone's got to pay the piper. And when this happens, the federal government will re-write their own rules and apply them retroactively to anyone who made a lot of money."

In 1984, Alan and I gave up trying to buy, or charter, an S&L, although at the time, it seemed that we were missing the opportunity of a lifetime.

I took what I had learned about S&Ls and became a frequent media guest, exposing the subject. I appeared regularly on ***Larry King Live!***, CNN, NPR, and anywhere else I could, warning viewers about the coming S&L crash.

I found an ally in then-Vice President George H. Bush, who invited me to testify before Congress in November 1985 at hearings for the Bush Task Force on Financial Reform. My speech before Congress, "Taking Uncle Sam for a $200 Billion Ride," was initially criticized for overstating the amount. Eventually, that number came in at $300 billion, $100 billion more than I predicted. My 1985 speech before Congress became a lead story the following year in the academic journal, ***Real Estate Review.***

In the end, Alan was 100% correct. The initial S&L entrepreneurs did make billions, immorally but legally at the time. But there were many bad actors who didn't operate legally, so that when the dust began to settle in the late 1980s, the federal government didn't care who operated an S&L legally or illegally; anyone who had operated an S&L was a suspect. The government moved hundreds of prosecuting attorneys to Dallas, considered the epicenter of S&L crime. The special prosecutors stayed more than a decade investigating anyone they could and putting people in jail, mostly for doing something that was technically legal at the time they did it.

Other People's Money: The Inside Story of the S&L Mess

In 1986, my dear friend in Dallas, Jan Miller, suggested I write a book on the S&L crisis. Jan, a literary agent who was already representing Arnold Schwarzenegger and Anthony Robbins, went on to become one of the best-known literary agents in the United States. Today Jan represents Dr. Phil, Oprah, Tony Robbins, Joel Osteen, and many other major non-fiction authors. Jan suggested that Allan J. Mayer at Simon & Schuster, then the largest book publisher in the United States, become the editor of my book on the crisis.

Allan is brilliant and well-educated, with an amazing resume. At age 26, while working for ***Newsweek*** in London, he wrote ***Madam Prime Minister: Margaret Thatcher and Her Rise to Power***. Today, after multiple careers, he is a real-life Ray Donavan—*Variety* described him as "Hollywood's most prominent crisis specialist," and ABC News called him "the man to call if you're a star facing scandal."

In 1986, Allan got me excited about what he could contribute as my editor on a book about the S&L crisis and what Simon & Schuster could do for me as my publisher. We went back and forth for months putting together an outline and table of contents and finished by early 1987. Each time I got an invitation to appear on a television or radio show, I'd call Allan, and he'd help prep me for the interview. I became the go-to person on the S&L crisis on CNN and NPR, who both called me a commentator. Allan became my media coach.

I particularly recollect the first time I briefly appeared on the *Larry King Live!* Television Show in 1987. Allan phoned me early the next morning. "Paul, he began, "it's such a pleasure to work with you because you're so brilliant and mostly self-educated, but being self-educated, you know so many big words but don't know how to pronounce them.

Last night, twice, you pronounced 'ubiquitous' as 'u-bi-quite-us.' Of course, I doubt anyone noticed, especially Mr. King since he's also self-educated and comes from the same neighborhood as you do in Brooklyn!"

Throughout all this activity, Allan kept promising Jan and me that he would have an offer to publish my S&L book "this week" or "tomorrow," but by the end of 1987, there was still no offer.

Then, in early 1988, Allan went dark, which made both Jan and me pretty angry. I was not used to being ghosted.

For the past two years, Jan and I had acted as if Allan was our editor and S&S was our publisher, but Jan had never stopped pitching the book to other publishers, none of whom were interested after an initial meeting.

I appeared again on the *Larry King Live!* television show in September 1988 to discuss the savings and loan crisis. The next morning, Allan called me on my home number.

"Paul, you did great on the *King* show last night! We're all ready to go at Simon & Schuster and publish ***Other People's Money.***"

"You worthless piece of [expletive]," I responded and probably said a few more choice words. "Now you're ready to publish after it's no longer hot news. We've missed the window to break the story! Everyone knows about the S&L crisis. Where were you the last two years?" I went on and on until there was dead silence on the line. "Are you still there, Allan?"

He responded. "Let me know when you are done cursing at me. Jan just received our offer for your book, and she should be calling you any minute. So-"

"What? How can I believe you?" I interjected.

"Let me explain," he said. "Paul, I now have on my desk four solid proposals to write a book on the S&L crisis. Two of them are from former chairmen of the Federal Reserve, one is from a U.S. Senator, and one is from one of our most popular authors and media personalities. Everyone wants to write this book."

He had my attention as he continued:

"How did Simon & Schuster become the largest publisher in the world? By publishing what people want to read when they want to read it. I liked you and your proposal right from the start. But I'm not the audience. If we had published your book two years ago, it would have flopped because few people back then needed or wanted to know about the coming S&L crisis—it wasn't affecting their lives. But it's front-page news now. S&Ls are being closed down every day with millions of people losing their life savings. People's lives are being affected, and some of them are ready to read an in-depth analysis that I believe you can provide them even though you've never written a book before."

"Moreover, the fact that S&S has five credible proposals on this subject, and our competition, combined, probably has 20 more such proposals, tells me more than anything else that the world is ready to read about the S&L crisis. I remembered that you were the first person who ever told me about the coming crisis and because you were the first—out of loyalty—I wanted to give you the first shot before I respond to our other four S&L crisis book proposals."

I calmed down and thought about how much publishing a book was like starting a company. A venture capitalist once told me that he loved hearing about my latest startup proposal but that he'd learned to listen, take notes, and then say "no" for a year or more.

"We want to invest in something on the cutting edge," he said, "but you're so far ahead, Paul, that you're often on the 'bleeding edge'—as in lots of red ink (losses) if we invest now."

Allan and Jan worked on the contract and we signed a deal later that afternoon. S&S would pay me an advance against book royalties and commit to a 12-city publicity tour and $100,000 in national advertising.

Allan and I began working on the manuscript the next day. The cover design was completed in October 1988, in time to be in S&S' 1989 catalog.

Sadly for me, Allan Mayer left S&S to start his own magazine, Buzz, in June 1989, three months before the publication of ***Other People's Money.*** While I was thrilled for Allan, I felt he had deserted me. I was assigned a new editor, Bob Asahina, who I already knew because he was the editor for my friend Anthony Robbins.

Bob called me one day to discuss the manuscript. "Paul, this is going to be a big book, and I'm glad to be your new editor, but there's something we need to discuss. This is a business book for a financial audience. But you've got too much God in the book! The first chapter is titled 'God Loves Savers,' and you spend two chapters on why S&Ls look like churches and the history of savings and faith—all before you even get to the crisis."

"What do you want to do?" I replied. "The manuscript has already gone to galleys, and some reviewers have already read it."

"Oh, it's too late to change any of the text, but I look forward to coaching you with the media and wanted to suggest that we play down the God stuff in your interviews." I acted like I agreed with Bob on the call, but I made a note to myself that we had theological differences.

Other People's Money was published in September 1989 and was reviewed by Tony Solomon, the former President of the Federal Reserve Bank of New York, on the cover of the ***New York Times Book Review*** on October 29, 1989.[27] Here are excerpts from his review:

> *"Now the whole disgraceful episode, though far from over, has spawned a flock of carefully researched, well-crafted books chronicling the fiasco. Three particularly good ones are Other People's Money, by Paul Zane Pilzer*

27. Solomon, Anthony M. "The Risks Were Too Good to Pass Up." ***New York Times Book Review***, October 29, 1989

with Robert Deitz; Inside Job, by Stephen Pizzo, Mary Fricker, and Paul Muolo; and The S&L Insurance Mess, by Edward J. Kane.

"Of the three books, this [Other People's Money] one is probably the best all-around treatment, despite sometimes irritating over-generalizations and hyperbole."

Two months later, Other People's Money was reviewed by John Kenneth Galbraith, the world's most prominent living economist at the time, in the ***New York Review of Books***. Galbraith, the author of 101 books, including ***The Affluent Society*** (1958), was a primary architect of many of the world's 20th Century economic policies.

I appeared in hundreds of articles, reviews, and on television shows. ***Other People's Money*** was a big hit!

One Monday night in January 1989, after my classes had ended at NYU, Jan Miller phoned to tell me she was taking the S&S team and me to celebrate at Elaine's Restaurant on Second Avenue, then one of the nation's most prestigious places for authors and movie personalities. The opening dinner scene in Woody Allen's ***Manhattan*** (1979) was filmed there, and Billy Joel (1978) had immortalized the restaurant in his songs. I accepted but then realized that I wouldn't be able to get through the line at the door. I immediately called Jan back to ask under which (famous) name had she booked the reservation? Jan laughed and said, "Paul, the reservation is under the name of Paul Zane Pilzer, the world-famous author, whose book is featured this week in the ***New York Review of***

Books! We are all getting in tonight because of you!"

Unlimited Wealth

While I enjoyed the recognition I received from ***Other People's Money***, I was more interested in using my newfound fame as an author to launch my next book and my new economic theory based on abundance, ***Unlimited Wealth***.

In October 1989, Jan took my proposal for ***Unlimited Wealth*** to market with the New York publishers. We were not able to make a deal with Simon & Schuster, partly because of differences over the religious references in the manuscript. S&S' marketing team felt they would limit sales of the book.

Instead, we made a deal with S&S' archival, Random House.

Unlimited Wealth was published in October 1990 under Crown Publishing, a Random House imprint. Its sales were much larger than sales of ***Other People's Money***. Soon after its publication, I received a call from Bob Asahina.

"Hello, Paul, this is Bob at Simon & Schuster. I'm calling to congratulate you on the success of ***Unlimited Wealth***. Our team messed up a little thinking about the impact of the religious references in your work. If you want to come back to Simon & Schuster for your next book ... hell, you can put 'God' on the [expletive] cover!"

In October 1993, Simon & Schuster published the sequel to ***Unlimited Wealth***, titled ***God Wants You to Be Rich: The Theology of Economics***.

It spent two years on the ***New York Times Business Bestseller List***, and its title was parodied by Andy Rooney on ***60 Minutes***.

BECOMING AN ENTREPRENEUR

PAUL ZANE PILZER

Chapter 22 - Learnings

1. Alan May stated that once the government understood the full consequences of what the Garn-St. Germain Depository Institutions Act of 1982 allowed, investors who had used S&L money in their investments would be retroactively prosecuted. The way in which people were abusing their depositors' money was legal, so why should people who had followed this law get into trouble after the fact? In your opinion, should prosecutors be allowed to pull this legal bait and switch?

2. A venture capitalist once told me that he loved hearing about my latest startup proposals but that he'd learned to listen, take notes, and then say "no" for a year or more. Do you understand what he was trying to accomplish by doing this? If not, go back and re-read the opening paragraph in italics in this chapter.

3. I was told there was too much "God" in my book ***Other People's Money.*** Examine the decisions you make in your business, whether it be mixing politics and business, religion and business, or pleasure and business. Why might doing this be costly to you? What's more important to you—your business life, politics, or religion?

4. Why do you think that people cannot come to peaceable agreements concerning differences in religious, political, sexual orientation, gender, finances, and so on? Why is it so hard to be accepting of another's lifestyle or choices that don't directly affect your life?

5. One of my books is titled ***God Wants You to Be Rich***. Understandably, this ruffles a few feathers of the devout. Why might people feel this is an offensive assertion? Why should or shouldn't God and money be talked about in the same sentence?

BECOMING AN ENTREPRENEUR

PAUL ZANE PILZER

CHAPTER 23

PRESIDENT REAGAN CALLS ME DISHONEST

Every event at the White House was a special treat for me, particularly because I played the dual role of fundraiser for national candidates and economic policy advisor on the issues of the week.

In the 1980s, I became involved in national politics and was close friends with legislators on both sides of the aisle. In 1988, while he was a leading candidate for President of the United States, House Majority Leader Dick Gephardt (D-MO) and his family spent a week in my Park City ski home.

Dick and I used to stay up late nights discussing (not debating) economic policy. Senator John Tower (R-TX) lived in my Dallas guest house for several months in 1989 during his failed confirmation hearing to become secretary of defense. And in the 1980s, Senator John Heinz (R-PA) and I ran fundraising events at my Dallas and Utah homes for Republican senatorial candidates from many states.

Tragically, Senator Heinz died on April 4, 1991 when his helicopter collided with an airplane. The next day Senator Tower died. Both of these deaths occurred weeks before each senator was scheduled to come to Dallas' Third Congressional District to campaign for me in my failed 1991 special election bid for Congress of the United States.

Dinner at The White House

One day in early 1988, in the midst of the Republican primaries, I was among about 60 Republican donors who were invited to attend a formal dinner in the East Wing of the White House. The featured guests included all the candidates who were running in the Republican presidential primary: George H.W. Bush, Bob Dole, Pat Robertson, Jack Kemp, and Pete du Pont. They were there to meet the major Republican donors to raise more money for their campaigns. I was particularly close at that time with Pat Robertson, who later became an important promoter of my books and speeches.

I had attended high-profile events like this before, and I almost always took someone with me because my invitation was for two. My dates were either someone I was dating, someone I wanted to be dating, or my mother. I was the 34-year-old bachelor entrepreneur who regularly took his 74-year-old mom to White House dinners.

My mom would always notice different things at these dinners than I did. That night, while my mom went to get something to eat, I spoke to Senate Majority Leader Bob Dole, who was doing a funny comedy routine about why he wanted to be President of the United States.

"When we came here to this dinner today, and we parked out front, I noticed they had valet parking," he said and then gestured toward his wife, United States Senator Elizabeth "Libby" Dole, who had also served in two White House Administrations. "So, I asked Libby, why don't we have valet parking where we live? Because it would be useful. Then I told her, Let's just move into this big white house on Pennsylvania Avenue!"

After his anecdote, he enumerated, one by one, the personal reasons he wanted to move into the White House (like daily maid service) as if he was shopping for a new apartment. Bob Dole had the timing of a seasoned comedian and told jokes like Bob Hope—they were actually good friends.

While I was listening to him, I saw my mother coming toward us with a serious expression as if she wanted to tell me something. I held up my finger as a signal for her not to interrupt, but she wasn't going to be deterred. She strode right up to me and spoke in a loud whisper that interrupted Senator Dole.

"Paul, Paul, look!" That immediately got the attention of everyone standing near her.

Mom was carrying a plate with four pieces of shrimp and a dab of cocktail sauce. Shrimp was a delicacy my mother rarely indulged in. She lived 48 years in the house I grew up in, which was strictly kosher, so she could never serve shrimp. Yet, at this point in her life, she had relaxed her rules to allow herself to enjoy shrimp and other *treif* (non-kosher) foods outside our home, especially when they were free of charge, like at a party. And she absolutely loved shrimp.

I looked to see what was causing her so much concern. She pointed to a large shrimp on her plate that still had a dark vein running through it. Then she said the most terrifying words ever spoken to me at the White House:

"Nancy needs to know about this!"

Mom then pointed toward Nancy Reagan, who was standing next to her husband. In my mom's mind, and as a sometime hostess herself, Nancy Reagan needed to be told that the person she had hired to clean her shrimp hadn't done a good job.

I was mortified, but Senator Dole found the situation highly entertaining. He called over the White House photographer and asked him to take a photo with me, my mom, and Libby. Then he turned to his wife.

"Libby, when we live here, will you promise you'll invite Mrs. Pilzer to dinner and that you'll always have clean shrimp?"

Libby agreed, but Senator Dole wasn't done. He then wrote on a piece of paper, "This paper is redeemable by the Pilzers for one dinner at President Dole's White House with clean shrimp," and handed it to me.

At the time, the situation was extremely embarrassing, but now it stands out as one of the funniest moments I've had in the White House.

The President of the United States Calls Me Dishonest

Later that evening, Senator Heinz was talking with President Reagan, and much to my surprise, he waved me over to join in the conversation. My mind was racing as I walked toward the Senator and the President—*what can I say that will be memorable and advance my career?* But as it turned out, I didn't have to come up with anything because Senator Heinz had a question for me.

"Professor," he said, referring to me by my Washington nickname, "you're one of the larger tax benefits syndicators. Please explain to President Reagan why we have real estate tax benefits and the function of tax benefits in the economy. The President was just asking me about this, but I know you'll do a better job explaining it than I can."

I turned to President Reagan, glad to be asked to explain something I knew so well.

"Oh, well, here's how they work, Mr. President," I began. "Throughout the United States, poor people need subsidies to afford housing, particularly low-income housing. Separately, some rich people pay too much in income taxes, which causes a drag on their businesses and our economy." President Reagan was listening intently, and feeling buoyed, I went on. "We go to Congress, but Congress won't allocate the funds that poor people need for housing, nor will they lower taxes on especially productive rich Americans, which would cause our GDP to rise and get poor people more jobs. So, what we do is come up with real estate tax benefits, where we carve the tax benefits out of an investment in low-income housing, and we sell those tax benefits to rich people. Let's say, for example, a rich person puts $100,000 in a tax syndication. They would get a $300,000 tax deduction, which to a taxpayer in a 50% tax bracket is worth $150,000 in cash off their income tax bill. Part of their $100,000 investment goes to landlords to subsidize the rent on low-income housing."

President Reagan looked straight at me and asked, "I'm confused. Why don't we simply go to Congress and explain why poor people need housing subsidies, and certain rich people need lower income tax rates?"

I smiled. "That would be ideal, Mr. President, but they won't pass it. So, we go around Congress and sell tax benefits to rich people and then use some of their investment to subsidize housing.

Congress doesn't even know about it since tax syndications don't show up in the federal budget or on people's tax returns—they just reduce their reportable taxable income!"

The President stood silent for a moment, then stared directly into my eyes with a look of disappointment that made me shrink on the spot. He said, "That's dishonest. If people need subsidized housing, we need to convince Congress to give them the subsidies they need, not go around them and do it without Congress knowing about it."

I could feel myself shaking. The President of the United States had just told me that my primary business was dishonest.

Fortunately, at this point in our conversation, a small crowd of about 12 guests waiting to speak to the President had gathered. They started jumping in as I slowly withdrew from the President and senator.

What he said haunted me. I was especially concerned because, in less than three months, I was scheduled to be in the Soviet Union, attending the Moscow Summit with President Reagan and Premier Gorbachev.[28]

I thought about what I had said wrong in explaining my business to the President. Then, after about four weeks of contemplation, I realized that the President was correct. My business syndicating tax benefits, although technically legal, was dishonest.

I didn't do any more tax syndications in 1988 or ever again. Instead, I threw myself into my next two ventures, creating Zane

28. YouTube video of President Reagan speaking at Moscow State University, May 31, 1988. Reagan Foundation. "Moscow State University: President Reagan's Address at Moscow State University - 5/31/88." ***YouTube***, April 21, 2009. https://www.youtube.com/watch?v=1lutYGxMWeA.

I was a lecturer from 1983-1989 at Moscow State University in the former USSR. After we returned to the U.S., President Reagan sent me this signed photo of him speaking in front of Lenin's bust on May 31, 1988. I consider the President's speech on that date at the university to be one of the finest of his career.

Publishing and developing an industrial park in Vladivostok. I founded Zane to improve K-12 education through technology, and, as you'll see in *Chapter 24: My Litigation with Apple Computer* (page 419), it grew to be one of the world's largest educational CD-ROM publishers.

BECOMING AN ENTREPRENEUR

PAUL ZANE PILZER

Chapter 23 - Learnings

1. When my mother pointed out the vein in the shrimp, I was embarrassed and wanted the floor to swallow me up. In retrospect, it was a funny moment and taught me not to take myself or the status of others too seriously. Reflect back on a time when you learned from a similar situation. What lesson did you walk away with?

2. President Reagan effectively told me that I was dishonest when I explained how rich people were sold tax benefits that were used to subsidize housing for the poor. What is your opinion of this strategy—if it benefits people in need, why wouldn't it be okay to continue it?

3. Think about a time you have encountered a situation where legally, you were in the right, but ethically, you might be in the wrong. How did you react in that moment?

4. Some of my most embarrassing moments with my mother are now my proudest moments—my own aging process has taught me how to lighten up. What moments in your life that were once embarrassing to you are you now proud of?

5. Looking back on my time in Washington in the 1980s, I am uncomfortable with the three roles I simultaneously played in fundraising for candidates, advising officials on national policy, and running my own businesses—some of which were dependent on public policy. How do you, with the benefit of 20/20 hindsight, view any possible conflicts of interest in my activities? Have you ever had conflicts of interest in your business, personal, or professional life?

BECOMING AN ENTREPRENEUR

PAUL ZANE PILZER

CHAPTER 24

MY LITIGATION WITH APPLE COMPUTER

How a potential lawsuit with Apple Computer turned a terrible adversary into a great partner!

In 1975, I was a graduate student at the University of Pennsylvania, spending most of my time working on my thesis in the computer center in the basement of Vance Hall. The mainframe computer I used was half the size of a school bus.

My thesis, technically called an advanced study project, or ASP, was on an interactive computer program that would teach the history of the Federal Reserve System using a mainframe computer. The computer would teletype information about the Federal Reserve System ending with a multiple-choice question. Then, based on the answer, type out different information ending with a different question. Just like the most skilled teacher of any subject, the computer would continually assess what you did and didn't know, and then it would teach it to you with unlimited patience—as only a robot can do.

Thomas Edison invented the phonograph in 1877, Lee de Forest invented the audio amplifier in 1912, the Lumiere brothers invented the first successful movie projector in 1894, and Guglielmo Marconi laid the foundation for radio broadcasting in 1895. These inventions changed the world for musicians, singers, and actors, allowing audiences worldwide to affordably enjoy their work and earning these creative artists great compensation.

Back then, I dreamed that my thesis, which I called an "interactive teaching machine," would one day help change the world for teachers and their students. I completed my thesis in January 1976 and wrote on the first page of teletyped text, "One day this technology will be used to affordably bring the best teacher of every subject to every student."

When I received my MBA from Wharton a few months later, I put this dream on the shelf and pursued multi-disciplined careers as an executive with Citibank, an economist in the White House, and an adjunct professor at NYU. But I never forgot about my dream of using technology to scale education. Fourteen years later, I knew it was time to take my dream off the shelf and bring it to actualization.

Multimedia CD-ROMs

I realized this in 1990, the moment that I saw a demo of a Microsoft CD-ROM called "Multimedia Beethoven." It was an entertaining and educational experience about Beethoven's Fifth Symphony, interactively combining art, music, video, and text with a seemingly unlimited search engine.

It was nothing short of revolutionary!

I was sure that this was the future of education and thought that this interactive, multimedia technology would one day make the giant entertainment industry pale in comparison.

Multimedia CD-ROMs were a huge paradigm shift for

computers as well as for education. Prior to 1990, people got their information from newspapers, books, meetings, movies, radio, and television, then manually typed the information into a computer to process it. The computer was a tool for manipulating but not obtaining information.

Then, thanks to the enormous amount of data you could economically put on a CD-ROM that cost less than a dollar, an incredible 680 megabytes per disc, the computer was instantly the best vehicle possible for obtaining information as well as for processing it. Unlike information obtained from print, radio, or television, information on a CD-ROM could be accessed instantaneously in a variety of forms ranging from text to full-color videos.

I started a new company to actualize my dream called ZCI: Education Through Technology. We changed the name to Zane Publishing in 1991. Zane began publishing interactive, robust learning experiences on CD-ROMs. These were multimedia presentations with text, audio, images, and video. By working with the world's leading traditional publishers, we created 176 original CD-ROM titles. They included the ***Encyclopedia of Postage Stamps*** with the U.S. Post Office and the ***Encyclopedia of Endangered Species*** with the World Wildlife Fund. We published complete multi-disc sets like ***The History of Art*** and Isaac Asimov's ***Library of the Universe.*** We even teamed up with Merriam-Webster for reference books and with educational publisher Prentice Hall to create multimedia versions of their most popular college and K-12 textbooks.

PowerCD CD-ROM Operating System

All the CD-ROMs we published starting late in 1990 were powered by our exclusive PowerCD technology, which uniquely allowed our CD-ROMs to run on any Apple or PC computer.

At that time, about 90% of personal computers for home or business were based on the IBM PC standard and called simply "PCs," and just 10% were Apple. However, in schools across America, this statistic was flip-flopped. Ninety-five percent of computers used in classrooms were Apple. At the time, programs developed for PCs could not run on Apple computers, and vice-versa.

We called our operating system "PowerCD" and filed a trademark for the name with the United States Patent and Trademark Office (USPTO) in 1991. PowerCD was the only CD-ROM operating system that allowed a single CD-ROM disc to run on both Apple and PC computers.

We also created a powerful HyperText Markup Language (HTML) that allowed us to author multimedia CD-ROM titles at a fraction of the cost of building completely new PC and Apple operating systems for each CD-ROM title.

While other CD-ROM publishers were spending millions of dollars to produce each CD-ROM title with its own unique integrated data and operating system architecture, each PowerCD CD-ROM disc separated the data and contained two independent operating systems to display it—one for PC and one for Apple personal computers.

The World Wide Web (www) was created in 1989, and Mosaic became the first web browser in 1993. But PowerCD was, in effect, the first browser, although we only used it to browse the CD-ROM itself instead of the entire web.

PowerCD was the backbone of our company.

PowerCD and Tony Robbins

Our first best-selling CD-ROM was ***Multimedia Powertalk!*** in 1991. It was a 65-minute audio-video presentation of my two books, ***Other People's Money*** and ***Unlimited Wealth***, along with Tony Robbins' two bestsellers, ***Awaken the Giant Within*** and ***Unlimited Power***. It included 4,000+ pages and 300 related articles, as well as hypertexted contents of the four books, questions with hypertexted explanations, quizzes, and a customized electronic glossary. This was some pretty cool stuff back then!

Multimedia Powertalk! caught the attention of ***PC Magazine***, then the must-read magazine for computer enthusiasts. John Dvorak was the lead writer for the magazine and the No. 1 computer writer in the world. He wrote an article about Zane Publishing and ***Multimedia Powertalk!*** calling PowerCD the future of education in America. He came to visit us in Dallas and eventually joined the board of our company.

By the end of 1991, we had several CD-ROM titles being sold in major computer stores and bookstore chains like Computer City, CompUSA, Barnes & Noble, and Borders, with each opening whole new departments featuring PowerCDs. The ***New York Times*** and various other magazines wrote articles about us and reviewed our latest PowerCD CD-ROMs. ***Success Magazine*** featured Zane Publishing and me on their cover. Twice!

Zane Publishing sales were taking off, and our customers loved our products. Then Apple became aware of our PowerCD operating system.

PowerCD and Apple Computer 1990-1993

Today, most people associate Apple Computer with the late Steve Jobs, and Apple is known for exciting, cutting-edge technology products. But Steve Jobs was forced out of the company in 1985, and from 1990 to 1993, Apple sales declined rapidly—the innovation for which Apple was known was nowhere to be found.

The company was also embroiled in lawsuits over its intellectual property. The most high-profile one was a six year long lawsuit filed in 1988 with Microsoft over who owned the Graphical User Interface (GUI) system on which Apple, and now Windows PC, computers were based. The Apple suit claimed that Microsoft stole the GUI elements in Windows from the Apple Lisa. The U.S. Court of Appeals ultimately dismissed the case in September 1994, noting that Apple itself had actually taken the GUI elements used in its products from Xerox. Steve Jobs returned to Apple in 1997 and built the company into the technology powerhouse it is known as today.

But back in 1991 and 1992, the lawyers at Apple were assuring stockholders that the courts would ultimately rule that Apple effectively owned Microsoft Windows. When Apple wasn't busy with litigation, the company was focused on a new product they had released in 1991: the PowerBook.

The PowerBook was a laptop computer, and the chip that ran it was called the PowerPC. But Apple had miscalculated how popular

CD-ROM discs would become, so none of their PowerBooks came with a built-in CD-ROM player. To sell their Powerbooks in 1991 Apple fast-tracked the manufacture of 50,000 external CD-ROM players that plugged into the PowerBook with a retail cost of $500 each. And guess what Apple called their external CD-ROM player that plugged into the PowerBook?

They named it the "PowerCD."

That changed everything for Zane Publishing and me.

Zane Publishing had its exclusive PowerCD technology, Apple had its PowerCD external CD-ROM player. The stage was set: David vs. Goliath. Apple had just produced $25 million worth of their external PowerCD players. And Apple, a company back then run by lawyers rather than engineers, could never conceive that its lawyers might have made a mistake.

Apple's lawyers immediately went into attack mode. I received a cease-and-desist letter telling Zane Publishing and me, personally, to stop using the term "PowerCD" and to destroy all our inventory. Our distributors received similar letters warning them of millions in potential damages if they didn't stop selling Zane Publishing PowerCDs.

I was floored. Zane Publishing was my lifelong passion, and I had invested millions of my own money into developing our PowerCD technology. I called our attorney at Paul Weiss Wharton and Rifkind, the same attorney who had filed our registration of PowerCD with the USPTO. She was as stunned as I was to hear about the demand letters and promised to get back to me right away.

She called back an hour later. "Very interesting," she said. "Before they sent all those letters threatening you and your distributors, they should've called the United States Patent and Trademark Office."

"What do you mean?"

"I filed your registration for the trademark PowerCD 11 days before Apple filed theirs," she replied, a smile in her voice. "They didn't even check to see if we had filed first. They always assume they're right because they're Apple."

Obviously, the news was a great relief, but I wanted to know how she was going to stop them from continuing their attack on me and my distributors and how much this was going to cost Zane Publishing in legal fees and damage to our reputation.

"Well," she said. "Let me have a little fun. I'll get back to you with a plan."

Today, I'm not proud of what happened next. But in 1992, I was young and cocky and had a lot to learn about business relationships. Moreover, I had disliked Apple since 1976 because of its refusal to share Apple's personal computer technology with third party hardware and software developers. In contrast, developers of the first IBM PC computers used open architecture that allowed third parties to make software and peripherals and even allowed companies like Dell, Compaq, and HP to make complete clones of the IBM PC computers themselves.

The plan our attorney came back with was for her to contact Apple and demand $250,000 in damages, worth about $500,000 today. This was a lot of money for a startup with no investors, and I knew I could use it to hire the editorial and multimedia teams needed to push more PowerCD CD-ROM titles into production.

Our attorney contacted Apple and went back and forth with

their lawyers during the next few days. Apple apologized and asked us not to make them destroy their 50,000 PowerCD external CD-ROM players. But our attorney was having so much fun; she suggested I give them a new demand. I agreed, and she made the following call to Apple's lawyers:

"Mr. Pilzer is quite upset and thinks you should be taught a lesson. This Sunday, he is flying to New York to have dinner with his mother and then teach the next day, Monday, at New York University. On Tuesday, he'll fly from New York to DFW Airport before proceeding to his office at Zane Publishing.

"Mr. Pilzer requests that John Sculley, the CEO of Apple, meet him on Tuesday at 10:00 a.m. at Gate 11 at DFW Airport to apologize and hand him a cashier's check for $250,000."

Apple accepted these terms, except they refused to have their humiliated CEO fly to Dallas to apologize. Instead, a senior financial officer would make the trip and meet me at the airport to apologize and hand over the check.

And so, on Tuesday morning, January 14, 1992, I flew to Dallas and met an Apple senior financial officer at Gate 11. He apologized and handed me a cashier's check for $250,000 made out to Zane Publishing.

Now that would be a good story on its own, but it gets much, much better.

Turning a Conflict into a Win-Win

After I received the cashier's check, I drove from DFW Airport to Zane Publishing's office in Dallas in the Infomart, a beautiful office building modeled after London's Crystal Palace. When I arrived at about 11:30 a.m., my noon appointment, a man named John Grillos was waiting for me in the reception area.

John was a nationally renowned venture capitalist with a firm that invested billions in technology companies throughout Silicon Valley.

"Mr. Pilzer," John said, once we were back in my office, "our firm backs the best companies in Silicon Valley. We'd like to make you an offer to invest $3 million on a $10 million valuation for a 30% equity interest."

Still feeling a little proud from my Apple encounter, I replied, "There's no way I'd take your money. I'm wealthier than the amount of money you're offering me, and the only reason I'd sell you equity is if I didn't believe in my product. This company is headed for the moon. Look what I have here!"

I opened my briefcase, took out the $250,000 cashier's check from Apple, and held it up for him to see.

John's eyes lit up. He leaned forward and looked closely at the check. "Apple is already buying your product?"

I shook my head and shared with John what had just transpired that morning at the airport. When I finished, John jumped up and started screaming at me.

"You have to be the dumbest [expletive], the [expletive] stupidest [expletive] ever. I'm so glad we didn't invest any of our money with somebody as [expletive] dumb as you."

I sat there speechless, my mouth hanging open, as he continued.

"According to John Dvorak, you make good educational CD-

ROMs that could change K-12 education as we know it. And the hardware to play all these CD-ROMs is almost entirely based on Apple computers because Apple owns the school market for personal computers. No school is going to play your CD-ROMs if they're not running on an Apple computer. And you just [expletive] the biggest potential distributor of your product, Apple Computer, in a way they will always, always remember. Do you realize what you've done to a public company, and how they're going to have to report the way you just [expletive] them?!"

After a moment of watching me sit there without saying a word, John calmed down. "I'm going to help you out," he said, sitting back down. "Since I'm already here anyway, I might as well help you apologize before I fly home."

He picked up the phone on my desk, pressed 9 for an outside line, and then punched in a 10-digit number from memory. A voice came over the speakerphone: "Apple Computer." John asked to be transferred to Apple's chief financial officer, the superior of the senior financial officer I had just met at the DFW airport. His conversation with the CFO went something like this:

JOHN: How are you?

CFO: Hi, John. Where are you?

JOHN: Dallas, Texas.

CFO: I almost had to go to Dallas this week. What brings you there?

JOHN: I'm in the office of someone you know, Paul Zane Pilzer.

CFO: [Silence]

JOHN: Paul Zane Pilzer.

CFO: [Dead silence]

JOHN: Yeah, you guys really, really [expletive] up at Apple, and you tried to put Mr. Pilzer out of business. You took his CD-ROM titles off the shelf at Barnes & Noble and everywhere else. He is really, really mad. But he made a really bad mistake. He listened to his lawyer and didn't think about what's going to happen when you two are done fighting. So, I'm here now to tell you that Mr. Pilzer is very, very sorry, and he wants to apologize. The first thing he's going to do is return this check your colleague delivered this morning. It hasn't been cashed yet. I'm going to bring this check back with me to Hillsborough tonight. I'll call you from the car when I land at SFO Airport. You can come to your front door, and I will hand you this check tonight for you to destroy.

CFO: [Pause] Go ahead, John. Tell me the rest of this story.

JOHN: Well, the rest of the story is that you're going to give me a new check. It doesn't need to be a cashier's check because we believe in Apple, and you're not going out of business. But it does need to be a quarter-million-dollar check from Apple attached to a contract that my assistant will draft today while I am flying from Dallas to San Francisco. The contract will state that Apple Computer is licensing $1.25 million worth of Zane Publishing's PowerCD titles and paying a $250,000 non-refundable deposit on the $1.25 million purchase.

CFO: When do I get to see the titles?

JOHN: You can't. Mr. Pilzer hasn't built them yet, but I'll tell you that our firm is going to invest $3 million in Mr. Pilzer's company to make sure they get built. And the reason we are going to invest $3 million is that we know they will produce great titles. And our first major customer is you: Apple. You're going to take the CD-ROMs that Mr. Pilzer builds you and bundle them with every Apple computer you ship to schools.

CFO: When do I have to pay the $1 million balance on the purchase contract?

JOHN: About a year from now.

CFO: What if we don't like the PowerCD titles?

JOHN: That's the best part. If you don't like the PowerCD titles, you don't have to pay for them. You give us the $250,000 deposit

> now, and if you don't like them a year from now, you don't have to pay the $1 million balance—you would just lose your $250,000 deposit on your $1.25 million purchase, which is no worse off than where you are right now. Except right now, your accountants are trying to figure out how to write up the expense of a quarter-million-dollar [expletive]-up by Apple Computer. After I get your new check tonight for $250,000, your accountants can write up your purchase of $1.25 million worth of new, exciting educational PowerCD titles, to be bundled with every Apple computer sold to schools. Which story do you want to put in your 1991 annual report from last year?

It turned out that John and the Apple CFO were members of the same country club and lived blocks away from each other in Hillsborough, one of the richest neighborhoods in the San Francisco Bay area.

After John hung up, he dialed his assistant to get her started on the contract. When he was done talking to her, he turned to me.

"You didn't deserve that, but I got you out of your mess. Now let's talk about the terms of my $3 million investment."

"Who the hell are you?" I asked.

"I'm pretty good, huh?" he replied. It was clear from the look on his face that he felt like the smug one now.

"John, I think I'm smart, especially when it comes to finance. My whole resume says I'm smart. But when it comes to structuring financial deals, I'm not even on the same planet as you are!" I shook my head and chuckled. Then John explained his terms.

Frankly, before meeting John Grillos on January 14, 1992, I didn't think I had anything left to learn about finance. Boy, was I wrong. But I had more to learn that day than just how a public company accounts for its mistakes.

"You can always turn every conflict into a win-win," John said to me that fateful day, "because you've already got all the parties sitting at the table. Getting everyone together is often the hardest part of resolving a conflict. You have to believe there's a win-win, and you don't get to that win-win until both parties fully understand each other's financial structure and mechanisms for reporting to their investors."

While I could not have been happier with the outcome, one little detail still nagged at me.

"What if, a year from now, Apple doesn't like the PowerCD titles we just agreed to develop?" I asked John.

"Don't worry Paul, it'll be great," he replied. "Apple will love your PowerCDs."

"How can you be so sure?"

He explained that if Apple decided they didn't like the PowerCDs, someone would have to go to the accounting department and retroactively convert a 1992 quarter-million-dollar asset on their books—the deposit—into a 1993 quarter-million-dollar expense due to their incompetence. Moreover, reversing this transaction could possibly expose their managers, including CEO John Sculley, to charges of fraud from their shareholders.

"I doubt anyone at Apple will ever not like your PowerCD titles, and I'm 100% confident that Apple will approve the $1 million balance for payment," John assured me.

A few weeks later, Zane Publishing received a $3 million investment from John Grillos, and in 1993, Apple Computer bundled our catalog and several of our PowerCDs with hundreds of thousands of Apple personal computers sold to schools. Over the next few years, my team at Zane Publishing created hundreds more educational CD-ROMs, and we became the distributor for many more CD-ROM titles that we licensed from our competitors.

This all happened because of John Grillos, who has been my friend and business associate since that first day in Dallas. Years later, when John left DFJ to start his own venture capital firm, I was one of his first investors.

***** **POSTSCRIPT** *****

Entrepreneurs Don't Wear Suits

One more story about John. One month after investing $3 million in Zane Publishing in 1992, John told me to attend our first board meeting in San Francisco. The morning of the meeting, I got on a plane dressed in my usual travel clothes of jeans and a T-shirt, carrying a suit bag with a brand new Brioni suit I had bought just for the meeting. It cost me $3,000, twice the amount I had ever spent before on a suit. When I landed in San Francisco, I took a taxi straight to John's office at the top of the Bank of America building. John greeted me when I arrived in the reception area, pointed to a nearby glass conference room, and told me to wait there for the meeting to begin.

After he left, I went into the bathroom and put on my Brioni suit, shirt, and a tie. Then I waited in the conference room. Shortly before the meeting was to begin, John saw me through the conference room window and burst through the doors.

"What the [expletive] are you doing?!" he screamed.

Startled, I replied, "Waiting here like you told me to do."

"No!" he growled as he grabbed my brand new $3,000 Brioni suit by the lapels,. "What the [expletive] are you doing with this?"

I didn't know how to reply, and any response I would have given would have been lost under the thunderous message he delivered next. He released my lapels and stated emphatically:

"This is [expletive] Silicon Valley! *We*, venture capitalists, have money! *We* wear suits! *You, entrepreneurs*, take our money. *You* build companies. *You* don't wear suits! *You* wear [expletive] jeans and T-shirts!"

I stared at him.

"None of my partners would ever [expletive] invest in anybody who wears [expletive] suits."

I changed back into my jeans and T-shirt. When the meeting began, it was unsettling to sit at the conference table in a T-shirt next to the other board members in their nicely tailored suits—even the women wore suits.

But it was another win-win. Our board members learned about my dream of using technology to scale education, and I learned how to dress appropriately as an entrepreneur in Silicon Valley.

Chapter 24 - Learnings

1. Accounting is the universal language of business—you can never know too much about accounting, especially as it pertains to the accounting rules governing your investors, your suppliers, and your customers. Do you know everything you need to know about these parties in your business?

2. Looking back today, although the deal with Apple helped launch our company, I can't believe how much we left on the table. I focused on the $250,000 deposit and $1.25 million order and what they meant to Zane Publishing. I should have focused on the $25 million of built, packaged, and branded PowerCD CD-ROM players Apple had already built and how much it would have cost Apple to destroy them if we hadn't made a deal. What business mistake have you made by selling yourself short, and how did you rectify it to never happen again?

3. When making a proposal to anyone—an investor, a supplier, a customer, or a prospective employer—take time to understand how your proposal looks to them, especially if they are a different type of legal entity, such as a public company governed by FASB Generally Accepted Accounting Principles. Make time to go through your proposal and calculate how the other party will report it on their books.

4. Venture capitalists can be a tremendous asset to growing your business, supplying much more than just money. If a venture capitalist came to you and presented you with a large check, what would be the smartest way to apply that to your business?

5. Every conflict can be turned into a win-win once the parties focus on resolution. Challenge yourself to walk back into a conflict and resolve it to your liking. How can you apply doing this in your life now?

BECOMING AN ENTREPRENEUR

PAUL ZANE PILZER

CHAPTER 25

CUTTING IN LINE

As the father of four young adult Gen Zers, I am constantly reminded of how much things are changing as they take over our world. Gen Zers, born between 1999 and 2012, currently make up about 20% of the U.S population, with an estimated 70 million individuals. The baby boomers, born between 1946 and 1964, currently make up the largest generation in the U.S., with an estimated 71 million individuals. However, as the baby boomer generation ages and passes away, the Gen Z population is projected to continue growing, eventually surpassing the baby boomers in overall numbers[29]

I realized Gen Zers were different about five years ago during what began as a typical night out with one of my children. One evening, sometime in December 2016, I decided at the last minute, and without a reservation, to take my daughter out to a nice dinner at her favorite restaurant on Main Street before we had to meet the rest of the family for a movie. It was peak ski season, the busiest time of the year in our ski town, and the restaurants were overcrowded with tourists.

When my daughter and I arrived about an hour before the movie,

---

29. Statista Research Department. "U.S. Population Share by Generation 2019." ***Statista***, January 20, 2021.

the restaurant was packed, and the line was out the door. I explained to the hostess that we didn't have a reservation, and had one hour to get seated, order food, eat, and leave the restaurant in order to make the movie on time, and I pointed out that we were regulars and knew the manager. The hostess nodded unapologetically and told us the wait was at least an hour and fifteen minutes, and added that the kitchen was running slow.

My daughter wanted to leave, but I told her to wait a moment as I took out my phone.

"Dad, what are you doing?" my daughter wanted to know.

"Getting us a table," I replied as I contacted the manager of the restaurant, sending him a text message explaining our dilemma.

We were regulars at this restaurant and I had even rented out the entire place a few times for work events. And since it had been my go-to spot after mountain biking, I naturally developed a friendly relationship with the manager of the restaurant. So, it didn't come as a surprise when, just moments later, that same hostess came outside to find us, calling out loudly, "Mr. Pilzer, Mr. Pilzer, your table is ready!"

My daughter glared at me. Ignoring her attitude, I pleadingly motioned her to follow the hostess. To get to our table, we had to awkwardly walk past the same line of people waiting who were clearly hungry and annoyed. The hostess smiled knowingly as she handed us menus and told us she would send our server over right away because she knew we were in a hurry.

Cutting in Line

When the hostess left, my daughter turned to me and with an exasperated sigh, she explained, "Dad, I know you meant well, but what you did was really not fair to all those people and families with little kids standing out there, waiting their turn because they want to eat here too. And we cut right in front of them. We took the seats of people who had been waiting for over an hour! Cutting in line is *not* cool. We should have waited in line like everybody else. I wish you could be more patient and considerate. Why does *everything* with you have to be so urgent?"

I couldn't believe my ears—her explanation went right through me. That's when I had a stark realization: *I've been cutting in line my whole life!* It's what I learned to do in business, and in life, to get ahead from as early as I can remember. Whether I wanted tickets to an oversold Broadway show, or a reservation at a popular restaurant, I became a master at getting to the front of the line (legally, of course).

When I was a nineteen-year-old undergrad, I applied to Wharton Graduate Business School for my MBA and I got rejected. I was beyond crushed. With nothing to lose, I requested a meeting with the director of admissions and one week later, I got accepted. When my children read this story in one of my previous books, they accused me of taking a coveted spot on the waiting list away from another applicant. Honestly, until they accused me of "cutting the line" for admissions, I had never thought that my acceptance meant that someone else had been denied a spot in the class because of my actions.

When my wife was pregnant with our fourth child and began having complications with her pregnancy, we didn't just show up at the emergency room and wait our turn. I used all my connections to make sure her doctors were waiting and ready for us at the ER when we arrived.

I did the same thing once when my mother was dying of a stroke on the evening of Yom Kippur. My mother was in the North Shore Hospital run by NYU in New York, and her surgeon couldn't get the surgical team he needed to stay late at the hospital to help her. As an adjunct professor at New York University, I had an NYU ID badge, so I pulled out my badge and implied that I was a professor at the med school at NYU (not just economics). I was able to talk them into keeping the team members in the hospital to care for my mother. She had a subdural hematoma, and she survived, thanks to the trauma team that left their families that night to take care of her.

None of these things ever seemed wrong. I was using my resources to get the service that my family and I needed. That's not how my young adult Gen Z daughter saw it. She pushed the menu aside in protest and said she wasn't going to eat *anything*.

"Of course, you are," I said. "We're here and we're seated. Not eating is not going to change anything for the people who are still waiting outside."

I attempted to explain to my daughter why it was okay to ask the restaurant manager or owner for a favor and to get us seated right away. We live fulltime in Park City, a popular ski resort destination, and we eat here all the time, but most of the people who were at the restaurant that night were tourists on vacation. That meant the odds of them coming back to Park City—let alone coming back to this restaurant—were quite low. I emphasized that as loyal customers, we deserve special treatment.

"As a restaurant owner, or any entrepreneur, the best thing you can do is take care of your existing customers," I told her. "Because when I have a good meal and a good experience here, I'm going to keep coming back here. And maybe, if they didn't seat us right away, we could have gone to another restaurant, one of their competitors. And maybe this place would've lost us, one of their best year-round customers, *forever.*"

My daughter was not convinced and refused to order when the server arrived. I ordered for both of us, choosing her favorite dish on the menu and figured she would give in once it arrived at the table. When the food arrived, she pushed it aside and didn't touch anything on the table.

Transparency

We continued our debate about cutting in line. I pointed out that asking the restaurant manager for a favor because we were regulars was no different than Delta Air Lines giving us complimentary upgrades to first-class or Comfort+ because of my frequent flier status.

"That's *completely* different," she argued. "Delta is transparent. Everyone knows about getting free upgrades the more you fly. People can choose whether or not to fly Delta, and they can pay more for first class if they want. That's not what you did here. *You* basically cheated."

Gen Zers

It was then that I realized we were coming from two very different places. The world that I was raised in was all about working hard, going to college, learning skills, and making contacts. It made sense to take advantage of every legal opportunity available to us. We maintained friendships and business contacts not for the purpose of gaining an advantage over others, but to improve our relationships and better serve our customers. Many of my closest friendships started as business contacts. But to my daughter, it was a matter of ethics and social equity.

In my daughter's eyes, I had used influence to gain an unfair advantage. My daughter explained that Gen Zers believe in waiting their turn and earning their place, ensuring that everyone has the same opportunities. If you worked hard to get ahead, while everyone else was offered the same opportunity, and everything is transparent, then there is nothing wrong with being more successful than someone else. For Gen Z, an undisclosed advantage that's not available to all is unethical. As a result, cutting in line breaks an unspoken code, and using influence to gain an unfair advantage is cheating.

That conversation was eye-opening for me. It made me realize that Gen Z is already changing the way we do business. I could see that ethics are not absolute, but rather a moving target, and what's right and what's wrong depends largely on what lens something is being viewed through. I grew up in a world with a clear-cut view of ethics based on Judeo-Christian values. However, Gen Zers have a more fluid view of ethics, and it is essential to understand their perspectives in order to do business with them.

If you're around my age, you probably remember tipping a maître d' or hostess to get a nice table or slipping them some cash after your meal so they'd remember you next time. When I had an exceptional meal, I even asked for a business card and had my secretary write them a personalized thank you on Citibank letterhead. Gen Zers tend to value fairness and social justice, and they have a stronger sense of empathy for others. Waiting in line for an hour seemed like a fair and just way to make sure that everyone had an equal chance at getting a table, while texting the manager to jump the line felt like a violation of that principle. (Gen Zers working in service jobs do accept tips.)

Gen Zers will soon exceed baby boomers in actual numbers and in purchasing power. As the largest generation, they will dominate the workforce, the economy, and politics. It's crucial to recognize that they're changing the way we approach work-life balance and they are disrupting old, tried-and-true principles of the business world. Gen Zers are sometimes criticized for being disengaged and entitled but admired for being generous and grounded. Whether or not you are a Gen Zer now, and whether or not you agree with their philosophies, soon most of your customers are going to be Gen Zers. The sooner you understand their ideologies and values, and the way they think, the better it will be for your business and your continued success.

BECOMING AN ENTREPRENEUR

PAUL ZANE PILZER

Chapter 25 - Learnings

1. I secured a table for my son and me by sending one text to a restaurant manager—when the waiting line was out the door. Do you think this was appropriate? In what situation is cutting the line acceptable?

2. Is there a difference between upgrading to first class legitimately, paying an exorbitant fare, or cutting a line through leveraging a relationship of someone you know? Did my son Richard blow things out of proportion? This example on airplane upgrades may no longer be relevant now that airlines have transparent algorithms for upgrading to first class.

3. Are there ways to get ahead in life and business without cutting the line? What are some examples? Or does the very act of "getting ahead" mean that you are pushing an ethical envelope by getting ahead?

4. Why or why not was it ethical of me to allude to being a medical professor at NYU? If you were facing the same circumstances and trying to save the life of a loved one, would you do the same? Do the rules change when it concerns health, your family, or other extraordinary circumstances?

5. If we all operated with full transparency, would that even out any supposed edge individuals or entities have over each other? Is social media about to make us fully transparent?

BECOMING AN ENTREPRENEUR

PAUL ZANE PILZER

CHAPTER 26

FIXING THINGS THAT AREN'T BROKEN

By 1994 I had learned that my strengths lie in inventing products and starting companies to develop them, but then stepping away to allow professional managers to scale my creations. Here's how I first learned this about myself.

When I landed at LAX the week before Christmas in December 1994, I was met at the airport by John Grillos, the venture capitalist who led the venture capital investment in Zane Publishing described in *Chapter 24: My Litigation with Apple Computer* (page 419).

One of John's investors in Zane Publishing was Draper Fisher Jurvetson (DFJ), which rebranded itself as Threshold Ventures in January 2019, one of the world's leading venture capital firms. Some credit its founder, Tim Draper, along with his father, Bill Draper, as being the originators of the modern venture capital industry. In 1992, DFJ and Grillos' firm invested $3 million in Zane Publishing, Inc., and John Grillos joined the company's board of directors.

At a board meeting in San Francisco a week prior, we had discussed DFJ upping its investment in the company. In the middle of the discussion, John said, "Before we go any further, Professor, let's you and me take this offline and meet next week over lunch in Los Angeles. I'm working there all week." Today was the day of that meeting. I had flown down to LA from Park City just to meet John, missing snowboarding on a great powder day in Utah because I could tell John had something important on his mind. I remember it was a powder day because I almost missed my flight driving in a snowstorm to the Salt Lake City airport.

After using our cell phones at LAX to confirm I had landed and where John was waiting—using a cell phone to find people at airports was still a novelty in 1994—I jumped into John's Mercedes convertible, which was waiting upstairs in the drop-off area. We drove up Lincoln Highway to get on I-10 westward, which took us underneath the freeway into darkness and then out onto Pacific Coast Highway (PCH), heading north in a spectacular explosion of California sunshine.

Girls played volleyball on the famous Santa Monica beach to on our left. Even the view of sand dunes and beach houses on our right was beautiful. I assumed John was driving somewhere nearby to have lunch.

We drove past Santa Monica, Pacific Palisades, Topanga, Malibu, and more hamlets along the beach as the homes got larger and larger. John kept pointing out, "Barbara Streisand lives there ... Cher lives over there ... the best surfing is right here ..." Finally, he said, "You can teach here," as we pulled off PCH and stopped in a parking area in front of a gigantic sign that read "Pepperdine University." John turned off the engine and faced me.

"Paul," he began—I knew something was up because he normally called me by my nickname—"we can't keep going on like this. See all those beach houses and all those pretty girls on the beaches? You've got to leave Dallas, buy yourself one of these beach houses, and move out here."

John went on to explain how disruptive my presence was at Zane Publishing headquarters in Dallas. "Paul, you're like a hurricane in the office. Look, we like Zane Publishing and your current model for success—that's why we invested three years ago and why we're ready to invest more. But we can't stand you jumping in every week to *fix things that aren't broken*—especially when the existing strategy is working. You've got to get out of the office and move here or anywhere else where you are thousands of miles away from the company!"

John laid out the plan. I would resign as CEO and become chairman of the board, only visiting the company in Dallas once a month for board of directors' meetings. DFJ would lead the search to hire a professional CEO who would report to the board of directors and whose equity and salary package would come mostly out of my compensation. I would remain a resource for the company for major sales calls and acquiring new content to publish, working from Malibu or anywhere else I desired that was away from Dallas. And DFJ would invest more money and explore plans to eventually take the company public, which could potentially make me hundreds of millions of dollars.

John finished and was silent. At first, I didn't know what to say—I didn't want to seem too eager. I was thrilled with everything John had presented, especially the idea of me leaving the company where I had worked for five years, moving to Malibu, and beginning a new life on the beach. At age 40, I sometimes felt I had missed out on *something* by never having lived in California. Now, I was going to get the chance to find out what that something was. I told John that I agreed and would move to California.

A few months later, in 1995, I purchased a rundown 1920s-era beach house on a cliff overlooking the ocean in Pacific Palisades—17810 Castellammare Drive, nine miles down the street from Pepperdine. It took me almost a year to renovate it into a five-bedroom, five-bathroom beach house that I loved, with a great office for "working" at Zane Publishing.

I moved in 1996, sure that I was retiring to a life of snowboarding, mountain biking, writing books, teaching, and giving commencement speeches worldwide, particularly in China, where my books were becoming popular. To fully embrace the "Southern California" experience, I tried surfing most mornings out of my backyard, and I enrolled at UCLA in acting and screenwriting classes. I wanted to see if I could turn my success as a ***New York Times*** bestselling book author into success as a Hollywood screenwriter. I couldn't, primarily because I knew absolutely nothing about the business of making movies, and the scripts I wrote were totally uneconomical to produce.

Actually, I found success beyond my dreams in Los Angles, but a kind of success I wasn't looking for ... I met my wife Lisa. We now live full-time in Utah, where we have four out-of-the-box-thinking children!

Chapter 26 - Learnings

1. Examine your role in your business. Are there any areas where you struggle with control? What can you do to change this?

2. I stepped down as the CEO of my own company to take on a less visible role on the board. As it pertains to your company, would you rather be more involved, or are you more inclined to build and sell or build and delegate?

3. In my life, I have moved through multiple, sometimes overlapping disciplines. What other industries or fields would you like to learn about, and what can you do to take a step forward?

4. Where in your life have you experienced a major surprise, and how did you handle it? Do you believe that planning for the worst-case scenario helps you prepare, or is this a counterproductive use of your time?

5. Is a true work-life balance even possible?

BECOMING AN ENTREPRENEUR

PAUL ZANE PILZER

CHAPTER 27

ADVENTURES IN PROGRESS

For the past 22 years, I have focused on being a husband and father of four children, and on the four areas in business where I can add value:

- *Health Insurance*
- *K-12 Education*
- *Wellness*
- *Sino-U.S. Relations*

My newfound retirement in Los Angeles lasted three years until 1999. The seeds had been planted long before, in 1975 and in 1985, for my next 20 years of entrepreneurial adventures

Here's a brief summary of what I've been doing since 1999 in Health Insurance, K-12 Education, and China with an explanation of how and why I got involved in each venture. The complete details of each company or activity are still being written.

ADVENTURES IN PROGRESS: HEALTH INSURANCE

Learning About U.S. Health Insurance in the Soviet Union

I have always been fascinated by the Cold War, which defined much of my family's existence. In 1914, my father emigrated from a part of Russia (then) called Galicia at age eleven. In 1976, my wife was born in Saigon (now Ho Chi Minh City) while her father was a prisoner in a North Vietnamese prison camp. In 1968, at age 14, I competed in a Soviet-American high school chess tournament in Moscow. There, I met several Russian friends I had been playing chess with through ham radio for years.

In 1983, the USSR shot down a Korean Airlines Boeing 747 airliner flying from Anchorage to Seoul, killing all 246 passengers and 23 crew, including a powerful U.S. congressman. Fearing nuclear holocaust and wanting to do anything I could to help keep the peace, I started developing more contacts in the USSR and ended up lecturing at Moscow State University from 1983-1989.

In 1985, my Soviet hosts asked me to give a lecture series explaining sovereign debt. Premier Gorbachev had just visited South America, and several Latin nations were in default on their debts to the West. After one of these lectures, a Soviet economist stood up and asked, "How can you, the son of a God-fearing Russian family, work for such an evil nation as the United States?"

I responded aggressively, pointing out Soviet activities in Afghanistan and Nicaragua, and we went back and forth on the bad deeds of the U.S. versus the USSR. Finally, he said, "I hear that in the United States if you lose your job, even if it's not your fault because your employer goes out of business, they take away the health insurance of you, your children, and your wife, even if she is pregnant!" I assured him that wasn't the case and took another question on a different subject. But his question bothered me all the way home.

When I got back to Washington, I realized that he was correct. Most Americans get their health insurance from their employer and lose their health insurance when they lose their job, even if they lose their job because of illness. This realization began my now 37-year quest to separate a person's health insurance policy in the U.S. from their employer, just like their auto, home, and life insurance policies, which have nothing to do with their employer.

Later that year, I supported COBRA, a law enacted by Congress which allows a person to stay on their employer's health plan after employment, although only for 18-36 months and at an enormous cost. But this issue of temporary employer group health insurance hit home for me personally 14 years later in 1999 when I left my position as director at a Wall Street firm when my wife was pregnant, and our entire family lost our employer-provided health insurance. The issue was about more than money; I could afford to pay our medical bills even if we had a prematurely born child. The issue was that in some states, at any price, even if you pay with cash, you can't get good healthcare without having health insurance and being part of a local network of medical providers. Failed employer-provided health insurance is the number one cause of U.S. personal bankruptcy, affecting more than one million U.S. families (four million Americans) each year.

Fortunately, our baby was born healthy, and I solved my family's problem by purchasing an economical individual health insurance policy. But I found it terribly unfair that I had to pay for this policy with after-tax dollars, whereas if my employer had provided my health insurance, the cost would have been tax-deductible to them, and the benefit would have been tax-free to me.

Many, if not most, of the problems with U.S. health insurance stem from a 1945 directive by President Roosevelt that allowed employers and unions to evade wage and price controls by providing tax-free health benefits to employees. This gave employer-provided health benefits a 2-to-1 financial advantage over giving employees money to buy their own health insurance, and made employer-provided health insurance in the U.S. virtually ubiquitous for large employers.

Extend Health, IRS Regulations, Two Books, and PeopleKeep

Since 1999, I've made reforming U.S. health insurance one of my top four priorities as follows:

1. ***1999-2012, Extend Health*** – In 1999, I founded Extend Health (formerly Extend Benefits) with my close friend Anthony Meyer to offer individual health insurance policies to employees reimbursed by their employers. Due to regulatory challenges spurred on by group health insurance providers, our company switched to serving mostly retirees willing to trade their former employer-provided benefits for a supplemental Medigap individual policy. I left my position as the company's chairman and founder in 2006, placing it in the good hands of Bryce Williams as CEO. Bryce was the son of Don Williams, the CEO of Trammell Crow, whom I met after I got Trammell Crow to manage our Memphis properties in

1983 (see *Chapter 21: Memphis: My First $100 Million Deal*, page 341). In 2012, Tony and Brandon managed the sale of Extend Health to the largest U.S. provider of group employer health benefits, Towers Watson, for $435 million.

2. ***1995-Today, U.S. Tax & IRS Regulations*** – In 1985, I began lobbying Congress and the IRS to allow Health Savings Accounts (then called Medical Savings Accounts), which were similar to IRAs but for medical expenses. In 2002, I began lobbying the IRS to interpret the U.S. tax code to allow employer tax-free reimbursement of medical expenses, including individual health insurance premiums. Since then, the IRS has gone back and forth on this issue, depending on who is in the White House.

3. ***2005, The New Health Insurance Solution by Paul Zane Pilzer (Wiley Press, 2005)*** – I wrote this book in 2005 which explained, in print and on a companion website, how to obtain an individual health policy in each state and get your employer to pay for it. This book launched my career in the press as a healthcare economist.

4. ***2006-Today, PeopleKeep (PK)*** - I founded this company (originally called Zane Benefits) in 2006 after leaving Extend Health. PK offers technology-only solutions for employers wishing to reimburse their employees tax-free

for medical expenses and individual health insurance premiums. The company, along with a dog-eared caricature of me, was featured July 30, 2007, on the front page of the ***Wall Street Journal*** in a lengthy article extolling individual policies and my work to promote them. I left the PK management team in 2010 but remained a shareholder and member of the board of directors.

The largest shareholder is W. James. Tozer, the same person who, 45 years ago, was the head of Citibank's New York Banking Division and whose firing in 1977 forever sealed my fate as an entrepreneur versus a corporate employee (see *Chapter 15: My Career at Citibank Takes Off*, page 175).

5. ***2012, The End of Employer-Provided Health Insurance, Paul Zane Pilzer with Rick Linkquist (Wiley Press, 2012)*** – I wrote this book with Rick, the CEO of PK, to explain to employers how to offer their employees lifetime individual health insurance policies in lieu of group policies that end when their employment is terminated. This was the first time I used my background as an author to promote one of my businesses, and I found it most enjoyable since I've always believed so much in the companies I have founded.

ADVENTURES IN PROGRESS: WELLNESS

On September 7, 1996, I was getting ready to give a speech on ***God Wants You to Be Rich*** to 45,000 people at the RCA Dome in Indianapolis. I should have been elated. But instead, I felt guilty. As I watched the audience file into the stadium and began my speech, I felt as if I were about to rip them off.

Like much of America, half of the audience was unhealthy and overweight, a direct consequence of diet and lifestyle as evidenced by the fatigued look on their faces and the size of their waistlines. Nothing I was about to say about economics was going to improve the quality of their lives until they first learned how to care for their bodies.

A strange urge seized me to scrap my prepared speech and tell my audience that good health was more important than any riches they might acquire, but I chickened out. I didn't want to offend my hosts, and I didn't know back then what action people should follow to take control of their health.

On the flight home early the next morning, I wrestled with this question: why would intelligent people spend time and money to improve their lives in every area *except* the one in which they most obviously needed improvement? And, more significantly, what should a person who is unhealthy and overweight do to begin taking control of their life?

I arrived in Los Angeles around 10:00 a.m. that Sunday and rushed to Pacific Palisades to meet the contractor who was renovating my beach house. As we stood outside discussing the construction, neighbors jogged or biked by on their way to the beach. I was struck by how fit and healthy everyone appeared. Compared to some of the people I had seen in Indianapolis, these neighbors looked like inhabitants of a different planet.

This conundrum launched my now 27-year quest into defining and contributing to the wellness industry. To get started, beginning in 1996, I first had to redefine the existing then $1 trillion medical industry into two parts:

> ***Sickness industry:*** Products and services provided reactively to people with existing disease(s), ranging from a common cold to cancerous tumors. These products and services seek to either treat the symptoms of a disease or eliminate it.

> ***Wellness industry:*** Products and services provided proactively to healthy people (those without an existing disease) to make them feel even healthier and look better, to slow the effects of aging, or to prevent diseases from developing in the first place.

Speeches, Four Books, Fitness Industry and Planet Fitness

Here are some of the things I've been doing in the Wellness Industry since first defining the term "wellness" in 1996. Prior to my books and speeches on the business opportunity in the wellness industry, "wellness" meant "cancer care" at a time when cancer was a terrifying, unspoken word. I'm pleased I've helped the industry define itself and capture its current name.

1. ***1996-Today, Speaking*** – I've delivered more than 250 keynote speeches worldwide on wellness before live audiences typically ranging from 1,000-100,000 people and sometimes introduced by the head of state in the host country. I helped launch a powerful industry that is improving the lives of tens of millions of people who have followed my research. The wellness industry has grown from $200 billion in 1996 to $1-2 trillion today, and it's been exciting for me to participate in its growth.

2. ***1999-Today, Four Books*** – I've written four books on wellness which continue to be bestsellers in 25 languages. Two of these books have been substantial upgrades of prior editions since the industry has grown so fast it's been hard to keep up.

3. ***2003-Today, Fitness Industry*** – In 2003, I was the keynote presenter at the annual convention of the International Health, Racquet & Sportsclub Association (IHRSA), the trade association for 30,000 fitness clubs in the U.S. with about 50 million members. I used this opportunity to take the industry to task, chastising them for, in the middle of an obesity crisis, tailoring their fitness clubs to mostly serve already-fit people. They loved the criticism, especially my strategies for how to attract new

In 1985, despite my criticism of fitness clubs for catering mostly to fit, already healthy members, I was the keynote speaker for the International Health, Racquet & Sportsman Association (IHRSA).

customers who were not fitness club members anywhere, versus competing with each other for existing customers. IHRSA invited me back the following year and eventually put my picture on the cover of their monthly magazine (***Prophet of New Profits***, Club Business International, May 2008).

4. ***2009-Today, Planet Fitness*** – In 2009, I was asked to be the keynote speaker at the first annual convention of Planet Fitness (PF) franchisees, then a 200-unit affordable fitness chain with one million members that prided itself on serving overweight people who weren't already members

of a fitness club. The owner and founder, Mike Grondahl, had watched me talk about ***Unlimited Wealth*** on ***Larry King Live!*** in 1991; he claims that show gave him the idea to re-engineer his (then one) fitness club for a 5× increase in membership and drop his price to $10 month. Mike promised himself back then that if PF ever could afford a keynote speaker, it would be me. Eighteen years later, in 2009, the audience of 200 PF franchisees loved my presentation almost as much as I loved meeting them—they were mostly successful businesspeople dedicated to using PF to improve the lives of ordinary people in their local communities.

In 2010 my wife asked me if PF was an honest company since my name was being used to help sell new franchises, and people were coming up to her asking if we owned part of Planet Fitness. "Lisa," I replied, "now you're getting *me* worried. Why don't you fly out to their headquarters in New Hampshire, meet some of their franchisees, and check out the parent company?"

Lisa flew there the next month and had a wonderful visit, so wonderful that she purchased a five-store Area Development Agreement for the west side of Salt Lake City near our home. Today, we still own two PF stores that, even after Covid-19, earn a significant annual profit, and the company has grown from 200 to 2,050 locations with 13 million members in the U.S. alone—the parent company (PLNT) is listed on the NYSE and is worth approximately $7 billion! And you ain't seen nothin' yet—I expect Planet Fitness to grow in the next decade to 3,000 locations and have a market cap exceeding $15 billion. I'm proudest that PF and their business practices have spawned competition similarly dedicated to affordably improving wellness in their communities worldwide.

Planet Fitness, like most of the companies described in this chapter, is still a work in progress. I look forward to one day writing a full chapter on Planet Fitness and how it has affected people's fitness more than any other company on the planet (no pun intended).

ADVENTURES IN PROGRESS: K-12 EDUCATION

In 1975, as I explained in *Chapter 24: My Litigation with Apple Computer* (page 419), I worked on my graduate thesis of using a mainframe computer for education. Today, I still use the algorithms I developed back then in my continuing passion of using computers to scale education. More than ever, I believe that online interactive education can do for teachers in the next decade what the phonograph and movie camera did for singers and actors in the last century—

affordably bring the best teacher of every subject to every student. I have created three companies that have served millions of customers to help make this happen. I feel good about this field, especially since the COVID-19 lockdowns of 2020-2021 forced every teacher and school district to embrace online education.

Zane Publishing, Graduation Alliance, and Zaniac Learning

1. ***1989-2005, Zane Publishing, Inc.*** – The story of this company is told in *Chapter 24: My Litigation with Apple Computer* (page 419). I consider this venture a great public policy success—we produced millions of educational CD-ROMs, helped define an industry of electronic education, and educated a decade of K-12 and college students in the 2000s—even though the company was unable to transition from CD-ROMs to the Internet. The traditional educational publishers licensed us copies of their textbooks for publication on CD-ROMs, but they refused to allow their monopoly products to go online. Even today, many educational publishers still force students and school districts to purchase print version textbooks for 1,000% or more of what they might cost electronically. Zane survives today as a legacy company based in Australia.

2. ***2004-Today, Graduation Alliance*** – In 2004, Governor of Utah, Ambassador Jon Huntsman introduced Anthony Meyer and me to the Utah Electronic High School

(UEHS), which back then was nothing more than a state-run correspondence school using many of my Zane Publishing CD-ROM titles for their curriculum. The UEHS served mainly as a remedial program for high school students needing to complete a missing credit or for those who were medically incapable of attending regular school. It was free to Utah high school students and similar to other programs in 23 states. As we examined the operation, we realized the larger opportunity was to 1) serve the 1.2 million U.S. high school students who become dropouts each year and to keep those at risk from becoming dropouts, and 2) serve the existing 75 million U.S. citizens who have already dropped out of high school, to help them earn a high school diploma and get a better job.

In 2005, Anthony Meyer and I partnered with UEHS to form the American Academy, later called NoDropouts and then Graduation Alliance (GA). Graduation Alliance has spent tens of millions of dollars over the past 15 years developing models to serve high school dropouts and those at risk for dropout. The company grew to be one of the leading online high schools in the nation and, in 2020, having served millions of students, was sold to KKR & Co. for more than $100 million.

3. ***2009-Today, Zaniac K-8 Learning*** – In 2008, when one of my four children had difficulty in elementary school, I visited their public school and was shocked at how much time was devoted to taking standardized tests. I was even more shocked to discover what was done with the test results that took my children hundreds of hours to produce—nothing. I personally led the development for one year of a complete K-8 math curriculum we call Zane Math. With Zane Math, incorrect responses identify subject matter deficiencies, that computers then use to produce additional lessons in the deficient areas.

This allows the test takers to learn from their mistakes, rather than be punished for them. We distributed Zane Math, along with other STEM-based curriculums in Zaniac K-8 learning centers. By 2016, Zaniac had 11 centers open in Connecticut, Florida, North Carolina, Kentucky, New York, and New Jersey. The company is owned primarily by the former CEO of Zane Publishing, Reed Bilbray. Reed started out as a Zaniac franchisee in Asheville, N.C., but got so excited about the impact on his own children that he purchased a majority interest in the parent company and became its CEO and owner of two campuses. Unfortunately, the business lockdowns of 2020-2021 proved devastating to Zaniac's "high touch" in-person learning experience, and the future of the

Hong Kong University, established by the British in the 19th Century, is one of my favorite colleges. The only language spoken on campus is English, and it attracts the best and brightest students from around the world who are dedicated to improving our planet.

company is now uncertain. Fortunately, the software-based, all-STEM curriculum is outstanding and should eventually find a new home with a different distribution model.

ADVENTURES IN PROGRESS: CHINA

I have written my next book, ***The New Roaring Twenties*** *(BenBella, 2023), which will examine much further my relationship with China and my prediction for its future—from my speech in The Great Hall of the People in 2009 to my lecturing at NYU Shanghai in 2019.*

Since 2009, I've been speaking and working in China, the richest nation on earth (adjusted for purchasing power parity). One of the biggest changes in the world economy in the next decade will be the emergence of China as the largest consuming nation on earth, in addition to already being the largest producing nation on earth. China, and more specifically U.S.-Chinese relations, will significantly impact what happens in the U.S. on Main Street as well as on Wall Street.

The enormous wealth China has created is continually cycled back into the U.S. economy: five million Chinese immigrants live in the U.S., and 400,000 Chinese students attend college in the U.S. Whatever your business is in the West, one key to your future success lies in how you purchase your goods from, or sell your goods and services to, China.

But China is not only the richest nation on earth—it is also one

December 9, 2009. Lecturing before 3,500 students and faculty at Peking University.

December 14, 2009. Lecturing at The Great Hall of the People—excerpts of this speech I'm told appeared the next morning on one billion devices.

of the unhappiest nations on earth.

In 1978, following the death of Chairman Mao, Deng Xiaoping became the leader of China. Deng instituted major reforms, and in 1997-2019, China's GDP rose from $962 billion to $27 trillion (that's $27,000 billion), an incredible 2,800% (28×) increase. Today, China and the U.S. combined account for almost 50% of the world's GDP with only 22% of the world's population.

Deng's Largest Reform: GDP vs. GNH

The largest reform Deng instituted will go down in world history as the best decision ever made in terms of Gross Domestic Product (GDP) and the worst decision ever made in terms of Gross National Happiness (GNH).

This is the adoption of the One-Child Policy (OCP).

The one-child policy was made into official law by Deng Xiaoping on January 1, 1980. It was abolished 35 years later in 2015 and had a major impact—it is estimated today that 400 million births were prevented by OCP. Or, as some of my Chinese colleagues remind me, 400 million of their unborn brothers, sisters, uncles, and aunts are missing from their lives.

Despite having achieved the modern Chinese dream—China is Tesla's second largest market—hundreds of millions of Chinese rue their family life situation where the majority of families have only one child.

Each productive Chinese citizen and their spouse fit what is commonly known at the "4-2-1 problem;" they each have two parents in their 50s-60s and four grandparents in their 70s-80s, which means that each couple together has twelve seniors to care for. When they plan a vacation or event with their immediate family, often one of their 12 senior charges has something come up and they have to cancel their plans.

Many high-earning Chinese feel trapped as caregivers. In China, as well as in much of Asia, children and grandchildren are still expected to take care of aging family members. But in China, there are relatively few children and grandchildren to share this burden because of OCP.

Today, China ranks number one in the world in terms of gross domestic product (adjusted for purchasing power parity), and ranks number eighty-four in the world in terms of gross national happiness. No wonder five million Chinese people live permanently in the U.S., and almost 400,000 Chinese citizens go to U.S. colleges.

I remain fascinated by the Chinese economic miracle, which has lifted one billion people out of poverty in just the last few decades. I expect to continue my fascination, and to return to teaching in China once the impact of COVID-19 on travel and work has subsided.

Chapter 27 - Learnings

1. There's only one major problem with the U.S. healthcare system: the cost. What do you think is the solution?

2. When I began my professional journey to help develop affordable fitness options, I found that the marketing of fitness was directed toward motivated and active people versus overweight and fatigued people. Why do you think this was so, and why is the distinction so vast between these two populations? Is it diet, exercise, or something else?

3. Many publishers of educational materials refuse to allow their monopoly products on the Internet, preventing students and school districts from saving significantly on their textbooks and other required resources. Do you think the government should step in and that these companies should not be afforded a choice in this matter? Should all material used in public schools be public domain?

4. Are standardized tests antiquated and meaningless? Do they pigeonhole the potential of children, or do they provide a helpful ranking for where students are in their learnings?

5. The OCP (one-child policy) in China allowed it to reset its economics that were keeping its citizens in abject poverty. Now, China is economically prosperous, but at what cost? Why or why not do you agree or disagree with the OCP?

BECOMING AN ENTREPRENEUR

PAUL ZANE PILZER

ACKNOWLEDGMENTS

Thank you, God, for each day with which you have blessed me. This book would not have been possible without the incredible relationships I've had with amazing people, teachers, business partners, students, friends, and mentors; you have believed in me, supported me, and provided opportunities for me to contribute to the world.

I am eternally grateful to my wife, Lisa, the love of my life, and our four incredible children, Miriam, Amethyst, Ashe, and Mark, who inspire me every day. I am also grateful to my brother-in-law, Brian Dang, my brother, Lee Pilzer and his wife Meryn, and my aunt Gerry Pilzer. I'd like to thank my literary agent Jan Miller and my business manager Reed Bilbray, who have been by my side since my first book almost 40 years ago.

I owe a great debt of gratitude to the incredible people who have shaped my life as an entrepreneur. In order as they appear in the book, they are:

Frank – first employer and owner of Frank's TV
Miriam Pilzer – mother
Elias Pilzer – father
Jerome Stern – mentor and father of my classmate Ronnie
Sam Walton – founder of Walmart
Menashe Kadishman – artist and friend
Stanley Marcus – mentor and founder of Neiman Marcus

Elsie and Stanley Pearle – founders of Pearle Vision
J.B. McFadden and Robert J. Sullivan – journalism professors at Lehigh University
Professor Richard Redd – art history professor at Lehigh University
J.I. Rodale and Robert Rodale – founders of Rodale Press
J. Brendan Ryan – marketing executive, Ogilvy & Mather CEO
W. James Tozer – mentor, Citibank executive, and friend
Ernie Bloch – professor, department chair at NYU
Peter Derby – SEC official, teaching assistant at NYU
George Stone and Morris Sutton – teaching assistants at NYU
Robert Petrucello – friend and student at NYU
Anthony Robbins – motivator, author, and friend
Murray Goodman – benefactor of Lehigh University
Alan M. May – partner, investor, and friend
Anthony M. Meyer – partner, investor, and friend
Richard Jaffe – partner and lifelong friend
Jeffrey Juster – investment banker
David Wallenstein – investment banker
President Ronald Reagan – my hero
John Grillos – venture capitalist

In addition, I would like to thank the following people, some of whom are no longer with us, for their unbounded friendship, inspiration, and contribution to my life: Christy and Jay Abraham,

Rick Alden, Ed Ames, Ayla and Fehmi Ashaboglu, Sheila and Michael Ashkin, Norman Beil, Ted Bloomberg, Farran and Robert Brown, Linda and Neill Brownstein, Lenny Cappe, Dr. Stacey Clardy, Ron Coase, Jerry Coffee, Ruth and Phil Davidson, Zack Davidson, Natalie and Peter Derby, Mark Dietzgen, David Drew, Kathy Drew, Julie and Randy Fields, Greg Friedman, Mitch Gaylord, Laurie and Patrick Gentempo, Roger Goldman, Mimi Kim and Kenny Griswold, Bobby Hahn, Meg and John Hauge, Allan Hunter, Scott Ingraham, Stephen Jarchow, Stuart Johnson, Larry King, Dr. Guillaume Lamotte, Cindy and Andy Levine, Eli Levine, Rabbi David Levinsky, Rick Lindquist, Ken Mabry, Sharon and Bill Macey, Ann Mather, Alan May, Aleda Toma and Mike McCoy, Eric Morgan, Mike Murray, Noreen and David O'Brien, Bob Petrucello, Uncle Charlie (Charles Jay Pilzer), Steven Pilzer, Lea and Barry Porter, Craig Primo, Russ Reiss, Larry Richman, Tony Robbins, Pat Robertson, Bari Nan Cohen and Jeffrey Rothchild, Paula Sepulvado, Richard Shaffer, Randy Sigman, Julian Simon, Michael Smerconish, Howie Spring, Lisa Evans and Hansell Stedman, Rabbi Yudi Steiger, Ralou and Ronnie Stern, In-Hei Hahn and Geoff Tabin, Stephen Taylor, Zibby and Jim Tozer, Art Warsoff, Brandon Williams, Jason Xu, Dexter Yager family, Caroline Zemmel, Susie Zemmel, Adamo Zweiback, and Rabbi Yoshi Zweiback.

Thank you to my team of editors: Judith Emmert, Paula Felps, Rachel Hecht, Hilary Jastram, Lisa Dang Pilzer, Zachary Primo, and cover designers Zeljka Vukojevic, Kim Baker, Lisa Dang Pilzer, and Mark Avi Pilzer. A special thank you goes to my interior book designer, Reid Kirby, who contributed his extensive expertise in creating the multiple editions of this book.

And finally, I am most grateful to my readers and students who have given me my professional *raison d'être*, the opportunity to do what I love most–teach.

Paul Zane Pilzer
Park City, Utah
March 1, 2023

ABOUT THE AUTHOR

Paul Zane Pilzer is a *New York Times* bestselling author, the founder of six companies, a world-renowned economist, a social entrepreneur, an adjunct professor, and the author of 13 books—including *The New Roaring Twenties 2023-2033* (BenBella Books 2023).

Pilzer received his BA from Lehigh University in three years and his MBA from Wharton Graduate Business School in 15 months at age 22. He became Citibank's youngest officer at age 22 and its youngest vice president at age 26.

At 24, he was appointed adjunct professor at New York University, where he taught for 21 years and was student-rated "best teacher" five times.

In commercial real estate, he co-founded Zane May Interests in 1981, which developed 66 projects in the U.S. and the former USSR.

In healthcare, he is the founder of Extend Health (1999) and PeopleKeep (2006), two leading U.S. suppliers of personalized health benefits to corporate America, including Walmart's Sam's Club.

In education, he is the founder of Zane Publishing (1989), Graduation Alliance (2005), and Zaniac Learning (2012), three pioneering companies in online education.

He was an appointed economic adviser in two White House administrations and warned of the impending $200 billion savings and loan crisis a—story that he later shared in ***Other People's Money*** (Simon & Schuster 1989), which was critically acclaimed by the ***New York Times Book Review***, John Kenneth Galbraith in the ***New York Review of Books***, and ***The Economist*** magazine.

Pilzer's ***Unlimited Wealth*** (Crown Publishing, 1991/1993) explains how we live in a world of unlimited physical resources because of rapidly advancing technology.

After reading ***Unlimited Wealth***, the late Sam Walton, founder of Walmart, said that he was "amazed at Pilzer's business capacity" and his "ability to put it into layman's terms."

Pilzer's ***God Wants You to be Rich: The Theology of Economics*** (Simon & Schuster, 1993/1995/2006) explains how the foundation of our economic system is based on our Judeo-Christian heritage—this ***New York Times*** business bestseller was featured on television shows ranging from ***60 Minutes*** to ***First Person with Maria Shriver***.

In ***The New Wellness Revolution*** (Wiley Press, 2007), Pilzer identifies the newly emerging wellness business—for this book, he received an Honorary Doctorate in Public Service and was called a "wellness guru" by the ***New York Times.***

The New Health Insurance Solution (Wiley Press, 2005) sets forth a bold new direction for U.S. health insurance and explains how individuals can now get affordable health insurance independent of their employer.

The Next Millionaires (Momentum Media, 2006) explains why the number of U.S. millionaires doubled and how the economy is creating one million millionaires a year.

The New Roaring Twenties 2023-2033 (BenBella Books 2023) explains our post-pandemic economy and how our new world order rests on 12 economic and social pillars.

Paul is a keynote and commencement speaker at business conferences and universities worldwide; clients include hundreds of private companies and Hong Kong University, Peking University, University of Nanjing, University of Utah, New York University Shanghai, and University of Pennsylvania. More than 20 million copies of his speeches have been sold.

A former commentator on National Public Radio and CNN, Pilzer and his companies have been featured on the cover of more than 100 publications including on the front page of the ***Wall Street Journal*** (July 30, 2007).

He lives in Utah with his wife Lisa and their four children.

BECOMING AN ENTREPRENEUR

PAUL ZANE PILZER

Let's Connect

Stay Current with Paul's Research

www.paulzanepilzer.com

wikipedia.org/wiki/Paul_Zane_Pilzer

Connect with Paul on Social Media

Paul Zane Pilzer
(facebook Paul Zane Pilzer Public Figure)

Paul Zane Pilzer
(LinkedIn Paul Zane Pilzer Economist/Author/Entrepreneur at ZCI)

Have Paul Speak at your Event

Bring Paul Zane Pilzer to your event and empower your team to understand the future and their paths to success. Paul will uniquely tailor his presentation to your specific needs and situation.

Visit www.paulzanepilzer.com or email reed@paulzanepilzer.com

Made in the USA
Coppell, TX
05 November 2026

11307330R00280